Third Workshop on Multimodal Artificial Intelligence (MAI 2021)

Online
6 June 2021

ISBN: 978-1-7138-3023-8

Printed from e-media with permission by:

Curran Associates, Inc.
57 Morehouse Lane
Red Hook, NY 12571

Some format issues inherent in the e-media version may also appear in this print version.

Association for Computational Linguistics
209 N. Eighth Street
Stroudsburg, Pennsylvania 18360

Phone: 1-570-476-8006
Fax: 1-570-476-0860

acl@aclweb.org

Additional copies of this publication are available from:

Curran Associates, Inc.
57 Morehouse Lane
Red Hook, NY 12571 USA
Phone: 845-758-0400
Fax: 845-758-2633
Email: curran@proceedings.com
Web: www.proceedings.com

NAACL-HLT 2021

Multimodal Artificial Intelligence (MAI)

Proceedings of the Third Workshop

June 6, 2021

The NAACL 2021 Workshop on Multimodal Artificial Intelligence (MAI-Workshop) offers a unique opportunity for interdisciplinary researchers to study and model interactions between (but not limited to) modalities of language, vision, and acoustic. Advances in multimodal learning allows the field of NLP to take the leap towards better generalization to real-world (as opposed to limitation to textual applications), and better downstream performance in Conversational AI, Virtual Reality, Robotics, HCI, Healthcare, and Education. We invite researchers from NLP, Computer Vision, Speech Processing, Robotics, HCI, and Affective Computing to submit their papers.

- Neural Modeling of Multimodal Language
- Multimodal Dialogue Modeling and Generation
- Multimodal Sentiment Analysis and Emotion Recognition
- Language, Vision and Speech
- Multimodal Artificial Social Intelligence Modeling
- Multimodal Commonsense Reasoning
- Multimodal RL and Control (Human-robot communication and multimodal language for robots)
- Multimodal Healthcare
- Multimodal Educational Systems
- Multimodal Affective Computing
- Multimodal Fusion and Alignment
- Multimodal Representation Learning
- Multimodal Sequential Modeling
- Multimodal Co-learning and Transfer Learning
- Multimodal Active Learning
- Multimodal and Multimedia Resources
- Creative Applications of Multimodal Learning in E-commerce, Art, and other Impactful Areas.

Amir Zadeh – Language Technologies Institute, Carnegie Mellon University
Louis-Philippe Morency – Language Technologies Institute, Carnegie Mellon University
Paul Pu Liang – Machine Learning Department, Carnegie Mellon University
Candace Ross – Massachusetts Institute of Technology
Ruslan Salakhutdinov – Carnegie Mellon University
Soujanya Poria – Singapore University of Technology and Design
Erik Cambria – Nanyang Technological University
Kelly Shi – Carnegie Mellon University

Table of Contents

Conference Program

No Day Set (continued)

Multimodal Weighted Fusion of Transformers for Movie Genre Classification

Isaac Rodríguez-Bribiesca and **A. Pastor López-Monroy**
Mathematics Research Center (CIMAT)
GTO, Mexico
{isaac.bribiesca,pastor.lopez}@cimat.mx

Manuel Montes-y-Gómez
National Institue of Astrophysics, Optics and Electronics (INAOE)
Puebla, Mexico
mmontesg@inaoep.mx

Abstract

The Multimodal Transformer showed to be a competitive model for multimodal tasks involving textual, visual and audio signals. However, as more modalities are involved, its late fusion by concatenation starts to have a negative impact on the model's performance. Besides, interpreting model's predictions becomes difficult, as one would have to look at the different attention activation matrices. In order to overcome these shortcomings, we propose to perform late fusion by adding a GMU module, which effectively allows the model to weight modalities at instance level, improving its performance while providing a better interpretabilty mechanism. In the experiments, we compare our proposed model (MulT-GMU) against the original implementation (MulT-Concat) and a SOTA model tested in a movie genre classification dataset. Our approach, MulT-GMU, outperforms both, MulT-Concat and previous SOTA model.

1 Introduction

Information on the internet has grown exponentially. Much of this information is multimodal (e.g. images, text, videos, etc.). For example, in platforms like YouTube and Facebook, multiple modalities can be extracted like video frames, audio and captions on different languages. In this context, it becomes increasingly important to design new methods that are able to analyze and understand automatically these type of multimodal content. One popular scenario is the movie streaming service (e.g. Netflix, Prime Video, etc.), where there is also an increasing interest in performing automatic movie understanding. In this paper we take as a case study the task of movie genre prediction. Our proposal exploits movie trailer frames and audio, plot, poster and a variety of metadata information, via Deep Learning techniques that have enough flexibility to fuse and learn to weight from all these modalities in a simultaneous way.

The success of the Transformer architecture (Vaswani et al., 2017) and its variants in NLP, has also inspired researchers to propose and extend these architectures in multimodal settings. Some examples include ViLBERT (Lu et al., 2019), MulT (Tsai et al., 2019), VisualBERT (Li et al., 2019), UNITER (Chen et al., 2020), MMBT (Kiela et al., 2019) and LXMERT (Tan and Bansal, 2019). However, the vast majority of these multimodal architectures were designed and tested only on bimodal data, more specifically, on text and visual information. Besides, models that only allow for early fusion, have the disadvantage that they rely solely on this mechanism that hinders the interpretability. While in models that output a feature per modality, an additional late fusion mechanism can be implemented to further fuse modalities and learn a richer representation, which is the case for the MulT model. Nonetheless, late fusion in this model was originally performed by means of concatenation, diminishing its fusion capacity.

Contributions of this work are twofold: We first adapt the MulT model (Tsai et al., 2019) to support additional number of modalities. Then, we consider a mechanism that learns to fuse all the modalities dynamically before making the prediction over each particular instance. This is a crucial step, given that for movies belonging to different genres, the relevant modalities could be quite different. For example, in Animation movies, visual information might be more relevant given the visual style, while for Drama movies, sound may be more helpful because of loud noises and screams.

In order learn to fuse the final representation of each modality we propose to adapt the GMU module (Arevalo et al., 2019). These units are highly interpretable gates which decide how each modal-

Proceedings of the Third Workshop on Multimodal Artificial Intelligence, pages 1–5
June 6, 2021. ©2021 Association for Computational Linguistics

ity influences the layer output activation units, and therefore, decide how relevant each modality is in order to make the prediction. This is a crucial step, given that for this task, not all modalities are going to be equally relevant for each observation, as has been shown is previous work like (Mangolin et al., 2020) and (Cascante-Bonilla et al., 2019). Our evaluation shows that our MulT-GMU model, which uses weighted fusion by GMU, can outperform SOTA results in the movie genre classification task by 4%-10% on all metrics (μAP, mAP and sAP).

We explore for the first time the use of the MulT in the movie genre prediction task. We demonstrate that the original MulT model, which uses late fusion by concatenation (MulT-Concat) can achieve SOTA results task for this . Then, we show that further improvements can be achieved by our proposed model with the GMU module (MulT-GMU). The contributions can be summarized as follows:

- We introduce the use of the Multimodal Transformer architecture (MulT) to the task of movie genre prediction.
- We improve the MulT model by including a GMU module on the top, which allows to successfully fuse more modalities and improve its prediction performance.
- We show that the interpretability of the MulT model increases by incorporating the GMU module, allowing to better understand the relevance of each modality for each instance.

2 Approach

In Sections 2.1 and 2.2, we briefly describe the MulT architecture and then explain how to adapt the GMU units at the top of the model to perform a more robust late fusion of modalities.

2.1 Multimodal Transformer (MulT)

In (Tsai et al., 2019) the MulT model was proposed in the context of human multimodal language understanding, involving a mixture of natural language, facial gestures, and acoustic behaviors. Thus, it operates with three different modalities, Language (L), Video (V) and Audio (A).

Each modality is represented as a sequence of features $X_\alpha \in \mathbb{R}^{T_\alpha \times d_\alpha}$ with $\alpha \in \{L, V, A\}$ being the modality. $T_{(.)}$ and $d_{(.)}$ are used to represent sequence length and feature dimension, respectively. Sequences are fused by pairs through crossmodal attention modules. These modules take two input modalities, $\alpha, \beta \in \{L, V, A\}$, and their respective sequences, $X_\alpha \in \mathbb{R}^{T_\alpha \times d_\alpha}$ and $X_\beta \in \mathbb{R}^{T_\beta \times d_\beta}$. The crossmodal attention block will try to adapt latently the modality β into α. To achieve this, queries from one modality are combined with keys and values from the other modality. D crossmodal transformer layers are stacked to form a crossmodal transformer. Another crossmodal transformer is used to provide the latent adaptation of modality α into β. Yielding representations $Z_{\beta\rightarrow\alpha}$ and $Z_{\alpha\rightarrow\beta}$, respectively.

In the case of three modalities (L, V, A), six crossmodal transformers are needed in order to model all pair interactions. Interactions that share the same target modality are concatenated. For example, the final representation of Language will be $Z_L = [Z^{[D]}_{V\rightarrow L}, Z^{[D]}_{A\rightarrow L}] \in \mathbb{R}^{T_{\{L,V,A\}} \times 2d}$. Finally, each modality is passed through L transformer encoder layers, separately. The last element of each sequence is concatenated and passed through fully connected layers to make predictions.

2.2 MulT-GMU: Extending MulT through GMU-based late fusion

The MulT model expects the inputs to be sequences of features, but there could be modalities that are not sequences but a fixed vector (e.g. an image). A simple approach would be to concatenate them alongside the MulT outputs (Z_L, Z_V, Z_A) just before the fully connected layers. We argue that this is not optimal given that the fully connected layers will not be able to properly weight the relevance of each modality. In this work, we propose to adapt the MulT model by changing the concatenation fusion with a GMU module, as shown in Figure 1.

The GMU module receives a feature vector $x_i \in \mathbb{R}^{d_i}$ associated to modality i. Then the associated gate, $z_i \in \mathbb{R}^{shared}$, controls the contribution of that modality to the overall output of the GMU module. For this, the first step is to calculate an intermediate representation, $h_i = tanh(W_i x_i^T) \in \mathbb{R}^{shared}$ with $W_i \in \mathbb{R}^{shared \times d_i}$, where all modalities have the same dimension so they can be added and weighted by z_i. The next step is to calculate the gates $z_i = \sigma(W_{z_i}[x_i]_{i=1}^N) \in \mathbb{R}^{shared}$ where N is the number of modalities and $[x_i]_{i=1}^N$ means the concatenation of vectors from x_1 to x_n. Finally, given the gates $z_1, z_2, ..., z_N$ and hidden features $h_1, h_2, ..., h_N$, fusion is performed through $h = \sum_{i=1}^n z_i \odot h_i$, where $\odot$ represents component-wise vector multiplication. This operation allows the GMU module to have a global view of all modalities, whereas MulT only allows for early fusion by modality pairs.

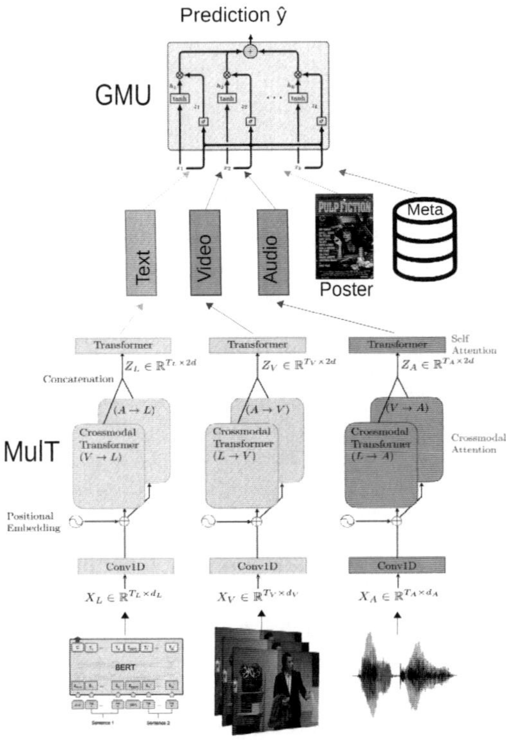

Figure 1: Proposed extension to the MulT architecture with a GMU module.

3 Evaluation

3.1 Datset

We base all of our experiments in the dataset Moviescope (Cascante-Bonilla et al., 2019). This is a large-scale datset comprising around 5,000 movies with corresponding movie trailers (video and audio), movie posters (images), movie plots (text), and metadata. The available data is already preprocessed. For the trailer video, we have 200 features vectors of size 4096, associated to 200 video frames subsampled by taking 1 every 10 frames. For the audio, log-mel scaled power spectrograms are provided. Poster images are provided in both, raw format and as a feature vector of size 4096. For the plot and metadata, raw data is provided. In the case of text, we use the pre-trained BERT-base model to extract features. For the metadata we follow (Cascante-Bonilla et al., 2019), extracting 13 different metadata values concatenated as a vector.

3.2 Experimental Framework

We compare three different models. The MulT model that works by concatenation of modalities (MulT-Concat), the extension of the MulT model with the GMU module (MulT-GMU), and the baseline model proposed in (Cascante-Bonilla et al., 2019), which is inspired by fastText (Joulin et al., 2017) to encode a sequence of features from text into a single vector, and a sequence of video features extracted from a pre-trained CNN also into single vector. The fusion of modalities is performed through a weighted regression, which could be considered as a form of modal attention. We refer to this model as Fast Modal Attention (Fast-MA).

In the case of the MulT-Concat and MulT-GMU, we show their mean performance over 5 runs with different random seeds. For the Fast-MA model we include the original results presented in (Cascante-Bonilla et al., 2019). The different modalities are denoted as V (Video), A (Audio), P (Poster), T (Text) and M (Metadata). The Fast-MA model was only tested in four of the presented settings (VA, VAP, TVAP and TVAPM). Furthermore, to investigate the impact of the GMU module we also include a more exhaustive list of experiments.

3.3 Results

We compared both baseline models, Fast-MA, MulT-Concat (late fusion by concatenation) with our proposed architecture MulT-GMU. Results on four different modality settings are shown in Table 1. They indicate that both MulT-Concat and MulT-GMU were able to outperform the state-of-the-art model Fast-MA when several modalities are considered. These results also show that Fast-MA outperformed both MulT-Concat and MulT-GMU in two of the modality settings, namely VA (Video and Audio) and VAP (Video, Audio and Poster). Note that these two settings are the only ones where Text (T) is not included, which confirms previous studies showing that for this task, text is the most relevant modality while audio is the least relevant (Mangolin et al. (2020), Cascante-Bonilla et al. (2019)). This explains in part, the low performance of the MulT models in these two settings. Once text is included, performance in MulT models increases dramatically. For example, from Table 2, we show that either bimodal MulT model that included text (TV or TA) already outperformed the best Fast-MA model (TVAPM).

Once we show the outstanding performance of

both MulT models, in Table 2 we further compare them on more modality settings. We can see that MulT-GMU outperforms MulT-Concat in almost all the settings except in TV (Text and Video). For example, from experimental settings TVPM and TVAPM, we can observe that MulT-Concat has difficulty handling the Metadata features, dropping quite considerably the performance. In contrast, MulT-GMU is able to handle these features and maintain or even increase its performance.

Modality	Model	μAP	mAP	sAP
VA	Fast-MA	**70.3**	**61.5**	**78.8**
	MulT-Concat	59.2±0.3	53.1±0.5	71.1±0.7
	MulT-GMU	58.9±0.7	52.5±0.6	70.6±0.6
VAP	Fast-MA	**70.4**	**61.7**	**78.8**
	MulT-Concat	63.1±0.5	54.3±0.5	73.9±0.5
	MulT-GMU	64.1±0.9	55.0±0.7	74.5±0.5
TVAP	Fast-MA	74.9	67.5	82.3
	MulT-Concat	78.9±0.3	75.7±0.5	85.6±0.3
	MulT-GMU	**79.8±0.4**	**76.0±0.9**	**86.1±0.4**
TVAPM	Fast-MA	75.3	68.6	82.5
	MulT-Concat	64.8±5.8	61.3±7.2	76.9±4
	MulT-GMU	**79.5±0.5**	**76.4±0.3**	**85.6±0.3**

Table 1: Comparison against MulT-Concat (Tsai et al., 2019) and Fast-MA (Cascante-Bonilla et al., 2019) on different modality combinations. Metrics reported correspond to average precision, micro (μAP), macro (mAP) and sample (sAP) averaged.

Modality	Model	μAP	mAP	sAP
TV	MulT-Concat	**77.5±0.5**	**73.5±0.2**	**84.4±0.2**
	MulT-GMU	76.9±0.3	73.2±0.2	84.2±0.4
TA	MulT-Concat	76.2±0.7	**72.4±0.8**	84±0.5
	MulT-GMU	**76.3±0.4**	71.1±0.4	**84.1±0.2**
TVA	MulT-Concat	77.2±0.7	74.8±0.4	84.2±0.5
	MulT-GMU	**78.2±0.5**	**74.9±0.5**	**85±0.3**
TVP	MulT-Concat	78.4±0.5	75.1±0.4	85.1±0.5
	MulT-GMU	**78.9±0.1**	**75.2±0.4**	**85.7±0.3**
TVPM	MulT-Concat	46.1±11	43.2±10.7	62.8±8.8
	MulT-GMU	**79.1±0.3**	**75.4±0.2**	**85.4±0.4**

Table 2: Comparison of the proposed model MulT-GMU and MulT-Concat (Tsai et al., 2019) with additional modality combinations. Metrics reported correspond to average precision, micro (μAP), macro (mAP) and sample (sAP) averaged.

4 Qualitative analysis

To understand how the GMU units are weighting the relevance of each modality according to each instance (movie) i, we inspected the gates z_i of the GMU module for all the observations in the test set. To achieve this, we selected the observations that contained each of the genres and averaged the gate activations per modality. We show results for 5 different movie genres in Figure 2, where each row already takes into account the average of all test movies of the corresponding genre.

In general, text and visual modalities were the most relevant according to the GMU module. We can see relatively low activations for the audio modality compared with the other ones. This is expected as it has been shown that audio modality is not as useful as the other ones, for this task (Mangolin et al. (2020), Cascante-Bonilla et al. (2019)). There is also a relationship between audio and video signals. In genres where video is the strongest, audio is the weakest.

Taking the Audio modality as an example, where Horror and Drama had the highest GMU activations overall, we could think that this was the case given that this kind of movies usually have loud noises like screams in the trailers, so this could be a good indicator that the movie is likely to belong to one of these two genres. There are other interesting scenarios, for example the text modality had the highest activation for genres like Comedy and Drama. In the case of the video modality, Comedy and Family genres had the highest activation.

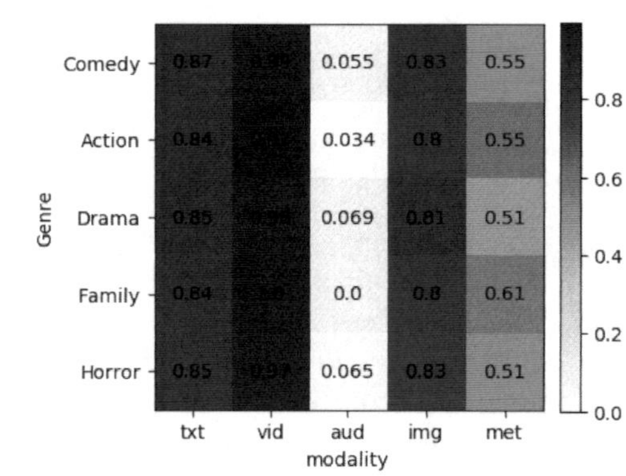

Figure 2: Average proportion of GMU unit activations normalized by genre for all the observations in test set. We only show the activations for 5 movie genres.

5 Conclusion

We proposed an adapted version of the Multimodal Transformer, MulT-GMU, by performing weighted late fusion with a GMU module. This approach achieved SOTA results in the multimodal movie genre classification task. Moreover, we improved the interpretability of the MulT model by performing a qualitative analysis, visualizing the activations of the GMU module, which allowed us to have a better understanding about relevant modalities for the model, depending on the genre of the movie. To the best of our knowledge, this is the first time multimodal transformer-based architectures are tested in the task of movie genre classification.

Acknowledgements

The authors thank CONACYT, INAOE and CIMAT for the computer resources provided through the INAOE Supercomputing Laboratory's Deep Learning Platform for Language Technologies and CIMAT Bajio Supercomputing Laboratory (#300832). Rodríguez-Bribiesca would like to thank CONACYT for its support through scholarship #952419.

References

John Arevalo, Thamar Solorio, Manuel Montes-y Gómez, and Fabio A. González. 2019. Gated multimodal networks. *Neural Computing and Applications*, 32(14):10209–10228.

Paola Cascante-Bonilla, Kalpathy Sitaraman, Mengjia Luo, and Vicente Ordonez. 2019. Moviescope: Large-scale Analysis of Movies using Multiple Modalities.

Yen-Chun Chen, Linjie Li, Licheng Yu, Ahmed El Kholy, Faisal Ahmed, Zhe Gan, Yu Cheng, and Jingjing Liu. 2020. UNITER: UNiversal Image-TExt Representation Learning.

Armand Joulin, Edouard Grave, Piotr Bojanowski, and Tomas Mikolov. 2017. Bag of tricks for efficient text classification. In *Proceedings of the 15th Conference of the European Chapter of the Association for Computational Linguistics: Volume 2, Short Papers*, pages 427–431. Association for Computational Linguistics.

Douwe Kiela, Suvrat Bhooshan, Hamed Firooz, and Davide Testuggine. 2019. Supervised Multimodal Bitransformers for Classifying Images and Text.

Liunian Harold Li, Mark Yatskar, Da Yin, Cho-Jui Hsieh, and Kai-Wei Chang. 2019. VisualBERT: A Simple and Performant Baseline for Vision and Language. (2):1–14.

Jiasen Lu, Dhruv Batra, Devi Parikh, and Stefan Lee. 2019. ViLBERT: Pretraining Task-Agnostic Visiolinguistic Representations for Vision-and-Language Tasks. pages 1–11.

Rafael B. Mangolin, Rodolfo M. Pereira, Alceu S. Britto, Carlos N. Silla, Valéria D. Feltrim, Diego Bertolini, and Yandre M. G. Costa. 2020. A multimodal approach for multi-label movie genre classification. pages 1–21.

Hao Tan and Mohit Bansal. 2019. LXMert: Learning cross-modality encoder representations from transformers. *EMNLP-IJCNLP 2019 - 2019 Conference on Empirical Methods in Natural Language Processing and 9th International Joint Conference on Natural Language Processing, Proceedings of the Conference*, pages 5100–5111.

Yao Hung Hubert Tsai, Shaojie Bai, Paul Pu Liang, J. Zico Kolter, Louis Philippe Morency, and Ruslan Salakhutdinov. 2019. Multimodal transformer for unaligned multimodal language sequences. *ACL 2019 - 57th Annual Meeting of the Association for Computational Linguistics, Proceedings of the Conference*, pages 6558–6569.

Ashish Vaswani, Noam Shazeer, Niki Parmar, Jakob Uszkoreit, Llion Jones, Aidan N. Gomez, Lukasz Kaiser, and Illia Polosukhin. 2017. Attention is all you need. *CoRR*, abs/1706.03762.

On Randomized Classification Layers and Their Implications in Natural Language Generation

Gal-Lev Shalev Bar-Ilan University, Israel gallev898@gmail.com

Gabi Shalev Bar-Ilan University, Israel shalev.gabi@gmail.com

Joseph Keshet Bar-Ilan University, Israel jkeshet@cs.biu.ac.il

Abstract

In natural language generation tasks, a neural language model is used for generating a sequence of words forming a sentence. The topmost weight matrix of the language model, known as the classification layer, can be viewed as a set of vectors, each representing a target word from the target dictionary. The target word vectors, along with the rest of the model parameters, are learned and updated during training.

In this paper, we analyze the properties encoded in the target vectors and question the necessity of learning these vectors. We suggest to randomly draw the target vectors and set them as fixed so that no weights updates are being made during training. We show that by excluding the vectors from the optimization, the number of parameters drastically decreases with a marginal effect on the performance. We demonstrate the effectiveness of our method in image-captioning and machine-translation.

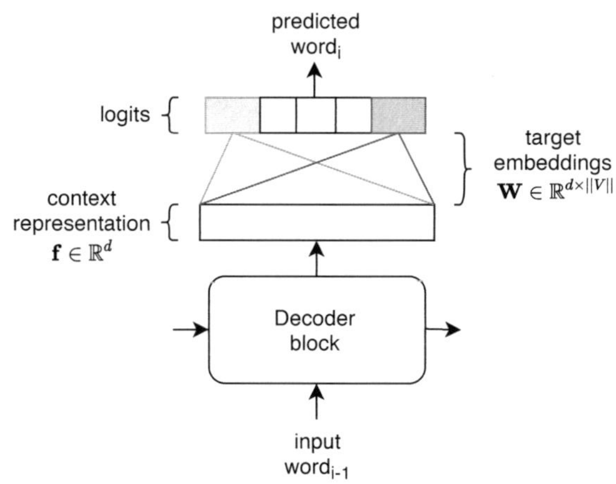

Figure 1: Scheme of a decoding step for predicting the i-th word. The colored boxes and edges represent the logits of two different target words and their corresponding embedding vectors, respectively.

1 Introduction

Deep neural networks enabled breakthroughs in natural language generation tasks such as machine-translation (Zhang and Zong, 2015), image captioning (Hossain et al., 2019), and more. Generating the text is done by employing a conditional language model as the decoder component, responsible for predicting the next word at each step during decoding, as depicted in Fig-1. For predicting the next word, the language model first encodes into a vector $f \in \mathbb{R}^d$, denoted as *context representation*, both the previously predicted words, and the task's related input (such as source sentence in machine-translation or input image in image-captioning). Then, at the classification layer, the context representation is projected onto a set of weight vectors, resulting in a vector termed as *logits vector*. Afterward, a softmax function is applied to output a distribution over the target vocabulary words. The set of weight vectors used for producing the logits, denoted here as matrix $W \in \mathbb{R}^{d\times|V|}$, where V is the target vocabulary. Matrix W can be viewed as $|V|$ vectors, where each is a d-dimensional vector representing a specific word from the target vocabulary, we term these vectors through the paper as *target word embeddings* and *target vectors*, interchangeably. The target embeddings, along with the rest of the model parameters, are estimated so as to minimize the loss function.

During training, an additional set of $|V|$ vectors are being learned to represent the previously predicted words when given to the decoding step. These vectors are referred as *input word embeddings*. Learning the input embeddings during training was shown to improve the performance of NLP classifers and allows achieving a level of generalization that is not possible with classical n-gram language models (Mikolov et al., 2013). Their main advantages are capturing the relationship between words and allowing similar words to have embedding vectors close in space. While a large amount

Proceedings of the Third Workshop on Multimodal Artificial Intelligence, pages 6–11
June 6, 2021.

of work has done to understand the properties and demonstrate the effectiveness of learning the input word embeddings, the benefits of learning the target word embeddings remain unexplored.

In this paper, we show that by randomly drawing the target word embeddings and excluding them from training, the number of trained parameters are drastically decreased with a marginal effect on the performance. By this, we show that the properties captured in the target word embeddings, such as word frequencies and relationships, are surprisingly redundant and may be ignored in low resource environments.

2 Background, Notations and Definitions

Consider a NLG task, such as machine-translation or image-captioning, where for a given input instance x_i, a corresponding sentence S_i should be generated. Typically, an encoder-decoder based neural network is trained for solving the task. The encoder is responsible for encoding the input instance into a vector, while the decoder responsible for generating the next word given the input vector and previously generated words. Commonly, an attention mechanism is incorporated during the decoding (Bahdanau et al., 2014; Xu et al., 2015).

Denote by $D_{train} = \{(x_i, S_i)\}_{i=1}^{N}$ a training dataset where x_i is the input to the model, S_i is the corresponding sentence, and N is the number of training examples. Training the model is done by maximizing the following objective function:

$$\underset{w_1,\ldots,w_{|V|},\theta}{\text{argmax}} \sum_{(x_i,S_i)\in D_{train}} \log P(S_i|x_i) \ ,$$

where θ and $w_1, ..., w_{|V|}$ are the learnable parameters of the model. Since S_i composed of a sequence of words $s_{i1}, ..., s_{ij}$, where j is the length of S_i, a chain rule is applied to model the joint probability over the sentence words as follows:

$$\log P(S_i|x_i) = \sum_{z=1}^{j} \log P(s_{iz}|x_i, s_{i1}, ..., s_{iz-1}) \ .$$

For generating the next word, a context vector $f_\theta \in \mathbb{R}^d$ is learned and is responsible for encoding the given input along with the previously predicted words. Then, the context vector is projected onto each of the target word vectors $w_j \in \mathbb{R}^d$ where $j = 1, ..., |V|$, by calculating the dot-product between the vectors. Afterward, a bias term $b \in \mathbb{R}^{|V|}$ is added, and a softmax function is applied, resulting in a distribution over the target words. Formally:

$$P(s_{iz}|x_i, s_{i1}, ..., s_{iz-1}) = softmax(W \cdot f_\theta + b)$$

Since $w_j \cdot f_\theta = ||w_j|| \cdot ||f_\theta|| \cdot \cos(\alpha_{w_j,f_\theta})$, where α_{w_j,f_θ} is the angle between the vectors, the predicted probability of the word s_j can be written as:

$$\frac{e^{||w_j||\cdot||f_\theta||\cdot\cos(\alpha_{w_j,f_\theta})+b_j}}{\sum_{m=1}^{|V|} e^{||w_m||\cdot||f_\theta||\cdot\cos(\alpha_{w_m,f_\theta})+b_m}} \quad (1)$$

Notice that both the angles and magnitudes of the target word vectors are influencing the predicted probability in Eq-1. The cosine of the angle between w_j and f_θ measures how well the word s_j fits into the context. Hence, interchangeable words have their corresponding target vectors directed at the same angle. The magnitudes of the target vectors control on the predicted probability, in a way that they have a stronger effect on words whose embeddings have direction similar to f_θ, and less effect or even a negative effect on words in other directions. Consider a case where the cosine of the angle between w_j and f_θ is close to 1, meaning that the angle between them is close to 0. In this case, increasing the magnitude $||w_j||$ would result in an increased probability for the word s_j. However, when w_j is directed in an opposite direction to f, the cosine of the angle between them would be close to -1, and therefore, increasing the magnitude would result in a lower probability. By fixing the target vectors and the bias term, the model can maximize the probability in Eq-1 **only by optimizing the vector** f_θ.

In recent work, Press and Wolf (2016) proposed tying the target and input embeddings by using the same vectors to represent both. The paper showed that the performance of weight tied models are on par with learning two separate vectors in machine-translation. However, the method forces the target vectors to have the same dimension as the input embeddings and adds additional computational costs. More recently, several works (Shalev et al., 2020; Hoffer et al., 2018; Shalev et al., 2018) explored the effects of fixing the classification layer in image classification models and demonstrated that the accuracy, number of parameters and out-of-distribution detection ability improve.

In this paper, we empirically show that randomly drawn, fixed target word embeddings allow models to achieve high performance in natural language generation tasks. From an efficiency perspective,

Model	B4	B3	VU	R-L	ME
Tell	27.28	36.59	721	49.72	23.09
Tell-Tied	27.11	36.23	699	49.21	22.83
Tell-Fixed	27.01	36.08	1378	49.34	22.99
Attend	29.12	38.51	784	50.91	24.02
Attend-Tied	29.01	38.11	773	50.76	23.90
Attend-Fixed	28.75	37.93	1026	50.96	23.91

Table 1: Image-captioning evaluation results. B3-4 refer to BLEU3-4. R-L refers to ROUGE-L. ME refers to METEOR. VU refers to vocabulary usage.

Dataset	Translation	Non-Fixed	Tied	Fixed
Multi30k	DE-EN	33.02	33.08	33.17
	EN-DE	31.63	31.49	32.12
IWSLT 2014	DE-EN	28.77	28.94	29.03
	EN-DE	25.48	25.66	25.97
WMT-14	EN-DE	25.84	25.62	25.49

Table 2: BLEU4 results for machine-translation.

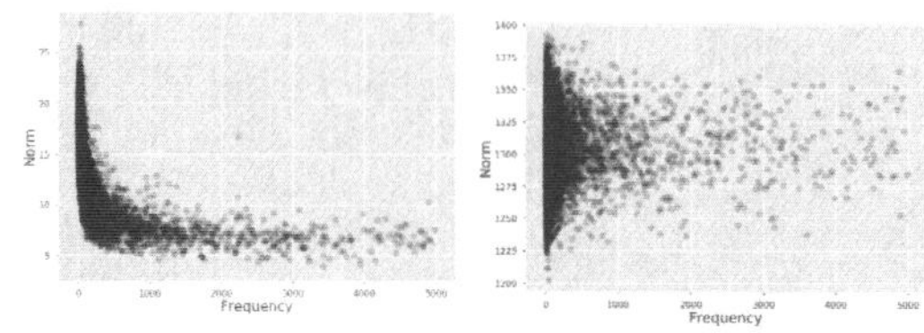

Figure 2: Left is the magnitude of the target vectors learned by *tell* model versus the corresponding word frequencies. Right is the magnitude of the randomly drawn vectors of the fixed *tell* model versus the word frequencies.

fixing these vectors decrease the number of parameters in the classification layer by $d \cdot |V|$. Since the target vocabulary typically contains thousands of words, and the dimension of the context vector f_θ is in hundreds or thousands, the reduction in parameters is significant.

3 Experiments

In this section, we present our experimental results. We evaluate our approach on image-captioning and machine-translation tasks. We start by describing the experimental setup; then, we present the results and analyze the target embeddings.

3.1 Experimental Setup

Image-captioning: For evaluating our approach in image-captioning, we implemented LSTM-based sentence generator as described in (Vinyals et al., 2015), denoted as *tell*. We also implemented an attention-based model as described in (Xu et al., 2015), denoted as *attend*. Additionally, we created identical models where the target embedding vectors are tied (*tell-tied* and *attend-tied*) and also the same models with randomly drawn target vectors without being updated during training (*tell-fixed* and *attend-fixed*). For the fixed target embeddings models, we randomly draw per each cell in the vectors a number in the range of [-10,10]. We evaluated the models on MSCOCO dataset (Lin et al., 2014) and used the standard, publicly available splits, as in previous work (Karpathy and Fei-Fei, 2015). For all models, we set a pre-trained Resnet-101 (He et al., 2016) as the image encoder, provided by the TorchVision package. Due to space limitations, we describe the training procedure in the appendix.

Machine-translation: For evaluating our approach in machine-translation, we used MultiK30 (Elliott et al., 2016), IWSLT 2014 (Cettolo et al., 2014) and WMT-14 datasets. For MultiK30 and IWSLT 2014 sets, we trained an attention-based encoder-decoder model, as described in (Bahdanau et al., 2014). We evaluated the models on English-German and German-English translations. For the WMT-14 EN-DE set we trained a convolutional sequence to sequence model as described in (Gehring et al., 2017). Additionally, we trained the same models with randomly drawn, fixed target vectors, and also with tied-embeddings. The training procedure described in detail in the appendix. We found that translation models with fixed target vectors perform best when the magnitude of the vectors is small, thus we normalized the vectors by dividing them with their L_2 norm.

3.2 Results

The results for image-captioning and machine-translation are shown in Table-1 and Table-2, respectively. Results suggest that our method of randomly drawing the target embeddings and fixing them during training allows the models to achieve high results in both tasks.

Next, we analyze the learned target word vectors. We find that the word frequencies are reflected in the magnitude of these vectors. As can be seen in Fig-2, target vectors with large magnitude are representing less frequent words. We measured the spearman's rank correlation coefficient between the magnitude of the target vectors ,$||w_j||$, and the number of appearances of the corresponding word s_j in the training set. We obtain a strong correlation between the two in all settings. In image-captioning, we obtain a correlation of 0.79 and 0.77 when considering the target vectors of *tell* and *attend*, respectively. In machine-translation, for Multi30K DE-EN and EN-DE, we obtain a correlation of 0.84 and 0.93, respectively. For IWSLT DE-EN and EN-DE, we find a correlation of 0.76 and 0.83, respectively. For WMT-14 EN-DE we find a correlation 0f 0.81.

In addition, we observe that the target vectors are able to capture word relationships. Recently, (Press and Wolf, 2016) showed that the target and input vectors of word2vec skip-gram are correlated similarly with human judgments of the strength of relationships between concepts. We followed the same experiment, and found that the target vectors correlate better with the human judgements than the input vectors in 3 out of the 4 tested models. Due to space limitations, results are shown in the appendix.

Interestingly, we noticed that the image-captioning models with fixed target embeddings had an increased vocabulary usage rate (see Table-1) and generated low-frequency words more often compared to the equivalent non-fixed models. In Fig-3, we demonstrate two images for which the non-fixed *tell* model generated the frequent word *bird* (appearing in 5135 training sentences), while the fixed model generated the words *seagull* (appearing in 201 training sentences) and *duck* (appearing in 263 training sentences). More examples can be seen in the appendix. We suspect that the increased usage of low-frequency words might be due to the randomization of the target vectors, which forces **visually similar concepts to have their target vectors far in space**. As a result, the model is encouraged to find a more discriminative representations to distinguish between the concepts. Recall that the cosine-similarity between f_θ and w_j measures how well word s_j fits into the context. If w_j and w_i represent concepts s_j and s_i which are **visually** close but the vectors are far in space, the model would have to find better representations for f_θ to determine whether it should be close in angle to w_j or w_i, as f_θ is the only term that can be optimized in Eq-1 when the target vectors are fixed. In the example above, the non-fixed *tell* model placed the vectors representing the concepts close in space. The cosine-similarity between w_{duck} and w_{bird} is 0.82, and is 0.81 between $w_{seagull}$ and w_{bird}. In contrast, the cosine-similarity between the equivalent target vectors in the fixed models are roughly 0 due to the randomization.

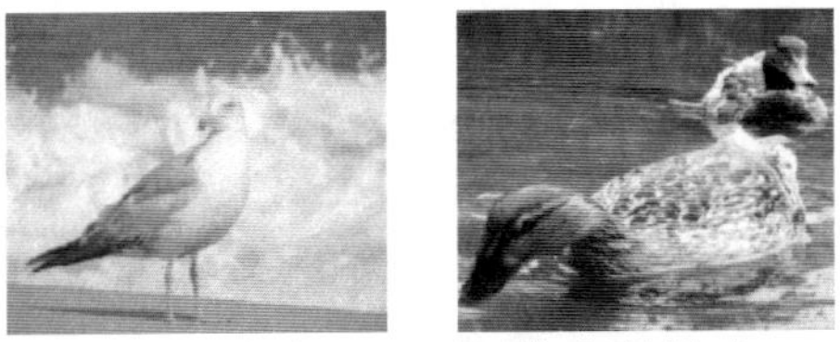

Non-Fixed: a bird that is flying over the water

Fixed: a seagull is standing in the sand on a beach

Non-Fixed: a bird that is standing in the water

Fixed: a duck swims through the body of water

Figure 3: Captions generated by fixed and non-fixed *tell* models.

Model	Non-Fixed	Fixed	%
Tell	18,001,171	13,142,291	27%
Attend	25,342,739	20,483,859	19%
Multi30K DE-EN	13,893,381	10,870,272	22%
Multi30K EN-DE	14,898,861	10,870,272	28%
IWSLT DE-EN	20,237,792	14,307,512	30%
IWSLT EN-DE	21,158,627	14,307,512	33%
WMT-14 EN-DE	36,267,832	28,043,832	21%

Table 3: The number of learnable parameters in each model with the relative decrease percentage.

3.3 Parameters and Computation Efficiency

Recall that the classification layers contains $d \cdot |V|$ parameters, where V is the target vocabulary and d is the dimension of the context vector f_θ. Table-3 demonstrates the significant reduction in the number of learnable parameters. Our method also results in improved computational efficiency compared to the tied-embeddings method (Press and Wolf, 2016). When using tied-embedding, the target vectors are the same as the input vectors, and therefor their dimensions are equal. As a result, the context vector, f_θ, should also be adjusted to have the same dimension as the input and target vectors. In contrast, our proposed method allows to set low dimensional representations, which results in increased computational efficiency at inference. Additionally, the fixed target vectors can be initialized with sparse vectors which can result in memory efficiency. An example is the Hadmard matrix, used by (Hoffer et al., 2018) as the last fully connected layer in image classification models.

3.4 Conclusions and Future Work

In this paper, we demonstrated that by randomly drawing the target embeddings, and setting them as fixed during training, the number of learnable parameters is significantly decreased while allowing to achieve high performance in machine-translation and image-captioning.

References

Dzmitry Bahdanau, Kyunghyun Cho, and Yoshua Bengio. 2014. Neural machine translation by jointly learning to align and translate. *arXiv preprint arXiv:1409.0473*.

Mauro Cettolo, Jan Niehues, Sebastian Stüker, Luisa Bentivogli, and Marcello Federico. 2014. Report on the 11th iwslt evaluation campaign, iwslt 2014. In *Proceedings of the International Workshop on Spoken Language Translation, Hanoi, Vietnam*, volume 57.

Bo Dai, Sanja Fidler, Raquel Urtasun, and Dahua Lin. 2017. Towards diverse and natural image descriptions via a conditional gan. In *Proceedings of the IEEE International Conference on Computer Vision*, pages 2970–2979.

Desmond Elliott, Stella Frank, Khalil Sima'an, and Lucia Specia. 2016. Multi30k: Multilingual english-german image descriptions. *arXiv preprint arXiv:1605.00459*.

Jonas Gehring, Michael Auli, David Grangier, Denis Yarats, and Yann N Dauphin. 2017. Convolutional sequence to sequence learning. In *International Conference on Machine Learning*, pages 1243–1252. PMLR.

Kaiming He, Xiangyu Zhang, Shaoqing Ren, and Jian Sun. 2016. Deep residual learning for image recognition. In *Proceedings of the IEEE conference on computer vision and pattern recognition*, pages 770–778.

Elad Hoffer, Itay Hubara, and Daniel Soudry. 2018. Fix your classifier: the marginal value of training the last weight layer. *arXiv preprint arXiv:1801.04540*.

MD Zakir Hossain, Ferdous Sohel, Mohd Fairuz Shiratuddin, and Hamid Laga. 2019. A comprehensive survey of deep learning for image captioning. *ACM Computing Surveys (CSUR)*, 51(6):1–36.

Andrej Karpathy and Li Fei-Fei. 2015. Deep visual-semantic alignments for generating image descriptions. In *Proceedings of the IEEE conference on computer vision and pattern recognition*, pages 3128–3137.

Tsung-Yi Lin, Michael Maire, Serge Belongie, James Hays, Pietro Perona, Deva Ramanan, Piotr Dollár, and C Lawrence Zitnick. 2014. Microsoft coco: Common objects in context. In *European conference on computer vision*, pages 740–755. Springer.

Tomáš Mikolov, Wen-tau Yih, and Geoffrey Zweig. 2013. Linguistic regularities in continuous space word representations. In *Proceedings of the 2013 conference of the north american chapter of the association for computational linguistics: Human language technologies*, pages 746–751.

Ofir Press and Lior Wolf. 2016. Using the output embedding to improve language models. *arXiv preprint arXiv:1608.05859*.

Gil Sadeh, Lior Fritz, Gabi Shalev, and Eduard Oks. 2019. Generating diverse and informative natural language fashion feedback. *arXiv preprint arXiv:1906.06619*.

Gabi Shalev, Yossi Adi, and Joseph Keshet. 2018. Out-of-distribution detection using multiple semantic label representations. *arXiv preprint arXiv:1808.06664*.

Gabi Shalev, Gal-Lev Shalev, and Joseph Keshet. 2020. Redesigning the classification layer by randomizing the class representation vectors. *arXiv preprint arXiv:2011.08704*.

Rakshith Shetty, Marcus Rohrbach, Lisa Anne Hendricks, Mario Fritz, and Bernt Schiele. 2017. Speaking the same language: Matching machine to human captions by adversarial training. In *Proceedings of the IEEE International Conference on Computer Vision*, pages 4135–4144.

Oriol Vinyals, Alexander Toshev, Samy Bengio, and Dumitru Erhan. 2015. Show and tell: A neural image caption generator. In *Proceedings of the IEEE conference on computer vision and pattern recognition*, pages 3156–3164.

Kelvin Xu, Jimmy Ba, Ryan Kiros, Kyunghyun Cho, Aaron Courville, Ruslan Salakhudinov, Rich Zemel, and Yoshua Bengio. 2015. Show, attend and tell: Neural image caption generation with visual attention. In *International conference on machine learning*, pages 2048–2057.

J. Zhang and C. Zong. 2015. Deep neural networks in machine translation: An overview. *IEEE Intelligent Systems*, 30(5):16–25.

4 Appendix

4.1 Training procedures

Image-captioning Training descriptions were preprocessed with basic tokenization, keeping all words that appeared at least 5 times in the training set. Words appearing less are map into *UNK* symbol. For training the models, we use Adam optimizer and set the initial learning rate to 0.0004. We multiply the learning rate by 0.8 for every 8 epochs without improvement in the BLEU score. Training is ended once the model achieves 20 epochs without improvement in the BLEU score. The batch size is set to 32 instances. At training, we apply *teacher-forcing* by feeding at each time step the ground-truth word. During decoding, we use beam-search as the decoding strategy, with a beam size of 10.

Machine-translation Training procedure for MultiK30 dataset is as follows: the training sentences were preprocessed with basic tokenization, keeping all words that appeared at least 2 times in the training set. Words appearing less are map into *UNK* symbol. For training the models, we use Adam optimizer and set the initial learning rate to 0.001. We multiply by 0.8 the learning rate for every 8 epochs without improvement in the BLEU score. Training is ended once the model achieves 20 epochs without improvement in the BLEU score. The batch size is set to 128 instances. At training, we apply *teacher-forcing* by feeding at each time step the ground-truth word.

For training the models on IWSLT we use the same procedure as in MultiK30 with the following modifications: We keep words that appeared at least 5 times in the training set, and filter data to have sentences with max length of 20. The initial learning rate is set to 0.002 and multiplied by 0.25 for every 8 epochs without improvement in the BLEU score. The batch size is set to 64 instances.

4.2 Word Relationships

For evaluating the quality of the non-fixed target vectors in both image-captioning and machine-translation, we follow the evaluation proposed in the *tied embeddings* paper. We calculate the pairwise (cosine) distances between embeddings and correlate these distances with human judgments of the strength of relationships between concepts. Results are shown in Table-4.

Model	Simlex999	MEN	MTurk-771
tell	**0.30**/0.24	0.26/**0.46**	0.20/**0.34**
attend	**0.38**/0.26	**0.49**/0.45	**0.40**/0.32
IWSLT DE-EN	0.07/0.07	**0.16**/0.07	**0.14**/0.11
MultiK30 DE-EN	**0.19**/0.04	**0.36**/0.01	**0.31**/0.06

Table 4: Spearman's correlation between word vectors and human judgments of the strength of relationships between concepts. The correlation of the target vector are in the left column. The correlation of the input vectors are in the right column.

4.3 Diversity

Despite the substantial progress in recent years, sentences produced by existing image captioning methods are still often overly rigid and lacking in variability. Several works (Shetty et al., 2017; Dai et al., 2017; Sadeh et al., 2019) address these issues with an alternative training and inference methods to generate more natural and diverse image descriptions. In Fig-4 we show how simple technique such as fixing the classification layer, which does not require any additional computational cost, might improve the diversity and accuracy of the generated captions.

Figure 4: Examples of captions generated by *tell* and *attend* models. NF and F refer to models with non-fixed and fixed target embeddings, respectively. Low-frequency words are underscored.

COIN: Conversational Interactive Networks for Emotion Recognition in Conversation

Haidong Zhang* and **Yekun Chai***
Institute of Automation, Chinese Academy of Sciences
haidong_zhang14@yahoo.com chaiyekun@gmail.com

Abstract

Emotion recognition in conversation has received considerable attention recently because of its practical industrial applications. Existing methods tend to overlook the immediate mutual interaction between different speakers in the speaker-utterance level, or apply single speaker-agnostic RNN for utterances from different speakers. We propose *COIN*, a conversational interactive model to mitigate this problem by applying state mutual interaction within history contexts. In addition, we introduce a stacked global interaction module to capture the contextual and inter-dependency representation in a hierarchical manner. To improve the robustness and generalization during training, we generate adversarial examples by applying the minor perturbations on multimodal feature inputs, unveiling the benefits of adversarial examples for emotion detection. The proposed model empirically achieves the current state-of-the-art results on the IEMOCAP benchmark dataset.

1 Introduction

Emotion recognition in conversation (ERC) has attracted extensive interests due to the prevalence of user-generated contents on social media platforms, such as conversational messages and videos (Poria et al., 2017; Hazarika et al., 2018b; Poria et al., 2019; Hazarika et al., 2021), which aims to detect the speaker's emotions and sentiments within the context of human conversations. Recent works on ERC adopted recurrent neural networks (RNNs) to firstly learn the sequential utterances in conversations and then leveraged high-level context extractor, such as CMN (Hazarika et al., 2018b), DialogueRNN (Majumder et al., 2019), DialogueGCN (Ghosal et al., 2019), to capture the global contextual representation for emotion detection.

This two-step scheme has proven to be effective to achieve success in ERC and can be divided into two categories: one is modeling each speaker with one RNN, such as (Hazarika et al., 2018b; Majumder et al., 2019); the other is speaker-agnostic, *i.e.*, modeling each utterance using one RNN irrespective of its speaker, such as (Poria et al., 2017; Majumder et al., 2019). However, there is no direct dyadic interaction between speaker-specific RNNs in previous work. Different RNNs corresponding to different speakers have been used without mutual interaction (Hazarika et al., 2018b) or interacting through a mediate global RNN (Majumder et al., 2019).

In this paper, the proposed **Co**nversational **I**nteractive **N**etworks (COIN) employs immediate coupling interaction at each state of different speakers and adopts a global extractor to capture the contextual and self-dependency representation for emotion classifier. To enhance the generalization and robustness of our model, we generate adversarial examples by applying minor perturbations on multi-modal embeddings for adversarial training (AT) (Goodfellow et al., 2014).

Our work illustrates that dyadic interaction advances the performance of multimodal emotion recognition in conversation by incorporating mutual interaction and applying adversarial training. Our key contributions are in threefold:

- We introduce state mutual interaction components to allow for the immediate state interaction between different speakers, and global stacked interaction to capture the contextual and inter-dependency representations.
- We unveil the importance of adversarial training in ERC by promoting the model performance with generated adversarial examples on extracted multimodal embeddings.
- We propose a competing model that achieves the state-of-the-art (SOTA) performance on the IEMOCAP dataset, showing that textual

*Equal contribution

Proceedings of the Third Workshop on Multimodal Artificial Intelligence, pages 12–18
June 6, 2021.

and audio features play the most important role in ERC.

2 Methodology

This section is orgnized as follows: Sec. 2.1 describes the definition of ERC task; Sec. 2.2 introduces the approach to extracting multimodal features; Sec. 2.3 gives a detailed description of the proposed model.

2.1 Task Definition

Let there be M parties or speakers $\{p_1, p_2, \cdots, p_M\}$ in a human conversation ($M = 2$ in our experiments). Given the utterances $\{u_1, u_2, \cdots, u_N\}$ from a conversation where the utterance u_t is from the corresponding speaker $p_{s(u_t)}$, the task of ERC is to detect the most likely class from emotion category set $\mathcal{C}$. Here s represents the mapping between the utterances and users.

2.2 Multimodal Feature Extraction

We extract multimodal features using the same setting as (Majumder et al., 2019) for a fair comparison. Multimodal features are simply concatenated along the feature dimension in our systems.

Textual Feature We employ multi-channel 1-D convolutional neural networks (CNNs) along the sequential dimension to extract n-gram lexical features with kernel sizes of $\{3, 4, 5\}$. Then a global max-pooling layer followed by a linear projection produces the utterance representation. This CNN is trained on emotion classification at the sentence level.

Acoustic Feature We use openSMILE (Eyben et al., 2010) toolkit[§] to extract speech features such as Mel-frequency cepstral coefficients (39 features) and pitch. Z-standardization is applied to normalize the low dimensional feature vectors.

Visual Feature 3D-CNN (Tran et al., 2015) is leveraged to obtain visual features from dialogue videos, followed by a ReLU and max-pooling operation.

2.3 Model Architecture

Fig. 1 illustrates the overview of proposed *COIN* architecture with the history length of $K = 6$. The multimodal inputs of utterances are firstly fed into feature extractor to obtain the multimodal features. Then we adopt Gated Recurrent Units (GRUs) (Chung et al., 2014) to capture the history dialogue of dyadic speakers A/B, followed by the mutual interaction for each state at utterance level. Afterward, the concatenated bidirectional mutual history vectors are fed into a stacked contextual interaction module to capture the inter-dependency between current and history dialogue states.

Speaker Mutual Interaction for Dialogue History Let $\mathbf{u}_i \in \mathbb{R}^d$ represent the extracted d-dimensional multimodal features for i-th speech uttered by speaker $\mathcal{P}$, K be the dialogue history length. We use GRUs in two directions to capture the utterance-level speaker dialogue context. For the forward GRU, we have: $\overrightarrow{\mathbf{h}}^i_{\mathcal{P}} = \overrightarrow{\mathrm{GRU}}^i_{\mathcal{P}}(\mathbf{u}_i), \mathcal{P} \in \{A, B\}, i \in [t-K, t-1]$, where $\mathbf{h}_{\mathcal{P}} \in \mathbb{R}^d$ indicates the hidden state of speaker $\mathcal{P}$ at the step i. The history utterance sequences for speaker $\mathcal{P}$ are denoted as $\mathcal{U}_{\mathcal{P}}$.

We compute the mutual interaction for each history step i by linearly regulating each output of GRU with the previous hidden state of another speaker. In the forward direction, we have:

$$\overrightarrow{\mathbf{m}}_i = \left\{ \begin{array}{ll} \overrightarrow{\mathbf{h}}^i_{\mathrm{A}} \sigma(\overrightarrow{\mathbf{h}}^{i-1}_{\mathrm{B}} \overrightarrow{\mathbf{W}}_{\mathrm{B}} + \overrightarrow{\mathbf{b}}_{\mathrm{B}}) & \text{if } \mathcal{P} = \mathrm{A} \\ \overrightarrow{\mathbf{h}}^i_{\mathrm{B}} \sigma(\overrightarrow{\mathbf{h}}^{i-1}_{\mathrm{A}} \overrightarrow{\mathbf{W}}_{\mathrm{A}} + \overrightarrow{\mathbf{b}}_{\mathrm{A}}) & \text{if } \mathcal{P} = \mathrm{B} \end{array} \right\}, \quad (1)$$

where $\mathbf{h}^0_{\mathcal{P}}$ represents the initial hidden state of speaker $\mathcal{P}$, the sigmoid function $\sigma(x) = 1/(1 + \exp(-x))$, $\{\overrightarrow{\mathbf{W}}_{\mathrm{A}}, \overrightarrow{\mathbf{W}}_{\mathrm{B}}\} \in \mathbb{R}^{d \times d}, \{\overrightarrow{\mathbf{b}}_{\mathrm{A}}, \overrightarrow{\mathbf{b}}_{\mathrm{B}}\} \in \mathbb{R}^d$ represent the trainable parameters. The identical but reversed operation is applied in the backward direction. The output of both forward and backward direction at step i are concatenated along the feature dimension, denoted as $\overleftrightarrow{\mathbf{m}}_i = [\overrightarrow{\mathbf{m}}_i; \overleftarrow{\mathbf{m}}_i] \in \mathbb{R}^{2d}$.

Stacked Contextual Interaction The contextual encoder consists of L identical stacks. In the l-th layer, we feed the history dialogue representations $\mathbf{M}^l$ into a bi-GRU followed by a self-attention (SA) layer to capture the inter-dependency semantics. In the first layer, $\mathbf{M}^l$ is the sequence of encoded context $\overleftrightarrow{\mathbf{m}}_i$, and is bi-GRU's output from previous layer for intermediate stacks, *i.e.*, $\mathbf{M}^{l-1}_g (l > 1)$.

Denoting the output of bi-GRU as $\mathbf{M}^l_g$, the

[§]https://www.audeering.com/opensmile/

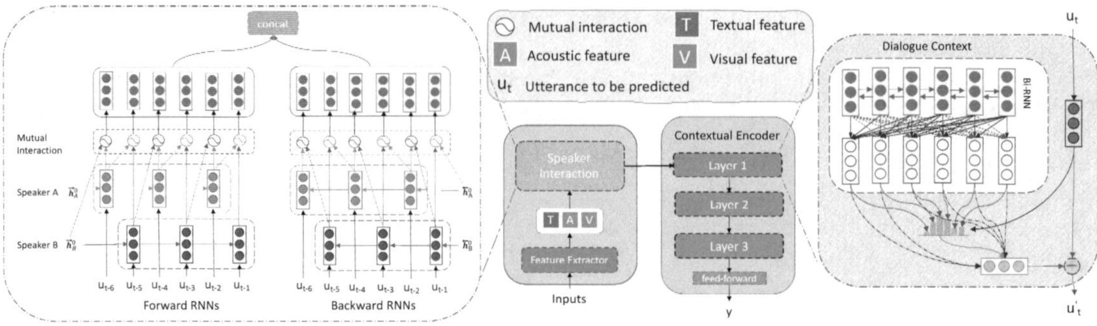

Figure 1: Schematic illustration of the proposed model.

scaled dot product self attention is calculated as:

$$\mathbf{Q}, \mathbf{K}, \mathbf{V} = \mathbf{M}_g^l \mathbf{W}_Q, \mathbf{M}_g^l \mathbf{W}_K, \mathbf{M}_g^l \mathbf{W}_V, \quad (2)$$

$$\mathbf{M}_{\text{att}}^l = \text{softmax}(d^{-1/2} \mathbf{Q} \mathbf{K}^\top) \mathbf{V}, \quad (3)$$

where $\mathbf{M}_{\text{att}} \in \mathbb{R}^{K \times 2d}$ is passed into the bi-GRU in the next interaction stack as the dialogue context.

Given the encoded utterance $\mathbf{u}_t^l \in \mathbb{R}^{2d}$ at l-th layer (linearly projected multimodal features when $l = 0$), we calculate the context vector for history dialogues:

$$\mathbf{c}^l = \mathbf{M}_{\text{att}}^l \text{softmax}(\mathbf{M}_{\text{att}}^l \mathbf{u}_t^l), \quad (4)$$

$$\mathbf{u}_t' = \tanh(\mathbf{u}_t^l + \mathbf{c}), \quad (5)$$

where the output $\mathbf{u}_t'$ is used as the input of $\{l+1\}$-th layer (*i.e.*, $\mathbf{u}_t^{l+1}$).

Emotion Classifier We use L-th stack's output vector $\mathbf{u}_t'$ to get the final emotion prediction through a linear transformation: $\hat{y} = \arg\max(\mathbf{W}_o \mathbf{u}_t' + \mathbf{b}_o)$, where $\mathbf{W}_o \in \mathbb{R}^{d \times |C|}$ and $\mathbf{b}_o \in \mathbb{R}^{|C|}$ are parameters.

2.4 Training

Let $\mathbf{u}$ represent the multimodal features. The cross entropy loss $\mathcal{L}_{\text{xe}}$ between $\hat{y}$ and golden label y is used for training. To improve the generalization, we generate adversarial examples using the model parameterized by $\boldsymbol{\theta}$ as in (Goodfellow et al., 2014)–adding perturbations on extracted multimodal features: $\mathbf{u}_{\text{adv}} = \mathbf{u} + \epsilon \frac{\mathbf{g}}{\|\mathbf{g}\|_2}$, where $\mathbf{g} = \nabla \mathcal{L}_{\text{xe}}(\boldsymbol{\theta}; \mathbf{u})$, $\epsilon \in \mathbb{R}$ is selected on the held out set. The final training objective is defined as:

$$\mathcal{L} = \mathcal{L}(\boldsymbol{\theta}; \mathbf{u}) + \mathcal{L}(\boldsymbol{\theta}; \mathbf{u}_{\text{adv}}). \quad (6)$$

3 Experiments

3.1 Experimental Setup

Dataset We evaluate our model on the IEMOCAP dataset (Busso et al., 2008) by reporting the accuracy (acc.) and F1 score on single and overall emotion class. IEMOCAP dataset contains dyadic dialogue videos for ten unique speakers, two of which are used for testing. We maintain the same 80/20 split for training/test set, consisting of 5,810/1,623 utterances respectively. The utterances are annotated as six emotion labels, *i.e.*, happy, sad, neutral, angry, excited, and frustrated.

Implementation Details We experiment using the batch size 512, contextual interaction layer number $L \in \{1, 2, 3, 4, 5, 6\}$, embedding size $d \in \{50, 100, 150, 200\}$, history context size $K \in \{20, 30, 40, 50\}$, the extracted textual/audio/visual feature dimensions of 100/100/512 respectively. We use Adam optimizer (Kingma and Ba, 2015) with initial learning rate of 1e-3. We employ the exponential annealing with base 2 to adjust the learning rate. For adversarial training, we select $\epsilon = 5$ using validation set. To avoid overfitting, we applies dropout keep rate $p \in \{0.2, 0.3, 0.4\}$ and early stopping patience of 10 epoch during training. The optimal hyperparameter settings are: $L = 3, d = 100, K = 40, p = 0.3$. We use an NVIDIA 2080 Ti GPU for experiments.

3.2 Results

Table 1 summarizes the performance of the proposed model compared with baseline models, in which our model overshadows previous baselines on both averaged accuracy and F1 metric. We found that the performance of our model ranks first for "angry" and "frustrated" sentiment prediction and achieves similar results on the other emotion classes.

Ablation Study We conduct ablation study on multi-modality (Fig. 2a), adversarial training and Speaker Mutual Interaction (SMI) module (Fig. 2b).

Model	Happy		Sad		Neutral		Angry		Excited		Frustrated		Average	
	Acc.	F1	Acc.	F1	Acc.	F1	Acc.	F1	Acc.	F1	Acc.	F1	Acc.	F1
CNN (Kim, 2014)	27.77	29.86	57.14	53.83	34.33	40.14	61.17	52.44	46.15	50.09	62.99	55.75	48.92	48.18
MemNet (Sukhbaatar et al., 2015)	25.72	33.53	55.53	61.77	58.12	52.84	59.32	55.39	51.50	58.30	67.20	59.00	55.72	55.10
bc-LSTM (Poria et al., 2017)	29.17	34.43	57.14	60.87	54.17	51.81	57.06	56.73	51.17	57.95	67.19	58.92	55.21	54.95
bc-LSTM+Att (Poria et al., 2017)	30.56	35.63	56.73	62.90	57.55	53.00	59.41	59.24	52.84	58.85	65.88	59.41	56.32	56.91
CMN (Hazarika et al., 2018b)	25.7	32.6	66.5	72.9	53.9	56.2	67.6	64.6	69.9	67.9	71.7	63.1	61.9	61.4
ICON (Hazarika et al., 2018a)	23.6	32.8	70.6	74.4	59.9	60.6	68.2	68.2	72.2	68.4	**71.9**	66.2	64.0	63.5
DialogueRNN (Majumder et al., 2019)	25.69	33.18	75.10	78.80	58.59	59.21	64.71	65.28	**80.27**	**71.86**	61.15	58.91	63.40	62.75
DialogueGCN (Ghosal et al., 2019)	40.62	42.75	89.14	84.54	61.92	63.54	67.53	64.19	65.46	63.08	64.18	66.99	65.25	64.18
IterativeERC (Lu et al., 2020)	-	53.17	-	77.19	-	61.31	-	61.45	-	69.23	-	60.92	-	64.37
COIN	**53.12**	42.50	85.71	73.07	60.05	62.23	66.48	**68.75**	69.13	69.01	61.73	**66.99**	**66.05**	**65.37**

Table 1: Overall performance of emotion recognition models on IEMOCAP dataset.

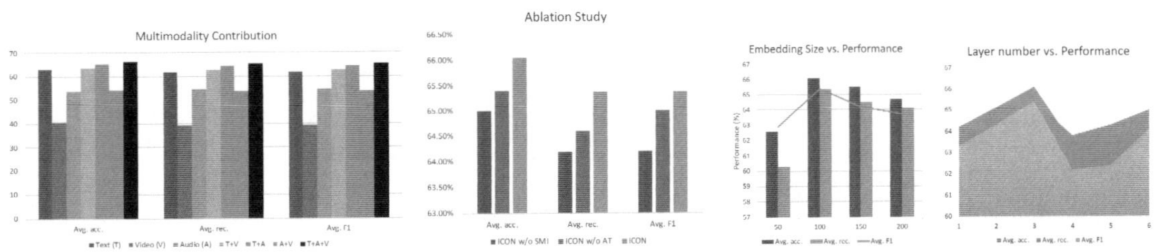

(a) Modality contribution (b) Ablation study (c) Embedding size (d) Layer number

Figure 2: Visualization of experimental analysis.

Fig. 2c and Fig. 2d show the influence of embedding size and stack number of context interactions. It can be seen model performance reaches its peak by taking the embedding size of 100 (Fig. 2c) and layer number $L = 3$ (Fig. 2d). Fig. 2b witnesses the influence of adversarial training and SMI on emotion detection. We further conduct experiments by applying adversarial training on various baselines, finding that our model achieves the best results among them. See Appendix B for discussion.

Fig. 2a show that among uni-modality, textual features contribute most followed by the acoustic setting whereas video features perform worst in our system. We guess high-level visual features extracted from CNN-3D lack of fine-grain facial representations, which requires further improvement. In dual modality settings, textual and acoustic features make the most contribution to predict emotion categories in comparison with tri-modal fusion settings.

Case Study Fig. 3 shows an instance of dialogue snippet, where our model captures the emotion dynamics of the male speaker during the conversation process. Using different RNNs to modeling various speaker utterances may circumvent the fluctuation of emotion transitions and effectively capture the emotion transition of disparate speakers. It is also observed in more examples in Appendix C.

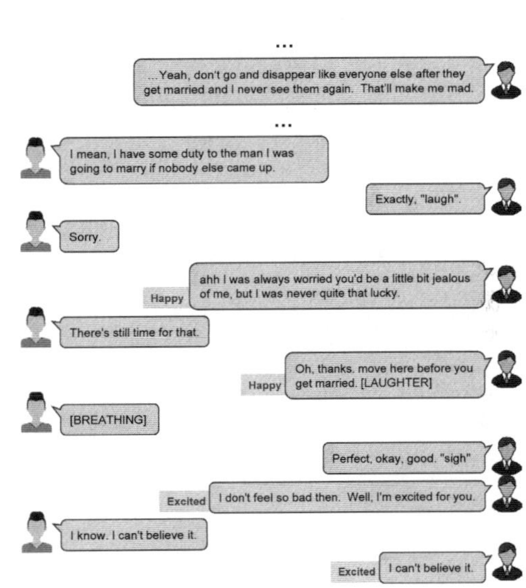

Figure 3: Case study.

4 Conclusion

We propose a new dialogue contextual interaction architecture to focus on the compact interaction for both speaker-level dialogue history and current utterance. By adopting adversarial training, our model achieves the SOTA performance on the IEMOCAP dataset for emotion recognition in conversation. In the future, multimodal fusion methods could be investigated to capture richer modelily-interactive representations at modality level.

References

Carlos Busso, Murtaza Bulut, Chi-Chun Lee, Abe Kazemzadeh, Emily Mower Provost, Samuel Kim, Jeannette N. Chang, Sungbok Lee, and Shrikanth S. Narayanan. 2008. Iemocap: interactive emotional dyadic motion capture database. *Language Resources and Evaluation*, 42:335–359.

Junyoung Chung, Çaglar Gülçehre, Kyunghyun Cho, and Yoshua Bengio. 2014. Empirical evaluation of gated recurrent neural networks on sequence modeling. *ArXiv*, abs/1412.3555.

Florian Eyben, Martin Wöllmer, and Björn W. Schuller. 2010. Opensmile: the munich versatile and fast open-source audio feature extractor. In *ACM Multimedia*.

Deepanway Ghosal, Navonil Majumder, Soujanya Poria, Niyati Chhaya, and Alexander Gelbukh. 2019. Dialoguegcn: A graph convolutional neural network for emotion recognition in conversation. In *EMNLP-IJCNLP*.

Ian J. Goodfellow, Jonathon Shlens, and Christian Szegedy. 2014. Explaining and harnessing adversarial examples. In *ICLR*.

Devamanyu Hazarika, Soujanya Poria, Rada Mihalcea, Erik Cambria, and Roger Zimmermann. 2018a. Icon: Interactive conversational memory network for multimodal emotion detection. In *EMNLP*.

Devamanyu Hazarika, Soujanya Poria, Amir Zadeh, Erik Cambria, Louis-Philippe Morency, and Roger Zimmermann. 2018b. Conversational memory network for emotion recognition in dyadic dialogue videos. *NAACL*.

Devamanyu Hazarika, Soujanya Poria, R. Zimmermann, and R. Mihalcea. 2021. Conversational transfer learning for emotion recognition. *Inf. Fusion*, 65:1–12.

Yoon Kim. 2014. Convolutional neural networks for sentence classification. In *EMNLP*.

Diederik P. Kingma and Jimmy Ba. 2015. Adam: A method for stochastic optimization. *CoRR*, abs/1412.6980.

X. Lu, Yanyan Zhao, Yang Wu, Yijian Tian, H. Chen, and Bing Qin. 2020. An iterative emotion interaction network for emotion recognition in conversations. In *COLING*.

Navonil Majumder, Soujanya Poria, Devamanyu Hazarika, Rada Mihalcea, Alexander Gelbukh, and Erik Cambria. 2019. Dialoguernn: An attentive rnn for emotion detection in conversations. In *AAAI*.

Soujanya Poria, Erik Cambria, Devamanyu Hazarika, Navonil Majumder, Amir Zadeh, and Louis-Philippe Morency. 2017. Context-dependent sentiment analysis in user-generated videos. In *ACL*.

Soujanya Poria, Navonil Majumder, Rada Mihalcea, and Eduard H. Hovy. 2019. Emotion recognition in conversation: Research challenges, datasets, and recent advances. *IEEE Access*, 7:100943–100953.

Sainbayar Sukhbaatar, Arthur Szlam, Jason Weston, and Rob Fergus. 2015. End-to-end memory networks. In *NIPS*.

Du Tran, Lubomir D. Bourdev, Rob Fergus, Lorenzo Torresani, and Manohar Paluri. 2015. Learning spatiotemporal features with 3d convolutional networks. *ICCV*.

A Qualitative Analysis

Fig. 4 illustrates the confusion matrix of predicted emotions. We found that negative sentiments such as "sad", "angry" can be easily mispredicted as "frustrated", and vice versa. "Happy" emotions exhibit the worst performance among all of six categories, which is difficult for the model to distinguish from "excited". This is in line with our manually observed prediction results because sometimes it is even not obvious for a human to distinguish the emotions with similar polarities, such as "sad" and "frustrated", "happy" and "excited". Further study on learning sentiments of similar polarity may be a solution to such misunderstanding.

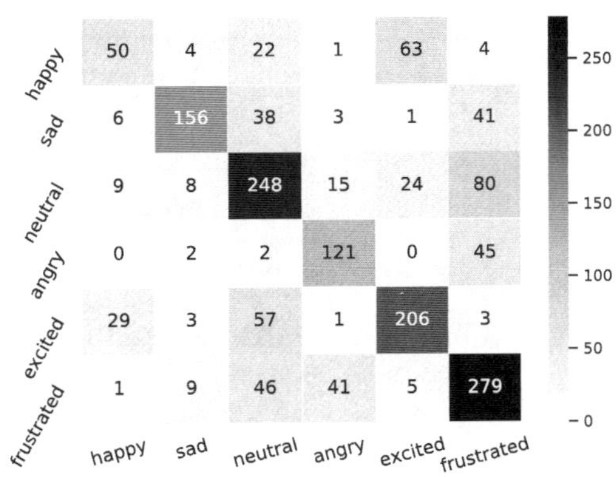

Figure 4: Confusion matrix of emotion predictions.

B Experiments on Adversarial Training

To verify the advantage of our model using adversarial training (AT), we further conduct experiments on different baseline models and report the result in Table 2. It is clear that our model outranks other models in terms of the overall performance, demonstrating the advantage of our model. Also, it is observed that emotion recognition models do not necessarily improve after incorporating the AT method. Specifically, models using single RNNs to simulate the speaker utterances, such as DialogueRNN and DialogueGCN, show the performance drop after adding AT, whereas models using separate RNNs to model different speakers, like ICON and ours, illustrate the advancement. We extrapolate that the emotion dynamics of different speakers may vary, thus the sensitivity of emotion models is affected by the adversarial noise derived from the conversational context. If different RNNs are adopted for various speaker utterance modeling, the noise would greatly rely on the current speaker's utterances despite the noise from noisy dialogue context, which eases the learning process of emotion transition.

C Case Study

Fig. 5 illustrates examples of our case study, which demonstrates that our model can capture the emotion dynamics during the conversation process.

Model	Happy		Sad		Neutral		Angry		Excited		Frustrated		Average	
	Acc	F1	Acc	F1	Acc	F1	Acc	F1	Acc	F1	Acc	F1	Acc	F1
ICON +AT	47.93	43.77	84.69	75.28	58.71	60.05	63.49	66.85	72.31	67.26	60.00	65.31	64.98	64.18
DialogueRNN +AT	36.04	31.17	91.10	79.82	53.53	55.35	65.32	65.89	65.65	65.09	55.08	59.22	61.48	60.72
DialogueGCN +AT	60.38	32.49	69.23	76.10	61.31	59.92	53.65	56.91	62.36	74.87	57.79	47.20	60.99	59.38
Ours (w/ AT)	53.12	42.50	85.71	73.07	60.05	62.23	66.48	68.75	69.13	69.01	61.73	66.99	**66.05**	**65.37**

Table 2: Performance of emotion recognition models with Adversarial Training (AT) on the IEMOCAP dataset.

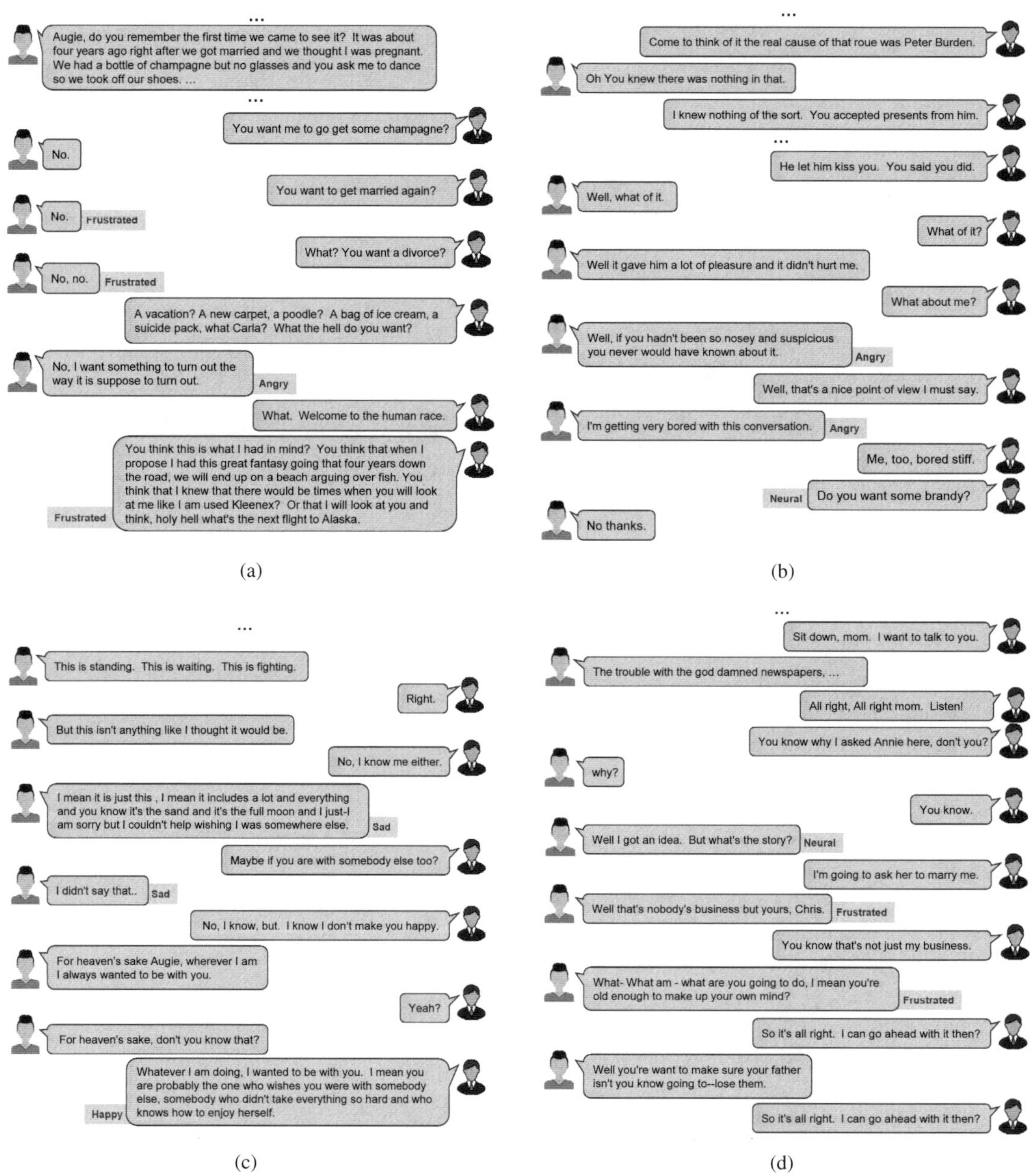

Figure 5: Case study examples.

A First Look: Towards Explainable TextVQA Models via Visual and Textual Explanations

Varun Nagaraj Rao [*†], **Xingjian Zhen** [*‡§], **Karen Hovsepian** [†], **Mingwei Shen** [†]
[†] PARS [¶], Amazon.com, Seattle   [‡] University of Wisconsin-Madison
varao@amazon.com, xzhen3@wisc.edu, {khhovsep, mingweis}@amazon.com
[*] Equal Contribution   [§] Work done while an intern at Amazon

Abstract

Explainable deep learning models are advantageous in many situations. Prior work mostly provide unimodal explanations through post-hoc approaches not part of the original system design. Explanation mechanisms also ignore useful textual information present in images. In this paper, we propose MTXNet, an end-to-end trainable multimodal architecture to generate multimodal explanations, which focuses on the text in the image. We curate a novel dataset TextVQA-X, containing ground truth visual and multi-reference textual explanations that can be leveraged during both training and evaluation. We then quantitatively show that training with multimodal explanations complements model performance and surpasses unimodal baselines by up to 7% in CIDEr scores and 2% in IoU. More importantly, we demonstrate that the multimodal explanations are consistent with human interpretations, help justify the models' decision, and provide useful insights to help diagnose an incorrect prediction. Finally, we describe a real-world e-commerce application for using the generated multimodal explanations.

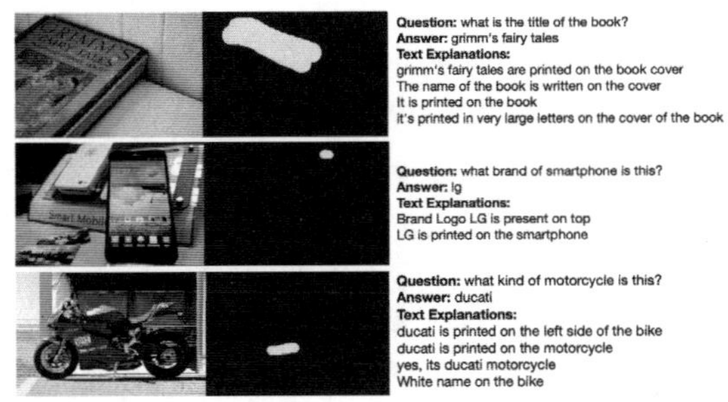

Figure 1: Sample Ground Truth Labels

1 Introduction

The ability to explain decisions through voice, text and visual pointing, is inherently human. Deep learning models on the other hand, are rather opaque black boxes that don't reveal very much about how they arrived at a specific prediction. Recent research effort, aided by regulatory provisions such as GDPRs "right to explanation" (Goodman and Flaxman, 2017), have focused on peeking beneath the hood of these black boxes and designing systems that inherently enable explanation. Explainable multimodal architectures can also be used to reduce the effort required for manual compliance checks of products sold by online retailers. Further, explanations can be provided as evidence to justify decisions and help improve customer and seller partner experiences.

We choose the TextVQA task proposed by Singh et al. (2019) for realizing the system, motivated by two reasons. First, the task is multimodal and is naturally suited for generating multimodal explanations. Second, the task specifically focuses on the text in the image, known to encode essential information for scene understanding and reasoning (Hu et al., 2020), and allows for better quality of explanations including the text recognized. Several approaches have been proposed for the TextVQA task (Singh et al., 2019; Hu et al., 2020; Mishra et al., 2019; Biten et al., 2019; Kant et al., 2020), but they do not include a means for explaining the model decision. In addition to allowing humans to interpret the model's decision, we believe the explanations can also provide valuable insight into what component could be improved.

Most prior explanation approaches (Hendricks et al., 2016, 2018; Li et al., 2018) have been unimodal and do not focus on the text in the image. Only recently, Huk Park et al. (2018) and Wu and Mooney (2019) generated multimodal explanations for the VQA and Activity Recognition tasks. They curated datasets (VQA-X, ACT-X) consisting of single reference ground truth textual explanations and relied on implicit attention-based visual expla-

[¶] Product Assurance, Risk, and Security https://www.amazon.jobs/en/teams/product-assurance-risk-security

Proceedings of the Third Workshop on Multimodal Artificial Intelligence, pages 19–29
June 6, 2021. ©2021 Association for Computational Linguistics

nations without any access to labeled visual ground truth. However, their models cannot read and incorporate text in the image into the explanations. In addition, it is debatable whether attention mechanisms are indeed explanations (Wiegreffe and Pinter, 2019; Jain and Wallace, 2019). Moreover, other works (Das et al., 2017) have shown that current VQA attention models do not seem to look at the same regions as humans, resulting in inconsistent explanations.

The goal of our work is two-fold. First, to collect a multimodal explanations dataset (TextVQA-X) thereby highlighting the need to curate datasets where explanations are not post-hoc but part of the initial interpretable model design. Non post-hoc explanations which may not be faithful to the model decision but are in line with human explanations are still beneficial to end users. Figure 1 provides a representative example. Second, to implement a multimodal explanation system that has the ability to not only read and reason about the text in the image, but more importantly justify its decision with natural language and visually highlight the evidence, useful to even non-experts (Miller et al., 2017). The explanations and model decision must be tightly coupled and mutually influence each other through an end-to-end trainable architecture. In summary, our contributions are as follows:

- We present TextVQA-X, a novel dataset of human-annotated multimodal explanations that includes ground truth segmentation maps and multi-reference textual explanations containing text in the image. The raw dataset is available publicly [1]. (Section 3)
- We propose the first end-to-end trainable MTXNet architecture that produces high quality textual and visual explanations, focusing on the text in the image. (Section 4)
- Qualitative and quantitative results show that textual and visual explanations help justify a model's decision and help diagnose the reasons for an incorrect prediction. (Section 5)
- We describe a real-world e-commerce system that can leverage the multimodal explanations and also highlight its challenges. (Section 6)

2 Related Work

VQA / TextVQA. The VQA task (Antol et al., 2015) has received a lot of research attention in terms of both datasets (Antol et al., 2015; Johnson et al., 2017; Hudson and Manning, 2019) and methods (Anderson et al., 2018; Ben-Younes et al., 2017; Lu et al., 2019). Oftentimes however, these models predict an answer without completely understanding the question and do not change answers across images (Agrawal et al., 2016). Further, they ignore the text in the image and tend to focus on visual components such as objects. To address this limitation, the TextVQA task was proposed by Singh et al. (2019) and has received recent research attention (Kant et al., 2020; Hu et al., 2020; Biten et al., 2019; Mishra et al., 2019). However, not having reliable explanation mechanisms that focus on the text in the image, as part of the system design makes it difficult to diagnose prediction failures. Our work, thus allows for better diagnosis of model failures through explanations in line with human interpretations and focus on the text in the image.

Explanations. Prior explanation approaches (Shortliffe and Buchanan, 1975; Van Lent et al., 2004; Zeiler and Fergus, 2014; Goyal et al., 2016; Ribeiro et al., 2016; Selvaraju et al., 2017; Das et al., 2017) focus on parts of the input that is relevant to the model's decision, but not on explicitly generating explanations as model predictions. Hendricks et al. (2016, 2018) were the first to generate natural language justifications for image classifiers. Unlike our model however, explanations are unimodal and there are no reference human explanations. Closer to our objective Huk Park et al. (2018) generate multimodal explanations and curate a new VQA-X dataset. Wu and Mooney (2019) extend their work to ensure explanations can be traced back to an object ensuring local faithfulness. However, their explanations do not contain the text in the image. They use implicit attention for visual explanations and have no access to visual ground truth during training. Further, they use a single textual explanation reference during training. In contrast, our work incorporates multimodal explanations which focuses on the text in the image.

3 TextVQA-X Dataset

To train and evaluate multimodal explanation models that focus on the text in the image, we collect the TextVQA-X dataset by human annotation of a subset of samples from the TextVQA dataset (Singh et al., 2019).

[1] https://github.com/amzn/explainable-text-vqa

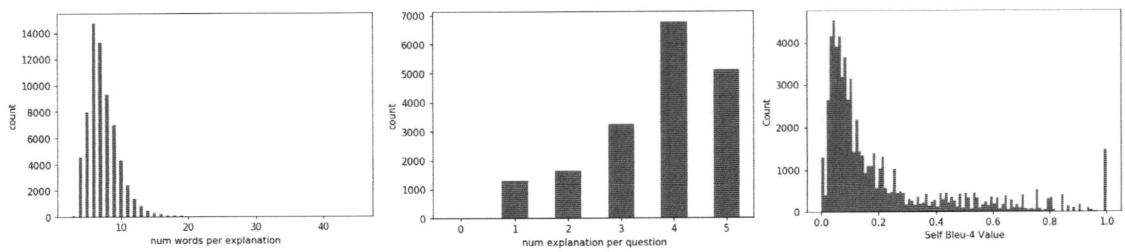

Figure 2: TextVQA-X Dataset Statistics

3.1 Ground Truth Label Collection

We used the Sagemaker Ground Truth (Amazon-AWS, 2018) platform to create a labeling task for gathering visual and textual explanations. Human annotators were asked to provide a single textual explanation that answers the question "Why do you think <answer> is the correct answer for the given question and image pair?". Specific instructions added that annotators should try to incorporate the answer and/or the text in the image as part of their explanation. The annotators were also asked to make use of a brush to segment image regions relevant to both the answer and written explanation. Sample annotations are shown in Figure 1. Each image and question pair can have up to 5 distinct human annotators allowing for multi-reference training and evaluation (Zheng et al., 2018). A single segmentation map is obtained by using a threshold of 0.5 obtained as an average over all annotations. Bad actors were identified and most were removed through a combination of heuristics and manual checks. Overall, we collected more than 67K explanations among over 800 unique workers.

3.2 TextVQA Explanation Dataset (TextVQA-X).

Dataset Statistic	Value
Num. Unique Images	11681
Num. Questions	18096
Num. Unique Questions	15374
Num. Visual Explanations	67055
Num. Textual Explanations	67055
Num. Unique Textual Explanations	61999
Avg. Num Textual Explanations per Question	3.71
Avg. Words per Textual Explanation	7.36
Avg. Characters per Textual Explanation	36.92
Textual Explanation Vocab Size	17910

Table 1: TextVQA-X Dataset Summary

In order to obtain a measure of the quality of explanations and to help filter out bad actors, we make use of the Self-BLEU-4 metric (Zhu et al., 2018). The Self-BLEU score is used to measure how one sentence resembles the rest in a generated collection by regarding one sentence as the hypothesis and the rest as references. A higher Self-BLEU score implies higher similarity of the hypothesis with all the references. A lower Self-BLEU implies higher diversity and lesser overlap. Although we would like to have several diverse textual explanations, we noticed that most good textual explanation annotations have overlap with others. The average Self-BLEU-4 across all annotations was 0.21 indicating consistent overlap and quality.

Comparison with VQA-X and VQA-HAT datasets. With respect to textual explanations, the TextVQA-X includes multi-references with an average of 3.71 explanations for each QA pair that can be utilized for both training and testing. In contrast, VQA-X (Huk Park et al., 2018) contains an average of 1.27 explanations with a single textual explanation for QA pairs in the training set and three textual explanations for test/val QA pairs. VQA-HAT (Das et al., 2017) does not include textual explanations. As far as visual explanations are concerned, there are a number of distinctions among these datasets. First, both VQA-X and VQA-HAT are defined on the VQA task, which does not require reading text in the. In contrast, the TextVQA-X is specifically designed to focus on the text in the image. Second, TextVQA-X includes one ground truth visual explanation for both training and testing (total 67K), whereas VQA-X includes explanations only as part of testing for a small random subset (total 6K). And third, similar to VQA-X, TextVQA-X annotators were asked to directly segment the relevant image region. On the contrary, VQA-HAT annotations were collected by having humans unblur the images and are more likely to introduce noise when irrelevant regions are uncovered.

4 Multimodal Text-in-Image Explanation Network (MTXNet)

We design our Multimodal Text-in-Image Explanation Network (MTXNet) to allow for end-to-end multitask training of answer prediction, text generation and semantic segmentation extending the M4C model proposed in (Hu et al., 2020). In the subsequent subsections we describe each of the individual components in more detail.

4.1 Graph Attention Network (GAT)

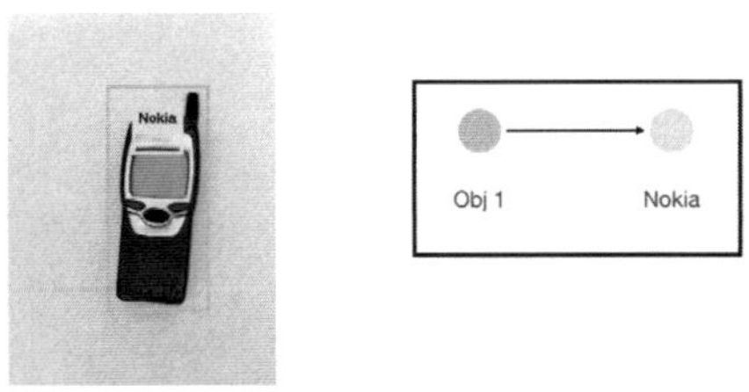

Figure 4: An example of how to build the graph

Many questions in the TextVQA dataset require the model to acknowledge the spatial relationship between objects and OCR tokens. To better encode the relationship between objects and OCR tokens and subsequently generate better quality explanations, we leverage graph neural networks. The ideal way to build the graph is to link together relevant components such as question words, OCR tokens and object labels. However, there are two limitations in the existing TextVQA dataset that prevent us from adopting this approach. First, the OCR tokens may be misspelled due to an inaccurate OCR system. And second, the object labels are not included and only the bounding box coordinates are present. Thus, for our model we build the graph using only the visual inputs (object and OCR region bounding boxes). Each object location and OCR token is treated as a node in the graph. Whenever the bounding box associated with node i is contained in node j, we add an edge from node j to node i. An example is presented in Figure 4. We then make use of the Graph Attention Network (GAT) (Veličković et al., 2017) to operate on the structured data. Unlike Graph Convolutional Networks (GCN) (Kipf and Welling, 2016) that treat each adjacent node equally, GATs incorporate attention into the layer-wise propagation rule and allows the model to variably weigh adjacent nodes based on relevancy.

4.2 Multimodal Transformer (MMT)

The multimodal transformer operates on three modalities - question words, visual objects and OCR tokens. The feature definitions are identical to that proposed in M4C (Hu et al., 2020) with the addition of textual explanation embeddings whose embedding process resembles that of the question words. The object embedding is obtained as a combination of the 2048-dim Faster R-CNN detector output and 4-dimensional relative location feature $[x_{min}/W_{im}, y_{min}/H_{im}, x_{max}/W_{im}, y_{max}/H_{im}]$. The OCR token embedding is obtained as a combination of 300-dim FastText vector (Bojanowski et al., 2017), 2048-dim output from fc6 features/ fc7 weights from Faster R-CNN detector for the bounding box region, 604-dim Pyramidal Histogram of Characters (PHOC) vector (Almazán et al., 2014), and 4-dim relative location feature $[x_{min}/W_{im}, y_{min}/H_{im}, x_{max}/W_{im}, y_{max}/H_{im}]$. Features are projected to a common d-dimensional semantic space used for decoding and prediction. The prediction takes place through a dynamic pointer network (Vinyals et al., 2015) that allows to either predict from a fixed vocabulary or from OCR tokens extracted from the image.

4.3 Multireferences for Textual Explanations

Neural text generation tasks such as machine translation, image captioning and summarization typically only consider a single reference for each example during training (Zheng et al., 2018). In our case however, considering just a single reference for training is insufficient because of the inherently subjective nature of textual explanations. Thus we leverage the multi-references we have collected in the TextVQA-X dataset during both training and evaluation. We use the *sample one* technique for incorporating multi-references during training. We randomly pick one of the available references in each training epoch.

4.4 Visual Explanations through Semantic Segmentation

Visual explanations are obtained through a semantic segmentation module (Feature Pyramid Network - FPN (Kirillov et al., 2017)). They are made an explicit and natural component of end-to-end training by leveraging ground truth label supervision. Incorporating explicit visual explanations is known to achieve state-of-the-art results on semantic segmentation benchmarks (Li et al., 2018).

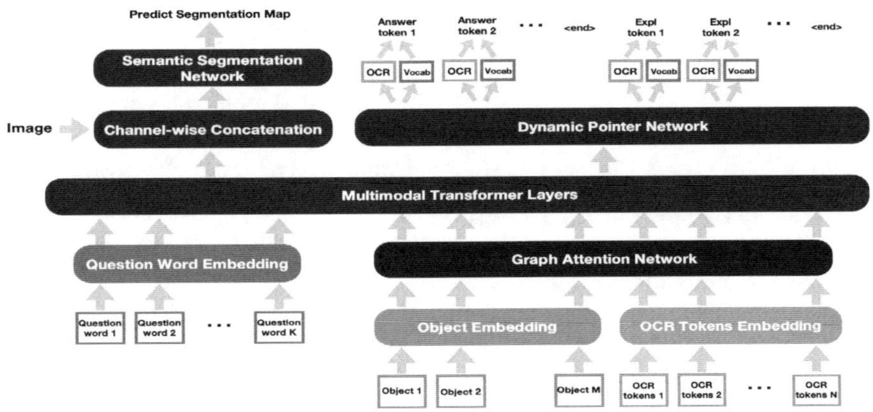

Figure 3: Our Multimodal Text-in-Image Explanation Model (MTXNet) architecture generates multimodal explanations. Explanations and Answers are utilized as a part of the iterative autoregressive decoding procedure.

Moreover, this allows the model to explain the image region in focus, while also providing a means for feedback. On another note, in the complimentary domain of NLP, the use of attention as a means of model explanation has been a topic of considerable debate (Wiegreffe and Pinter, 2019; Jain and Wallace, 2019). We thus leverage ground truth label supervision and explicitly ensure the visual explanation to be part of the training objective. To incorporate the multimodal embedding from the MMT into the segmentation module, we reshape, pad and concatenate the output with the raw input image along the channel. Thus, the overall input channels for the segmentation module increases to five, with 3 color channels and 2 multimodal channels. The output of the segmentation model is a continuous mask with a higher value implying greater relevancy to the inputs. The mask may be binarized through thresholding.

4.5 Training

The MTXNet architecture is end-to-end trainable with three distinct tasks (1) answer prediction (2) textual explanation generation and (3) visual explanation through semantic segmentation. We ensure cross-modal feedback between the textual explanations and predicted answers by leveraging a phased training process where we randomly choose between one of three choices (1) predict answer then textual explanation (2) predict textual explanation then answer and (3) predict both answer and textual explanation independently. Each task corresponds to an individual part of the training objective. For the losses of answer prediction ($\mathscr{L}_{\text{ans}}$) and textual explanation generation ($\mathscr{L}_{\text{text}}$) we use the *binary cross entropy with logits* [2]. For semantic segmentation ($\mathscr{L}_{\text{vis}}$) we use the *dice loss* (Sudre et al., 2017). The naive approach to combine multiple losses is to use a predetermined weighted linear sum of the individual losses. However, the model performance is sensitive to the weights which are hyperparameters and expensive to tune. We thus use a multitask learning loss with homoscedastic uncertainty as proposed by Kendall et al. (2018). The overall objective is present in Equation 1. The weights $\{w_{ans}, w_{text}, w_{vis}\}$ corresponding to the loss terms of the three individual tasks are learned.

$$\mathscr{L} = \sum_i \mathscr{L}_i exp(-w_i) + w_i, i \in \{ans, text, vis\} \quad (1)$$

5 Experiments

In this section, we detail the experimental setup, present quantitative results with ablations and finally analyze qualitative results.

5.1 Experimental Setup

This subsection discusses the dataset splits, model training, hyperparameter settings and evaluation metrics.

Dataset Splits. We use the TextVQA-X dataset described in Section 3. We choose a random 80/20 split for train and test. The dataset split statistics are present in Table 2. Each question is associated with a single image, one or more textual explanations and a single visual explanation. The OCR tokens and object regions are already present in the original TextVQA dataset.

[2] https://pytorch.org/docs/stable/generated/torch.nn.BCEWithLogitsLoss.html

Split	#Img.	#Ques.	#Text Expl.	#Vis. Expl.
train	10379	14475	53536	14475
test	3354	3619	13507	3619

Table 2: Train / Test Splits of TextVQA-X Dataset

Preprocessing. The dynamic pointer network is allowed to choose between a fixed 5000 word vocabulary and a maximum of 100 OCR tokens per image. For each image, we use the top 36 possible objects extracted by Faster R-CNN sorted in descending order of confidence score attribute. The average number of edges per image was 104. Each image included an average of 13 OCR tokens. The text explanations and answers are capped to a maximum length of 16 and 12 tokens respectively. For the visual explanations, we use a FPN decoder with ResNeXt50 encoder and $320 \times 320 \times 5$ input feature size. The MMT consists of 4 layers and 12 attention heads. The dimension of the joint embedding space is 184×768 which is padded and resized to $320 \times 320 \times 2$ and concatenated with the 3-channel image input.

Model training and hyperparameters. We train the MTXNet model end-to-end in a supervised setting using the Pythia [3] framework. We use a batch size of 128 and train for a maximum of 8500 epochs using Adam optimizer. The learning rate is set to $1e-4$ with no weight decay. The best model is chosen corresponding to the lowest train loss at an evaluation granularity of every 100 epochs. The entire training task varies from 14-20 hours on 8 Nvidia K80 GPUs.

Evaluation Metrics. Each question in the TextVQA dataset has 10 human-annotated answers, and the predicted answer accuracy is measured via a soft voting in accordance with the VQA task evaluation script [4]. We evaluate the textual explanations using the standard BLEU-4 (Papineni et al., 2002), ROUGE (Lin, 2004), METEOR (Banerjee and Lavie, 2005) and CIDEr (Vedantam et al., 2015) metrics computed with the `coco-caption` [5] code . All the text generation metrics account for multi-references by averaging the individual scores. Finally, we evaluate the visual explanations using IoU (Intersection over Union) score with a threshold of 0.5.

5.2 Ablation Study

We ablate MTXNet and compare quantitatively with a related model on our TextVQA-X dataset through automatic evaluations for answers and explanations. The results are present in Table 3.

Comparison with existing baselines. We compute the performance of the baseline model M4C (Hu et al., 2020) on the TextVQA-X test set (without explanations) and obtain an answer accuracy of 35.23%. Using the MTXNet architecture and evaluating on the TextVQA-X test set, we obtain an answer accuracy of 36.27%. The addition of explanations thus complements the MTXNet performance.

Unimodal vs. Multimodal explanations We notice that each modality mutually influences the other as the model learns to jointly optimize for both modalities of explanations and the answer prediction. Excluding visual explanations results in the largest drop of up to 7% in CIDEr scores of the textual explanations. Similarly, the absence of text explanations results in a 2% drop in IoU of visual explanations. More importantly, we notice that the multimodal explanations provide visual and textual rationale into a models decision. This further accentuates the value of designing multimodal explanation systems.

GAT better captures structural dependencies. The removal of GAT from the MTXNet architecture adversely impacts the quality of explanations and answers. The greatest drop of 7% is observed for the CIDEr metric. We believe the GAT helps better encode the relationship between objects and OCR tokens enhancing the relationship reasoning ability. The image region corresponding to the text is also highlighted better as seen in the 2% increase in IoU when GAT is included in MTXNet.

Multi-reference training improves text generation. Training with multi-references significantly outperforms training with a single randomly chosen sample fixed for all epochs. The largest increase of up to 25% was noticed in CIDEr score, with the increase being consistent across all text generation metrics. This underscores the benefits of having multi-references for both training and evaluation and designing systems that utilize this effectively.

5.3 Qualitative Samples

As can be seen in Figure 5, the MTXNet is able to accurately answer the given question while also justifying its decision through textual and visual

[3] https://github.com/facebookresearch/mmf

[4] https://visualqa.org/evaluation

[5] https://github.com/tylin/coco-caption

Ablation	Approach	Visual Explanation	Textual Explanation			
		IoU	B	R	M	C
No visual explanation (VE)	MTXNet (GAT + MR + TE)	-	25.16	47.63	21.76	88.43
No textual explanation (TE)	MTXNet (GAT + MR + VE)	16.10	-	-	-	-
No graph attention (GAT)	MTXNet (MR + TE + VE)	16.55	27.87	49.28	21.61	88.57
No multireferences (MR)	MTXNet (GAT + TE + VE)	17.52	5.92	28.05	11.65	70.60
Consolidated architecture	MTXNet (GAT + MR + TE + VE)	**18.86**	**31.07**	**53.87**	**22.06**	**95.07**

Table 3: Quantitative Evaluation of Answer and Explanations. All metrics are in %. VE: visual explanation, TE: textual explanation, GAT: graph attention network, MR: multi-references. Evaluated automatic metrics: Intersection over Union (IoU), BLEU-4 (B), METEOR (M), ROUGE (R), CIDEr (C).

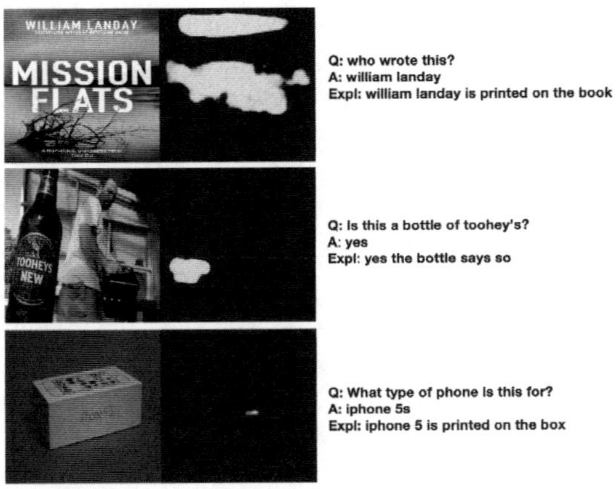

Figure 5: Examples where the MTXNet model produces high quality explanations.

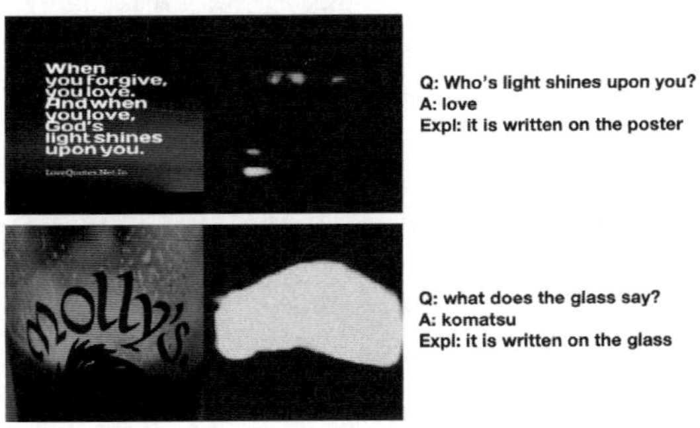

Figure 6: Examples where the MTXNet model fails.

explanations. In certain cases, the OCR engine could be inaccurate and lead to wrong tokens being predicted, but the overall answer and explanations are correct. Figure 6 depicts two failure cases. The upper subimage indicates this could be due to incorrect visual localization while the lower subimage indicates a potential OCR prediction error, although the visual explanation is correct. Despite being generic and dull the textual explanations are correct. In other cases, the model fails due to incorrect visual localization as seen in Figure 7.

Explanations help explain incorrect decisions of model. In Figure 7, we see that the right answer to the question is "target". However, the model

Figure 7: Example where the explanation is consistent with an incorrect prediction.

predicts "dollar tree". From the visual and textual explanations we see that the image region localized is incorrect and the model fails to grasp the meaning of "fading". This potentially results in it focusing on the more prominent "dollar tree" text. Such an analysis provides insights into the component of the system that is failing and deserves further attention.

6 Applications to E-Commerce Businesses

E-commerce businesses need to comply with industry-wide, and country-specific regulations, to provide accurate and useful information of products to improve customer experience that leads to more business. Our long-term goal with explainable multimodal architectures is to automate and reduce manual effort required for compliance and product detail checks. This will enable businesses to scale compliance and customer experience improvement efficiently without linear increases in cost. Further, these architectures help validate if models are performing as intended and used for the right purposes.

A potential customer experience issue arises when the physical product in a warehouse is different from that uploaded by a seller on the product details page. A possible reason could be that the seller or manufacturer labeled the product erroneously when they packaged it. Many sellers taking advantage of lower cost of manufacturing in a global supply chain, may not be able to audit every batch of product leaving the factory. Such discrepancies will almost certainly lead to product returns, because the customer didn't get what they wanted and increases costs. Such discrepancies may also be due to more nefarious reasons, such as opportunistic bad actors taking advantage of sellers that have successful products by introducing poorer quality or mismatched offers at a lower price to unsuspecting customers. Examples of compliance issues include detecting products that contain batteries and chemicals to comply with transportation and logistics regulations, as well as identifying products that require additional safety documentation and checks, such as products that may have unintended use by children (e.g. toys and products that may end up as toys should not have heavy metals or other poisons that cause illness or death when accidentally ingested). While not all answers can be obtained with product images alone, manual investigation processes utilize these images to identify potential risks that warrant additional steps in the process (e.g. lab testing).

Rather than manually auditing products in a warehouse, product images can be automatically captured at scale, and passed through models that detect such discrepancies. With the help of subject matter experts, attributes such as quantity, color and brand names, and other common misleading attributes are identified apriori. Relevant questions that target these attributes are formulated. The image and question are then inputs to a multimodal explainable system (such as MTXNet) that can provide an answer and justify its prediction through multimodal explanations. Answers can then be compared against the information extracted from the product detail pages on the website. Any discrepancies found can be noted and a selling partner can be provided evidence through the multimodal explanations to take corrective steps.

An example use-case is as follows. Given a large container of cereal, with smaller boxes within, a potential question is: "How many cereal boxes are within the container?" . This information is usually written on the larger container present in the warehouse and can be answered based on reading the text in the image. If there is any discrepancy encountered in the number of boxes of cereal in the warehouse and that listed on the website, appropriate action can be taken. Other similar questions include: "How heavy is the product?", "Is the chair red?", "Does the item contain allergens?", and "Did the product pass the lead test?".

The challenges with the use of such explainable systems are two-fold. First, since there can be multiple stakeholders with diverse expertise and expectations, we need to clearly define the level of abstraction at which they interact with the system. For instance, while a scientist can use the explanations to improve the model, a business operations associate may use the explanations to identify and audit product discrepancies. Second, we need fine grained evaluation methodologies and metrics that take into account the stakeholders as well.

7 Conclusion

A central tenet of explainable AI is to create a suite of tools and frameworks that result in explainable models without sacrificing learning performance and allow humans to understand and trust AI models. As Miller et al. (2017) argues, for explainable AI to succeed, we should draw upon existing principles and create strategies that are more people-centric. Unfortunately most prior explanation approaches have been post-hoc, unimodal, ignore text present in the image and not always in accordance with human interpretation. Further, there is a paucity of labeled multimodal explanation datasets. The research presented in this paper shows that existing TextVQA systems can be rather easily adapted to produce multimodal explanations that focus on the text in the image when given access to ground truth annotations. We curate the TextVQA-X dataset consisting of visual and textual explanations. We then present a novel end-to-end trainable architecture, MTXNet, that generates multimodal explanations focusing on the text in the image, in line with human interpretation and surpasses unimodal baselines (7% in CIDEr scores and 2% in IoU) while complimenting model performance. We also show how the system may be applicable in the e-commerce space to reduce effort for manual audit of compliance checks and improve customer experience. Results of this research open the door to design of explanainable models part of the original system design that effectively takes advantage of available ground truth multimodal explanation annotations. Future work involves incorporating visual features as part of the transformer architecture.

References

Aishwarya Agrawal, Dhruv Batra, and Devi Parikh. 2016. Analyzing the behavior of visual question answering models. *arXiv preprint arXiv:1606.07356*.

Jon Almazán, Albert Gordo, Alicia Fornés, and Ernest Valveny. 2014. Word spotting and recognition with embedded attributes. *IEEE transactions on pattern analysis and machine intelligence*, 36(12):2552–2566.

Amazon-AWS. 2018. SageMaker Ground Truth. `https://aws.amazon.com/sagemaker/groundtruth/`.

Peter Anderson, Xiaodong He, Chris Buehler, Damien Teney, Mark Johnson, Stephen Gould, and Lei Zhang. 2018. Bottom-up and top-down attention for image captioning and visual question answering. In *Proceedings of the IEEE conference on computer vision and pattern recognition*, pages 6077–6086.

Stanislaw Antol, Aishwarya Agrawal, Jiasen Lu, Margaret Mitchell, Dhruv Batra, C Lawrence Zitnick, and Devi Parikh. 2015. Vqa: Visual question answering. In *Proceedings of the IEEE international conference on computer vision*, pages 2425–2433.

Jimmy Lei Ba, Jamie Ryan Kiros, and Geoffrey E Hinton. 2016. Layer normalization. *arXiv preprint arXiv:1607.06450*.

Satanjeev Banerjee and Alon Lavie. 2005. Meteor: An automatic metric for mt evaluation with improved correlation with human judgments. In *Proceedings of the acl workshop on intrinsic and extrinsic evaluation measures for machine translation and/or summarization*, pages 65–72.

Hedi Ben-Younes, Rémi Cadene, Matthieu Cord, and Nicolas Thome. 2017. Mutan: Multimodal tucker fusion for visual question answering. In *Proceedings of the IEEE international conference on computer vision*, pages 2612–2620.

Ali Furkan Biten, Ruben Tito, Andres Mafla, Lluis Gomez, Marçal Rusinol, Ernest Valveny, CV Jawahar, and Dimosthenis Karatzas. 2019. Scene text visual question answering. In *Proceedings of the IEEE International Conference on Computer Vision*, pages 4291–4301.

Piotr Bojanowski, Edouard Grave, Armand Joulin, and Tomas Mikolov. 2017. Enriching word vectors with subword information. *Transactions of the Association for Computational Linguistics*, 5:135–146.

Mark G Core, H Chad Lane, Michael Van Lent, Dave Gomboc, Steve Solomon, and Milton Rosenberg. 2006. Building explainable artificial intelligence systems. In *AAAI*, pages 1766–1773.

Abhishek Das, Harsh Agrawal, Larry Zitnick, Devi Parikh, and Dhruv Batra. 2017. Human attention in visual question answering: Do humans and deep networks look at the same regions? *Computer Vision and Image Understanding*, 163:90–100.

Jacob Devlin, Ming-Wei Chang, Kenton Lee, and Kristina Toutanova. 2018. Bert: Pre-training of deep bidirectional transformers for language understanding. *arXiv preprint arXiv:1810.04805*.

David K Duvenaud, Dougal Maclaurin, Jorge Iparraguirre, Rafael Bombarell, Timothy Hirzel, Alán Aspuru-Guzik, and Ryan P Adams. 2015. Convolutional networks on graphs for learning molecular fingerprints. In *Advances in neural information processing systems*, pages 2224–2232.

Wenqi Fan, Yao Ma, Qing Li, Yuan He, Eric Zhao, Jiliang Tang, and Dawei Yin. 2019. Graph neural networks for social recommendation. In *The World Wide Web Conference*, pages 417–426.

Akira Fukui, Dong Huk Park, Daylen Yang, Anna Rohrbach, Trevor Darrell, and Marcus Rohrbach. 2016. Multimodal compact bilinear pooling for visual question answering and visual grounding. *arXiv preprint arXiv:1606.01847*.

Chenyu Gao, Qi Zhu, Peng Wang, Hui Li, Yuliang Liu, Anton van den Hengel, and Qi Wu. 2020. Structured multimodal attentions for textvqa. *arXiv preprint arXiv:2006.00753*.

Bryce Goodman and Seth Flaxman. 2017. European union regulations on algorithmic decision-making and a "right to explanation". *AI magazine*, 38(3):50–57.

Yash Goyal, Tejas Khot, Douglas Summers-Stay, Dhruv Batra, and Devi Parikh. 2017. Making the v in vqa matter: Elevating the role of image understanding in visual question answering. In *Proceedings of the IEEE Conference on Computer Vision and Pattern Recognition*, pages 6904–6913.

Yash Goyal, Akrit Mohapatra, Devi Parikh, and Dhruv Batra. 2016. Towards transparent ai systems: Interpreting visual question answering models. *arXiv preprint arXiv:1608.08974*.

Lisa Anne Hendricks, Zeynep Akata, Marcus Rohrbach, Jeff Donahue, Bernt Schiele, and Trevor Darrell. 2016. Generating visual explanations. In *European Conference on Computer Vision*, pages 3–19. Springer.

Lisa Anne Hendricks, Ronghang Hu, Trevor Darrell, and Zeynep Akata. 2018. Grounding visual explanations. In *Proceedings of the European Conference on Computer Vision (ECCV)*, pages 264–279.

Ronghang Hu, Amanpreet Singh, Trevor Darrell, and Marcus Rohrbach. 2020. Iterative answer prediction with pointer-augmented multimodal transformers for textvqa. In *Proceedings of the IEEE/CVF Conference on Computer Vision and Pattern Recognition*, pages 9992–10002.

Drew A Hudson and Christopher D Manning. 2019. Gqa: a new dataset for compositional question answering over real-world images. *arXiv preprint arXiv:1902.09506*, 3(8).

Dong Huk Park, Lisa Anne Hendricks, Zeynep Akata, Anna Rohrbach, Bernt Schiele, Trevor Darrell, and Marcus Rohrbach. 2018. Multimodal explanations: Justifying decisions and pointing to the evidence. In *Proceedings of the IEEE Conference on Computer Vision and Pattern Recognition*, pages 8779–8788.

Sarthak Jain and Byron C Wallace. 2019. Attention is not explanation. *arXiv preprint arXiv:1902.10186*.

Justin Johnson, Bharath Hariharan, Laurens van der Maaten, Li Fei-Fei, C Lawrence Zitnick, and Ross Girshick. 2017. Clevr: A diagnostic dataset for compositional language and elementary visual reasoning. In *Proceedings of the IEEE Conference on Computer Vision and Pattern Recognition*, pages 2901–2910.

Yash Kant, Dhruv Batra, Peter Anderson, Alex Schwing, Devi Parikh, Jiasen Lu, and Harsh Agrawal. 2020. Spatially aware multimodal transformers for textvqa. *arXiv preprint arXiv:2007.12146*.

Andrej Karpathy and Li Fei-Fei. 2015. Deep visual-semantic alignments for generating image descriptions. In *Proceedings of the IEEE conference on computer vision and pattern recognition*, pages 3128–3137.

Alex Kendall, Yarin Gal, and Roberto Cipolla. 2018. Multi-task learning using uncertainty to weigh losses for scene geometry and semantics. In *Proceedings of the IEEE conference on computer vision and pattern recognition*, pages 7482–7491.

Thomas N Kipf and Max Welling. 2016. Semi-supervised classification with graph convolutional networks. *arXiv preprint arXiv:1609.02907*.

Alexander Kirillov, Kaiming He, Ross Girshick, and Piotr Dollár. 2017. A unified architecture for instance and semantic segmentation.

H Chad Lane, Mark G Core, Michael Van Lent, Steve Solomon, and Dave Gomboc. 2005. Explainable artificial intelligence for training and tutoring. Technical report, UNIVERSITY OF SOUTHERN CALIFORNIA MARINA DEL REY CA INST FOR CREATIVE ....

Qing Li, Jianlong Fu, Dongfei Yu, Tao Mei, and Jiebo Luo. 2018. Tell-and-answer: Towards explainable visual question answering using attributes and captions. *arXiv preprint arXiv:1801.09041*.

Chin-Yew Lin. 2004. Rouge: A package for automatic evaluation of summaries. In *Text summarization branches out*, pages 74–81.

Jiasen Lu, Dhruv Batra, Devi Parikh, and Stefan Lee. 2019. Vilbert: Pretraining task-agnostic visiolinguistic representations for vision-and-language tasks. In *Advances in Neural Information Processing Systems*, pages 13–23.

Tim Miller, Piers Howe, and Liz Sonenberg. 2017. Explainable ai: Beware of inmates running the asylum or: How i learnt to stop worrying and love the social and behavioural sciences. *arXiv preprint arXiv:1712.00547*.

Anand Mishra, Shashank Shekhar, Ajeet Kumar Singh, and Anirban Chakraborty. 2019. Ocr-vqa: Visual question answering by reading text in images. In *2019 International Conference on Document Analysis and Recognition (ICDAR)*, pages 947–952. IEEE.

Kishore Papineni, Salim Roukos, Todd Ward, and Wei-Jing Zhu. 2002. Bleu: a method for automatic evaluation of machine translation. In *Proceedings of the 40th annual meeting of the Association for Computational Linguistics*, pages 311–318.

Colin Raffel, Noam Shazeer, Adam Roberts, Katherine Lee, Sharan Narang, Michael Matena, Yanqi Zhou, Wei Li, and Peter J Liu. 2019. Exploring the limits of transfer learning with a unified text-to-text transformer. *arXiv preprint arXiv:1910.10683*.

Marco Tulio Ribeiro, Sameer Singh, and Carlos Guestrin. 2016. " why should i trust you?" explaining the predictions of any classifier. In *Proceedings of the 22nd ACM SIGKDD international conference on knowledge discovery and data mining*, pages 1135–1144.

Ramprasaath R Selvaraju, Michael Cogswell, Abhishek Das, Ramakrishna Vedantam, Devi Parikh, and Dhruv Batra. 2017. Grad-cam: Visual explanations from deep networks via gradient-based localization. In *Proceedings of the IEEE international conference on computer vision*, pages 618–626.

Edward H Shortliffe and Bruce G Buchanan. 1975. A model of inexact reasoning in medicine. *Mathematical biosciences*, 23(3-4):351–379.

Amanpreet Singh, Vivek Natarajan, Meet Shah, Yu Jiang, Xinlei Chen, Dhruv Batra, Devi Parikh, and Marcus Rohrbach. 2019. Towards vqa models that can read. In *Proceedings of the IEEE Conference on Computer Vision and Pattern Recognition*, pages 8317–8326.

Carole H Sudre, Wenqi Li, Tom Vercauteren, Sebastien Ourselin, and M Jorge Cardoso. 2017. Generalised dice overlap as a deep learning loss function for highly unbalanced segmentations. In *Deep learning in medical image analysis and multimodal learning for clinical decision support*, pages 240–248. Springer.

Michael Van Lent, William Fisher, and Michael Mancuso. 2004. An explainable artificial intelligence system for small-unit tactical behavior. In *Proceedings of the national conference on artificial intelligence*, pages 900–907. Menlo Park, CA; Cambridge, MA; London; AAAI Press; MIT Press; 1999.

Ramakrishna Vedantam, C Lawrence Zitnick, and Devi Parikh. 2015. Cider: Consensus-based image description evaluation. In *Proceedings of the IEEE conference on computer vision and pattern recognition*, pages 4566–4575.

Petar Veličković, Guillem Cucurull, Arantxa Casanova, Adriana Romero, Pietro Lio, and Yoshua Bengio. 2017. Graph attention networks. *arXiv preprint arXiv:1710.10903*.

Oriol Vinyals, Meire Fortunato, and Navdeep Jaitly. 2015. Pointer networks. In *Advances in neural information processing systems*, pages 2692–2700.

Sarah Wiegreffe and Yuval Pinter. 2019. Attention is not not explanation. *arXiv preprint arXiv:1908.04626*.

Jialin Wu and Raymond Mooney. 2019. Faithful multimodal explanation for visual question answering. In *Proceedings of the 2019 ACL Workshop BlackboxNLP: Analyzing and Interpreting Neural Networks for NLP*, pages 103–112.

Matthew D Zeiler and Rob Fergus. 2014. Visualizing and understanding convolutional networks. In *European conference on computer vision*, pages 818–833. Springer.

Renjie Zheng, Mingbo Ma, and Liang Huang. 2018. Multi-reference training with pseudo-references for neural translation and text generation. *arXiv preprint arXiv:1808.09564*.

Bolei Zhou, Aditya Khosla, Agata Lapedriza, Aude Oliva, and Antonio Torralba. 2016. Learning deep features for discriminative localization. In *Proceedings of the IEEE conference on computer vision and pattern recognition*, pages 2921–2929.

Yaoming Zhu, Sidi Lu, Lei Zheng, Jiaxian Guo, Weinan Zhang, Jun Wang, and Yong Yu. 2018. Texygen: A benchmarking platform for text generation models. In *The 41st International ACM SIGIR Conference on Research & Development in Information Retrieval*, pages 1097–1100.

Multi Task Learning Based Framework for Multimodal Classification

Danting Zeng
Stanford University, Stanford, USA
dandan_9817@hotmail.com

Abstract

Large-scale multi-modal classification aim to distinguish between different multi-modal data, and it has drawn dramatically attentions since last decade. In this paper, we propose a multi-task learning-based framework for the multimodal classification task, which consists of two branches: multi-modal autoencoder branch and attention-based multi-modal modeling branch. Multi-modal autoencoder can receive multi-modal features and obtain the interactive information which called multi-modal encoder feature, and use this feature to reconstitute all the input data. Besides, multi-modal encoder feature can be used to enrich the raw dataset, and improve the performance of downstream tasks (such as classification task). As for attention-based multimodal modeling branch, we first employ attention mechanism to make the model focused on important features, then we use the multi-modal encoder feature to enrich the input information, achieve a better performance. We conduct extensive experiments on different dataset, the results demonstrate the effectiveness of proposed framework.

1 Introduction

With the easy-access of mobile devices, the world has witnessed the explosion of multimedia data, which contains various modalities, such as image, audio and text. Generally speaking, different modality can provide complementary information. However, many previous attempts focus on one single modality, as the multimodal data is more complex. The applications of multimodal data analysis seem to evident in several fields, such as, emotion recognition, medical diagnosis. Recently, the development of multimodal machine learning approaches has witnessed growing interest (Ngiam et al., 2011). On the other hand, deep learning has witnessed dramatically progress in various fields: ranges from computer vision, natural language processing and speech recognition (Oramas et al., 2018). Due to the great success of deep learning in single modality, great interests have been given for the multimodal deep learning framework (Xu et al., 2016; Radu et al., 2016). Despite of sustainable efforts have been made, multimodal deep learning is still far from been fully solved, using deep learning. Moreover, traditional approach train the classifiers on different modal and weighted average to generate the predictions, which is time-consuming and cannot model the interaction between different modal.

In this short paper, a general multimodal data classification task is proposed, leveraging multi task-based deep learning. The framework consists of two branches: multi-modal autoencoder branch and attention-based multi-modal modeling branch. The framework takes the interaction between different modals into consideration. To demonstrate the efficacy and robustness of proposed method, we conduct extensive experiments on different dataset and the results support our claims.

2 Dataset and Evaluation

In this paper, we use the Adoption Prediction Dataset from Kaggle[1] to do our research, which is a real world and challenging dataset. The dataset is composed of three different modal features: tabular features (the basic information about each pet), textual features (the pet description written by English) and visual features (the photo of each pet), and it aims to predict how quickly a pet is adopted. There are 14993 instances in this dataset, and the label is the categorical speed of adoption, there are five different classes from 0 to 4, in details, 0 means this pet was adopted on the same day as it was listed, 1 means this pet was adopted between 1 and 7 days after being listed. Figure 1 shows some example instances. Besides, in this classification task, due to the number of classes is balanced, we use accuracy

[1]https://www.kaggle.com/c/petfinder-adoption-prediction

Proceedings of the Third Workshop on Multimodal Artificial Intelligence, pages 30–35

to evaluate different models' performance.

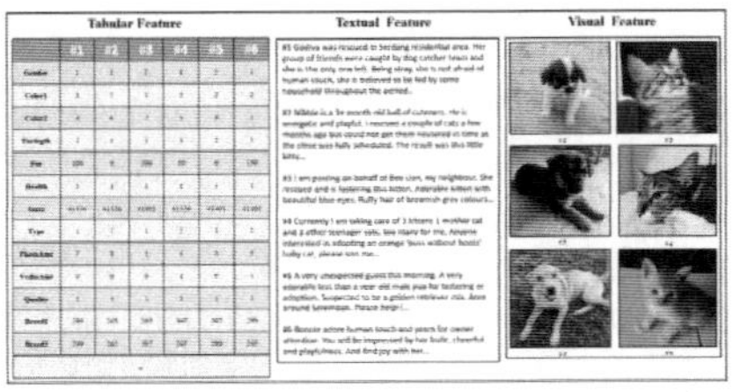

Figure 1: Six example instances from Adoption Prediction Dataset. The instance numbers are displayed as $\#1$ to $\#6$.

Tabular Features: These features are the basic information of each pet, there are 15 categorical variables and 4 continuous variables.

Textual Features: The textual features are the pet descriptions written by English.

Visual Features: The visual feature of each pet is a image whose size is from 240 pixels to 1024 pixels, in order to train our model, we reshape all the images to 512×512.

3 Proposed Approach

In this paper, our proposed approach has two parts: multi-modal autoencoder branch and attention-based multi-modal modeling branch.

3.1 Multi-modal Autoencoder

In the previous work, autoencoders receive a single modal feature and reconstitute it, with a goal to minimize the reconstruction loss between the input and output. However, if a task has multi-modal features, we can build a MMAE which can receive different modal features at the same time. MMAE first learns the encoder representation from each single modal feature, then concatenating them as a multimodal encoder feature, and finally this feature is used to reconstitute all the input. As can be seen in Figure 2, MMAE has two parts:

Input Layer: For the tabular features (represented as $x_{tabular}$), One-Hot Encoding for categorical variables and Max-Min Normalization for continuous variables. As for the visual features (represented as x_{visual}), we first reshape all the images size into 512×512, that is $x_{visual} = x_{visual}/255.0$. As for the textual features, every instance has a paragraph to describe the pet, for the i_{th} input paragraph with n words $w_1^i; w_2^i; :::; w_n^i$, we first padding the paragraph into fixed length $l = 100$.Then we us word embedding layer to transform paragraph into dense matrix X^i. All input paragraphs will be transformed into dense matrices whose size is 100×300, represented as $x_{textual}$. After the data preprocessing, the input layer will put $x_{tabular}$,x_{visual} and $x_{textual}$ into the next layer.

Multi-modal Interaction Layer: For each modal feature, we suppose $f(x)$ is the encoder function, $g(x)$ is the decoder function, in the previous work, we should build three independent autoencoders, each autoencoder can only encode a single modal feature. During encoding, the input data is compressed into a low dimensional vector, which we called encoder feature. During encoding, the autoencoder will reconstitute the input using encoder feature. The mathematical expressions are shown below:

$$h_{tabular} = f^1(x_{tabular}), \hat{x}_{tabular} = g^1(h_{tabular}) \quad (1)$$

$$h_{visual} = f^2(x_{visual}), \hat{x}_{visual} = g^2(h_{visual}) \quad (2)$$

$$h_{textual} = f^3(x_{textual}), \hat{x}_{textual} = g^3(h_{textual}) \quad (3)$$

where $h_{tabular}$,h_{visual} and $h_{textual}$are the encoder features of each modal input, they have the same length k, and during training, we minimize the reconstruction loss to optimize the parameters, the loss function is Mean Square Error (MSE). Take visual features as an example:

$$x_{visual} \approx \hat{x}_{visual} \quad (4)$$

In multi-modal interaction layer, in order to automatically obtain the interactive information between different modal features, we merge all the encoder features into a multi-modal encoder feature to reconstitute each input, rather than directly use corresponding encoder feature. In details, we first concatenate different encoder features to h_{mm}:

$$h_{mm} = [h_{tabular}; h_{visual}; h_{textual}] \quad (5)$$

Then $h_{mm} \in R^{1 \times 3k}$ is used to decode all the inputs:

$$\overline{x}_{tabular}, \overline{x}_{visual}, \overline{x}_{textual} = g(h_{mm}) \quad (6)$$

In fact, this could be treated as multi-task learning, and the loss in **MMAE** is shown as bellow:

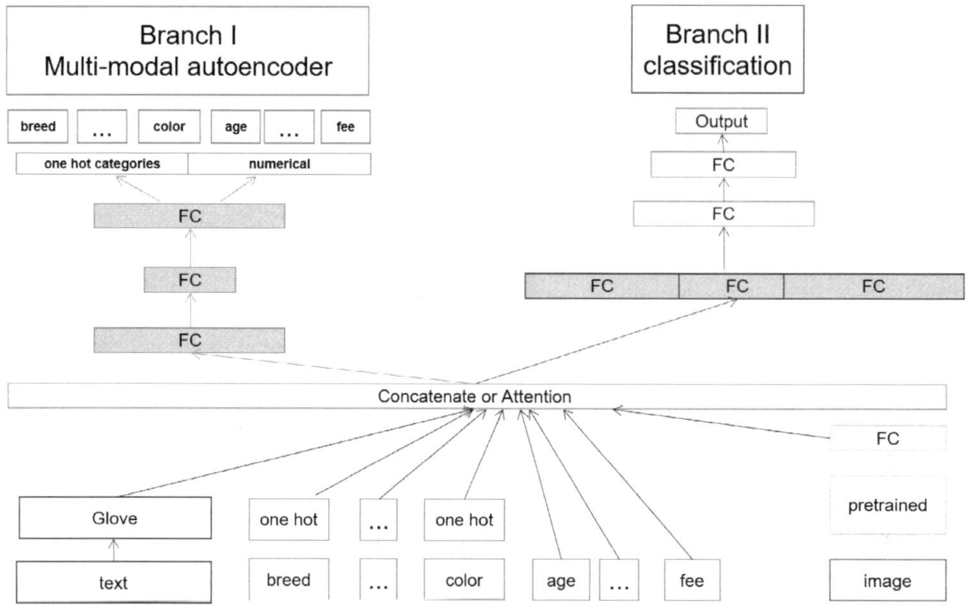

Figure 2: Framework of our solution.

$$Loss = \alpha * loss_{tabular} + \beta * loss_{visual} + \gamma * loss_{textual} \quad (7)$$

where $\alpha * loss_{tabular}$, $\beta * loss_{visual}$ and $\gamma * loss_{textual}$ are the reconstruction losses of different inputs, α, β and γ are the corresponding weights of different losses, they can adjust according to the practical scenario. In our experiments, we find that $\alpha = \beta = \gamma$ yields the best result. Besides, all the autoencoders in **MMAE** are four layers fully-connected neural networks. The multi-modal encoder feature we obtained from **MMAE** will be used in some downstream tasks to improve the performance, such as classification task.

3.2 Attention-based Multi-modal Modeling part:

In the previous work, a multi-modal model first receives different kind of inputs, then handles them separately to obtain high-level features, and do some simply interactions such as concatenate, finally a fully-connected layer is followed to get the prediction. However, in practical scenario, different modal features for a same task may have different importance, so simply concatenate those high-level features is not enough to help the model get key information. Inspired by the attention mechanism used in natural language processing and computer vision,we introduce attention mechanism into multi-modal model,which can make the model focus on the key information. Besides, we also add the multi-modal encoder feature from **MMAE** to enrich our input. The modeling part model mainly composed of four components:

Input Layer: This layer has the same function as the input layer in MMAE, so in this layer, we do the same thing as mentioned above.

Fully-Connected Layer and Convolutional Layer: In this layer, we use different neural networks for different input features. For the tabular features, we use a fully-connected layer to learn the high-level representation v_1, the activation function in each layer is ReLu (Glorot et al., 2011), and a dropout (Srivastava et al., 2014) is followed by each layer to prevent our model from over fitting. For the textual features, after word embedding layer, we use the same model architecture as TextCNN. Finally a fully connected layer is followed to obtain the final representation v_2. As for the visual features, we use the same architecture as DenseNet (Huang et al., 2017). DenseNet has some dense blocks, each layer in a dense block obtains additional inputs from all preceding layers. In our model, we use two dense blocks to obtain the final representation v_3.

Attention Layer: This layer is the core layer of Attention-based Multimodal Model. At the previous layer,we get the high-level one-dimensional features from each modal input: v_1, v_2 and v_3, these three representations have the same dimension $d^{1\times m}$. we employ soft attention mechanism to associate the important information between the given three high-level features. We compute the normalized attention weights as the similarity with Equation 8.

$$e_i = tanh(v_i \odot \mu^T), i \in [1, 2, 3] \quad (8)$$

where v_1 is one of the $v_{tabular}$, $v_{textual}$ and v_{visual}, μ is the weighted vector that we used to compute the similarity, it will randomly initialized and will be adjusted during the training stage. e_i is the un-normalized attention weights, $odot$ is the dot product between the two given vectors. Beside, in this equation, we use $tanh$ as the activation function. Next, we use softmax to get the normalized attention weights. For each element in v_i, it will multiply by its corresponding normalized attention weight to get the final attention output.

$$\hat{v}_i = \sum_{i=1}^{3} \frac{exp(e_i)}{\sum_{i=1}^{3} exp(e_i)} \cdot v_i, i \in [1, 2, 3] \quad (9)$$

where $\hat{v}_i$ is the attention output of each high-level feature. Finally we concatenate every $\hat{v}_i$ vi as this layer's output and pass on it to the next layer.

Merge and Classification Layer: In this layer, we not only use $\hat{v}_1$, $\hat{v}_2$ and $\hat{v}_3$ to predict the results,but also add the multi-modal encoder feature hmm which obtained from **MMAE** to improve model's performance.

$$h = [\hat{v}_1, \hat{v}_2, \hat{v}_3, h_{mm}] \quad (10)$$

where $h \in R^{1\times(3m+3k)}$. Because this is a multi-class classification problem,so we use $softmax$ to get the final results.

$$prediction = softmax(h) \quad (11)$$

4 Experimental settings and Results

In this section, we first introduce some baseline models and their experimental settings. In order to have a fair comparison and reduce the randomness of results, we use five-fold cross-validation. The batch size is set as 32. The neural networks are trained using the RMSprop optimizer with the learning rate 0.001.

4.1 Baseline models and Previous Work

$\#1$ **Tabular Only:** In this model,the input only has tabular features and will do data preprocessing mentioned above. Tabular Only model is a two layers fully-connected neural network,the number of hidden layer units in each layer is 256 and 128,the activation function is $relu$,and a dropout layer is followed to avoid overfitting,the dropout rate is 0.2.

$\#2$ **Textual Only:** This model is an application of **TextCNN**. In this model, we have the same parameter settings as **TextCNN**, the filter windows is 3,4,5 with 100 feature maps each, and dropout rate is 0.5, but we have a full-connected layer at then end before the classification layer.

$\#3$ **Visual Only:** This is an application of **DenseNet**. In this model, we have two Dense Blocks, each Dense Block has the same parameter settings, and we also have a full-connected layer at the end before the classification layer.

$\#4$ **Tabular (Continuous) + Textual + Visual with Concatenatey:** This is a common architecture for multi-modal dataset, this model has three independent parts which used to learn high-level features from different modal inputs. Continuous means the continuous features in tabular features only do Max-Min Normalization before put into the model. The parameters in these three parts are the same as baseline model **Tabular Only**, **Textual Only** and **Visual Only**. For the representations learned from different parts, this model will simply concatenate them before classification layer.

$\#5$ **Tabular (Discretized) + Textual + Visual with Concatenate:** This model is inspired by. The architecture and the parameters are the same as the model $\#4$, but this model will convert the continuous features to a discrete sequence of tokens to reduce the storage and prevent the model from overfitting.

4.2 Experimental Results

$\#6$ **Tabular(Continuous)+Textual+ Visual with Attention:** The architecture and the parameters in this model are the same as the model $\#4$, but we use soft attention mechanism to interactive the representations learned from different modal inputs instead of simply concatenating.

$\#7$ **Tabular(Continuous)+Textual+Visual+AE Feature with Attention:** In this architecture, we add the autoencoder features into our model. The autoencoder features has three parts from tabular features, textual features and visual features, they are trained from three in dependent autoencoders,all the autoencoders are four layers fully-connected neural network, and the hidden

	Model	Operation	Accuracy $\pm$ STD
#1	**Tabular only**	-	36.729$\pm$0.0061
#2	**Tabular only**	-	29.403$\pm$0.0032
#3	**Visual only**	-	29.252 $\pm$0.0031
#4	**Tabular(Continuous)+Textual+Visual**	Concatenate	37.080$\pm$0.0055
#5	**Tabular(Discretized) +Textual + Visual**	Concatenate	37.152$\pm$0.002
#6	**Tabular(Continuous) + Textual + Visual**	Attention	**37.381$\pm$0.0035**
#7	**Tabular (Continuous)+Textual+ Visual+ AE-Feature**	Attention	37.582$\pm$0.0032
#8	**Tabular (Continuous)+Textual+ Visual+ MMAE-Feature**	Attention	**37.883$\pm$0.0037**

Table 1: Accuracy between our models and some baseline models on different Multi-modal datasets. AE-Feature means the additional features obtained from three independent autoencoders, MMAE-Feature means the additional features learned from Multi-modal Autoencoder. As for the representations learned from different modals, concatenate means they are combined by simply concatenating, attention means they are combined using attention mechanism. Accuracy higher than the best baseline are in bold. Results are displayed as $mean \pm std$.

Feature	MSE (Normalized)
Visual Feature only	0.03786
+ Tabular Feature	0.03557
+ Textual Feature	**0.03468**

Table 2: The image reconstruction loss using different feature combination. Multi-model Autoencoder has a lower loss.

units size is 512-64-64-512. We concatenate them together with the attention output to predict the final results.

#8 **Tabular(Continuous)+Textual+Visual+MMAE Feature with Attention:** In this architecture, we add the multi-modal autoencoder features into our model. As introduced above, the multi-modal encoder feature is obtained from output of MMAE, which learns the interactive information between different modal features. In order to have a fair comparison with #7, the MMAE Feature has the same dimension with AE-Feature. Besides, MMAE also has three autoencoders, and the parameters in each autoencoders are the same as #7.

5 Conclusion

In this paper, we proposed the a novel framework for multimodal data classification. The framework consists of multi-modal autoencoder module and attention-based multi-modal modeling module. We evaluate the model on the large-scale multimodal datasets. Our framework shows an advantage on accuracy with compared to other approaches. In the future, we will try to extract more features, such as the semantic information of images, thus the similarity or dissimilarity between different modality can be calculated. Moreover, our framework could be adapted to other types of multimodal machine learning task, for instance, the detection task. On the other hand, we will conduct more experiments on larger dataset.

References

Xavier Glorot, Antoine Bordes, and Yoshua Bengio. 2011. Deep sparse rectifier neural networks. In *Proceedings of the fourteenth international conference on artificial intelligence and statistics*, pages 315–323. JMLR Workshop and Conference Proceedings.

Gao Huang, Zhuang Liu, Laurens Van Der Maaten, and Kilian Q Weinberger. 2017. Densely connected convolutional networks. In *Proceedings of the IEEE conference on computer vision and pattern recognition*, pages 4700–4708.

Jiquan Ngiam, Aditya Khosla, Mingyu Kim, Juhan Nam, Honglak Lee, and Andrew Y Ng. 2011. Multimodal deep learning. In *ICML*.

Sergio Oramas, Francesco Barbieri, Oriol Nieto Caballero, and Xavier Serra. 2018. Multimodal deep learning for music genre classification. *Transactions of the International Society for Music Information Retrieval. 2018; 1 (1): 4-21.*

Valentin Radu, Nicholas D Lane, Sourav Bhattacharya, Cecilia Mascolo, Mahesh K Marina, and Fahim Kawsar. 2016. Towards multimodal deep learning for activity recognition on mobile devices. In *Proceedings of the 2016 ACM International Joint Conference on Pervasive and Ubiquitous Computing: Adjunct*, pages 185–188.

Nitish Srivastava, Geoffrey Hinton, Alex Krizhevsky, Ilya Sutskever, and Ruslan Salakhutdinov. 2014. Dropout: a simple way to prevent neural networks from overfitting. *The journal of machine learning research*, 15(1):1929–1958.

Tao Xu, Han Zhang, Xiaolei Huang, Shaoting Zhang, and Dimitris N Metaxas. 2016. Multimodal deep learning for cervical dysplasia diagnosis. In *International conference on medical image computing and computer-assisted intervention*, pages 115–123. Springer.

Validity-Based Sampling and Smoothing Methods for Multiple Reference Image Captioning

Shunta Nagasawa[1] **Yotaro Watanabe**[2] **Hitoshi Iyatomi**[1]
[1]Department of Applied Informatics, Graduate School of Science and Engineering, Hosei University, Tokyo, Japan
[2]PKSHA Technology Inc, Tokyo, Japan
{shunta.nagasawa@stu., iyatomi@}hosei.ac.jp
y_watanabe@pkshatech.com

Abstract

In image captioning, multiple captions are often provided as ground truths, since a valid caption is not always uniquely determined. Conventional methods randomly select a single caption and treat it as correct, but there have been few effective training methods that utilize multiple given captions. In this paper, we propose two training techniques for making effective use of multiple reference captions: 1) validity-based caption sampling (VBCS), which prioritizes the use of captions that are estimated to be highly valid during training, and 2) weighted caption smoothing (WCS), which applies smoothing only to the relevant words the reference caption to reflect multiple reference captions simultaneously. Experiments show that our proposed methods improve CIDEr by 2.6 points and BLEU4 by 0.9 points from baseline on the MSCOCO dataset.

1 Introduction

Image captioning is a very challenging task that requires recognizing and understanding the objects in the image and then verbalizing the recognition results using natural language. This task is expected to have a wide range of practical applications, including use in text-based image retrieval systems and providing assistance for the visually impaired (Lin et al., 2014; Gurari et al., 2020). With the development of the field of deep learning, research in the area has primarily focused on the end-to-end method, which consists of an encoder that extracts information from images and a decoder that generates a description from the extracted information (Karpathy and Fei-Fei, 2015; Vinyals et al., 2015; Xu et al., 2015; Lu et al., 2017). For example, some of the recent models use pre-trained object detection models (Ren et al., 2015; Liu et al., 2016; Anderson et al., 2018) and self-attention mechanisms (Huang et al., 2019; Cornia et al., 2020) for encoders or decoders.

Image captioning is often a multi-reference task where multiple reference captions are used for training. MSCOCO (Lin et al., 2014), one of the most famous datasets of image captions, has about five reference captions for each image. Some of these reference captions are subject to uncertainty due to speculation, and may differ in subject matter and wording. Such label variance may affect the training of the model and the evaluation of the generated captions. In typical training for conventional models, one caption is randomly selected by uniform sampling at each training epoch, which means the validity and variance of reference captions are not considered. In addition, reference captions that were not selected in the training epoch are treated as incorrect. To address this problem, Yi et al. (2020) proposed a new metric that correlates well with human evaluation by taking into account the variance of captions. However, to the best of our knowledge, appropriate training methods that consider such variation in captions have not yet been sufficiently studied.

In this paper, we propose a simple and effective training method that uses multiple reference captions to generate appropriate captions. The proposed training method consists of two techniques: validity-based caption sampling (VBCS), which selects highly valid reference captions, and weighted caption smoothing (WCS), which reflects multiple reference captions simultaneously in training. We define that a highly valid caption has common phrases among reference captions. In VBCS, the validity score for each reference caption is estimated based on similarities among the reference captions. When training the model, the training captions to be used in each epoch are sampled, one per image, according to this score. In addition, WCS improves the generality of the model by applying soft labels only for highly relevant words based on their validity scores. By effectively utilizing multiple captions, the proposed method improves

Proceedings of the Third Workshop on Multimodal Artificial Intelligence, pages 36–41
June 6, 2021.

CIDEr by 2.6 points and BLEU4 by 0.9 points in the evaluation experiments using the MSCOCO dataset. Main contributions of this paper include:

- Validity-based caption sampling (VBCS) allows us to prioritize captions that are considered to be highly valid.
- Weighted caption smoothing (WCS) allows multiple reference captions to be reflected in training simultaneously.
- The proposed VBCS and WCS are architecture-independent and highly versatile for image captioning and can be applied to other NLP multi-reference tasks.

2 Related Work

2.1 Selection of Training Data

Preparing highly reliable training data is important, however open datasets often contain incorrectly labeled or mislabeled samples. In a typical supervised task, one training label is assigned to each piece of training data. In this common setting, several methods have been proposed to improve the performance of the model by selecting suitable data for training from a large amount of labeled data (Reed et al., 2014; Northcutt et al., 2021).

In the multi-reference task, on the other hand, we expect to improve the performance by selecting appropriate labels from among them in the training. The choice can be deterministic, choosing the best one, or probability-based, depending on the characteristics of the data, such as likelihood (Hastings, 1970; Casella and George, 1992). The latter can be taken as a sampling problem. The proposed method prioritizes the sampling of highly valid captions to reduce the influence of less valid captions (i.e., noisy samples) and improves the performance.

2.2 Soft Label

Label smoothing (LS) (Pereyra et al., 2017) is a widely used soft labeling technique that prevents overfitting by creating soft supervised labels (i.e., adding a uniform distribution to each class of training labels). The introduction of LS has also been reported to improve the performance in language generation tasks, such as machine translation (Vaswani et al., 2017) and image captioning (Huang et al., 2019). Although the LS may contribute to the diversity of generated words, it treats all words in the vocabulary equally without taking into account their relevance to the image. Our WCS further improves the performance by constructing a novel soft label from multiple reference captions given to the image. Our soft label focuses on only relevant words among the reference captions based on the validity score.

3 Methodology

3.1 Validity-Based Caption Sampling (VBCS)

The proposed VBCS can take into account the validity and variance of reference captions. We define that a high validity caption has common phrases among reference captions, and assign a validity score to each reference caption. Let $R^{(i)} = \{\mathrm{ref}_1^{(i)}, \mathrm{ref}_2^{(i)}, \cdots, \mathrm{ref}_{K^{(i)}}^{(i)}\}$ be the reference caption set for image $I^{(i)} (i = 1, 2, \cdots, N)$. $K^{(i)}$ is the number of reference captions for image $I^{(i)}$. The similarity $s_j^{(i)}$ of the reference caption $\mathrm{ref}_j^{(i)}$ to other captions for image $I^{(i)}$ is calculated as follows:

$$\mathrm{s}_j^{(i)} = \frac{1}{K^{(i)} - 1} \sum_{\substack{k=1\cdots K^{(i)},\\ k\neq j}} f_{\mathrm{metric}}(\mathrm{ref}_j^{(i)}, \mathrm{ref}_k^{(i)}), \quad (1)$$

where f_{metric} is a metric of the similarity of the reference caption. Possible metrics that use word n-grams or longest match sequence include BLEU (Papineni et al., 2002), ROUGE-L (Lin et al., 2014), and CIDEr (Vedantam et al., 2015). Finally, the sampling probability $p_j^{(i)}$ for the j-th reference caption of image $I^{(i)}$ is calculated as follows:

$$p_j^{(i)} = \frac{\exp(\mathrm{s}_j^{(i)})}{\sum_{k=1}^{K^{(i)}} \exp(\mathrm{s}_k^{(i)})}. \quad (2)$$

This probability represents the validity of the reference caption and is referred to as the validity score in this paper. This allows us to prioritize training captions that have a high degree of similarity to other reference captions and are considered to be highly valid.

3.2 Weighted Caption Smoothing (WCS)

The proposed WCS solves the problem that unselected captions are treated as incorrect by introducing a soft label. Our soft label generated by WCS consists of only the words in each position of multiple reference captions, weighted by the validity score obtained by VBCS. This technique can reflect multiple captions in the training simultaneously.

	Evaluation Metric					
	B@1	B@4	M	R	C	S
Anderson et al. (2018)†	76.0 ±0.2	34.9 ±0.1	27.3 ±0.1	56.2 ±0.1	111.7 ±0.0	20.5 ±0.1
+ **LS**	76.1 ±0.1	35.2 ±0.2	27.4 ±0.0	56.3 ±0.1	112.8 ±0.3	20.6 ±0.2
+ **VBCS (ours)**	76.2 ±0.1	35.2 ±0.1	27.4 ±0.1	56.4 ±0.1	113.1 ±0.5	20.7 ±0.1
+ **WCS (ours)**	76.9 ±0.3	35.7 ±0.2	27.4 ±0.1	56.6 ±0.1	113.7 ±0.7	20.7 ±0.1
+ **VBCS + WCS (ours)**	**77.2 ±0.1**	**35.8 ±0.1**	**27.5 ±0.1**	**56.7 ±0.1**	**114.3 ±0.3**	**20.8 ±0.1**

Table 1: Summary of image captioning performance for MSCOCO test data, where B@N, M, R, C, and S are short for BLEU@N, METEOR, ROUGE-L, CIDEr, and SPICE scores, respectively. For a robust evaluation, we run each method five times with different seeds. († are not the values given in the original paper, but the result of our best efforts to reimplement them.)

Specifically, our soft label $\tilde{y}_t^{(i)}$ used for predicting the t-th word of the image $I^{(i)}$ obtained by WCS is defined with two terms $y_{j,t}^{(i)}$ and $\hat{y}_t^{(i)}$:

$$\tilde{y}_t^{(i)} = (1-\alpha) y_{j,t}^{(i)} + \alpha \hat{y}_t^{(i)}, \tag{3}$$

where $y_{j,t}^{(i)}$ is the one-hot representation for the t-th word of the j-th reference caption selected by VBCS and α is hyperparameter that adjusts the smoothing. $\hat{y}_t^{(i)}$ is the weighted sum of the t-th word one-hot representation of multiple reference captions by the validity score and is obtained by:

$$\hat{y}_t^{(i)} = \sum_{k=1}^{K^{(i)}} p_k^{(i)} y_{k,t}^{(i)}. \tag{4}$$

Here, the length of each reference caption is padded or cropped according to the length of $y_j^{(i)}$.

The main difference between WCS and LS is the number of words to be smoothed. In our WCS, smoothing is not done uniformly for all words, but only for words that are in the same position in the assigned reference caption, weighted individually according to their validity score (i.e., words that are highly relevant).

4 Experiment

4.1 Dataset

We used the MSCOCO 2014 caption dataset (Lin et al., 2014), which contains 123,287 images labeled with five captions each. The "Karpathy" data split (Karpathy and Fei-Fei, 2015) was used for performance comparisons, and 5,000 images were used for validation, 5,000 images for testing, and the rest for training. As for pre-processing, we converted all sentences to lower case and dropped any words that occurred less than five times. To evaluate caption quality, we used several standard metrics, such as BLEU (Papineni et al., 2002), METEOR (Denkowski and Lavie, 2014), ROUGE-L (Lin, 2004), CIDEr (Vedantam et al., 2015), and SPICE (Anderson et al., 2016).

4.2 Models

For our evaluation, we used the Up-Down (Anderson et al., 2018) model as a baseline, which has a typical structure in the field of image captioning and has been reported to be highly accurate. We compared the following training methods: +**LS** with its uniform smoothing for all words; +**VBCS**, which prioritizes highly valid reference captions for training based on the validity score; +**WCS** with smoothing for highly relevant words based on the validity score; and +**VBCS**+**WCS**, which is our proposed method. To ensure robust evaluation, we ran each method five times with different seeds.

4.3 Implementation Details

In the Up-Down model, we used the Faster-RCNN model (Ren et al., 2015), which was pre-trained with ImageNet (Deng et al., 2009) and Visual Genome (Krishna et al., 2017), as a content vector generator. We used beam search when generating captions, and set the beam size to 5. In this study, we decided to select CIDEr for f_{metric}, as it is the most widely used in image captioning and is capable of focusing on the importance of caption phrases. In Section 5.2, we will discuss the effectiveness of other metrics for f_{metric}. The hyperparameter of LS was set to 0.2 according to Huang et al. (2019). This corresponds to α when $\hat{y_t}^{(i)}$ is regarded as a soft label equal to all words in Eq 3. In WCS, α was set to 0.2 for comparison.

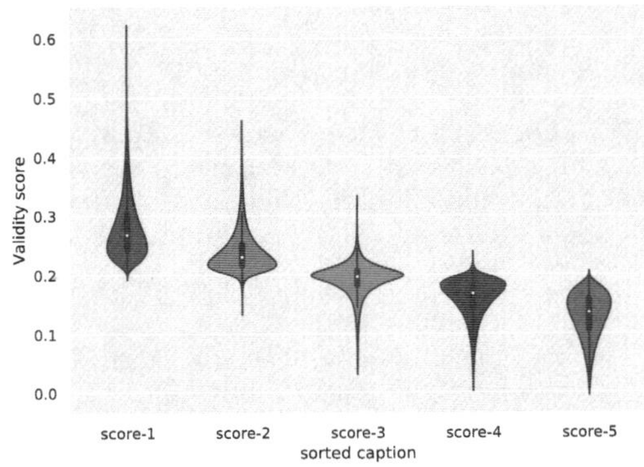

Figure 1: Distribution of the sorted validity scores in descending order.

	Evaluation Metric					
f_{metric}	B@1	B@4	M	R	C	S
baseline	75.8	34.7	27.2	56.1	109.4	20.1
BLEU4	**77.0**	**35.8**	27.2	**56.6**	111.4	20.3
ROUGE-L	76.6	35.2	27.2	56.5	110.7	20.4
CIDEr	76.7	35.4	**27.4**	**56.6**	**112.0**	**20.5**

Table 2: Comparison of scores for validation data under different f_{metric} choices in VBCS.

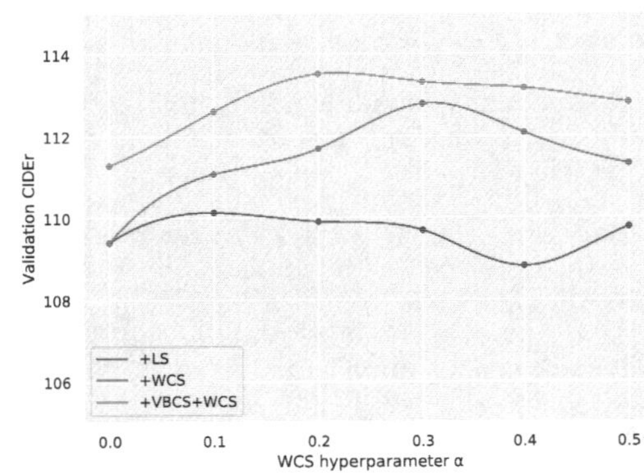

Figure 2: The effect of α, a smoothing hyperparameter of WCS for validation data. The proposed method achieves higher performance than LS with any α.

5 Results and Discussion

5.1 Quantitative Analysis

Table 1 demonstrates the performance of our proposed method with other comparable models. With the introduction of efficient caption sampling, our VBCS improved performance in all metrics against the baseline. In particular, the CIDEr score improved by 1.4 points. This confirmed that sampling using the validity scores contributes to improving the score for each metric. Figure 1 shows the distribution of the validity scores in descending order using the violin plot. Since the validity of each reference caption is different, the distribution from the validity score is very different from the commonly used uniform distribution.

Our WCS outperformed LS on all metrics and was 0.5 and 0.9 points higher on BLEU4 and CIDEr, respectively. Since WCS smooths only a limited number of relevant words, we believe that it can learn more efficiently than LS, which smooths all words uniformly. The proposed techniques (+ VBCS + WCS) scored the highest on all the metrics. The improvements in BLEU4, ROUGE-L, and CIDEr, which are based on n-grams and longest matching sequence are particularly clear.

5.2 Effect of Hyperparameters

In this section, we investigate the impact of hyperparameters in our proposed methods.

Effect of f_{metric} for Validation Data Table 2 demonstrates the performance with the validation data, where BLEU4, ROUGE-L, and CIDEr were applied to f_{metric}. Regardless of the choice of f_{metric}, the proposed method produces results equal to or better than baseline. These results indicate that CIDEr is superior to the others and can capture more important phrases than other metrics.

Effect of Hyperparameter in WCS Figure 2 demonstrates the effect of the hyperparameter α on the validation data in WCS. Our proposed +VBCS+WCS with $\alpha = 0.2$ performed the best. Since WCS applies to smooth to a limited number of words, it results in higher scores than those of LS with any α.

6 Conclusion and Future Works

In this paper, we proposed two novel techniques called VBCS and WCS that effectively utilize multiple references in image captioning tasks, and demonstrated their advantages. The former determines a sampling probability (i.e., validity score), for each caption based on similarities among the reference captions. The latter simultaneously reflects multiple reference captions in the training. In the future, we would like to consider the grammar in WCS and, extend the proposed method to be adaptable to reinforcement learning.

References

Peter Anderson, Basura Fernando, Mark Johnson, and Stephen Gould. 2016. Spice: Semantic propositional image caption evaluation. In *Proceeding of the European Conference on Computer Vision*, pages 382–398.

Peter Anderson, Xiaodong He, Chris Buehler, Damien Teney, Mark Johnson, Stephen Gould, and Lei Zhang. 2018. Bottom-up and top-down attention for image captioning and visual question answering. In *Proceedings of the IEEE Conference on Computer Vision and Pattern Recognition*, pages 6077–6086.

George Casella and Edward I George. 1992. Explaining the gibbs sampler. *The American Statistician*, 46(3):167–174.

Marcella Cornia, Matteo Stefanini, Lorenzo Baraldi, and Rita Cucchiara. 2020. Meshed-memory transformer for image captioning. In *Proceedings of the IEEE Conference on Computer Vision and Pattern Recognition*, pages 10578–10587.

Jia Deng, Wei Dong, Richard Socher, Li-Jia Li, Kai Li, and Li Fei-Fei. 2009. Imagenet: A large-scale hierarchical image database. In *Proceedings of the IEEE Conference on Computer Vision and Pattern Recognition*, pages 248–255.

Michael Denkowski and Alon Lavie. 2014. Meteor universal: Language specific translation evaluation for any target language. In *Proceedings of the Ninth Workshop on Statistical Machine Translation*, pages 376–380.

Danna Gurari, Yinan Zhao, Meng Zhang, and Nilavra Bhattacharya. 2020. Captioning images taken by people who are blind. In *Proceedings of the IEEE European Conference on Computer Vision*, pages 417–434.

Wilfred Keith Hastings. 1970. Monte Carlo sampling methods using Markov chains and their applications. *Biometrika*, 57(1):97–109.

Lun Huang, Wenmin Wang, Jie Chen, and Xiao-Yong Wei. 2019. Attention on attention for image captioning. In *Proceedings of the IEEE International Conference on Computer Vision*, pages 4634–4643.

Andrej Karpathy and Li Fei-Fei. 2015. Deep visual-semantic alignments for generating image descriptions. In *Proceedings of the IEEE Conference on Computer Vision and Pattern Recognition*, pages 3128–3137.

Ranjay Krishna, Yuke Zhu, Oliver Groth, Justin Johnson, Kenji Hata, Joshua Kravitz, Stephanie Chen, Yannis Kalantidis, Li-Jia Li, David A Shamma, et al. 2017. Visual genome: Connecting language and vision using crowdsourced dense image annotations. *International Journal of Computer Vision*, 123(1):32–73.

Chin-Yew Lin. 2004. ROUGE: A package for automatic evaluation of summaries. In *Text Summarization Branches Out*, pages 74–81.

Tsung-Yi Lin, Michael Maire, Serge Belongie, James Hays, Pietro Perona, Deva Ramanan, Piotr Dollár, and C Lawrence Zitnick. 2014. Microsoft coco: Common objects in context. In *Proceedings of the European Conference on Computer Vision*, pages 740–755.

Wei Liu, Dragomir Anguelov, Dumitru Erhan, Christian Szegedy, Scott Reed, Cheng-Yang Fu, and Alexander C Berg. 2016. Ssd: Single shot multibox detector. In *Proceedings of the European Conference on Computer Vision*, pages 21–37.

Jiasen Lu, Caiming Xiong, Devi Parikh, and Richard Socher. 2017. Knowing when to look: Adaptive attention via a visual sentinel for image captioning. In *Proceedings of the IEEE Conference on Computer Vision and Pattern Recognition*, pages 375–383.

Curtis G. Northcutt, Lu Jiang, and Isaac L. Chuang. 2021. Confident learning: Estimating uncertainty in dataset labels. *CoRR preprint arXiv:1911.00068v3*.

Kishore Papineni, Salim Roukos, Todd Ward, and Wei-Jing Zhu. 2002. Bleu: a method for automatic evaluation of machine translation. In *Proceedings of the 40th Annual Meeting of the Association for Computational Linguistics*, pages 311–318.

Gabriel Pereyra, George Tucker, Jan Chorowski, Łukasz Kaiser, and Geoffrey Hinton. 2017. Regularizing neural networks by penalizing confident output distributions. *CoRR preprint arXiv:1701.06548*.

Scott Reed, Honglak Lee, Dragomir Anguelov, Christian Szegedy, Dumitru Erhan, and Andrew Rabinovich. 2014. Training deep neural networks on noisy labels with bootstrapping. *CoRR preprint arXiv:1412.6596*.

Shaoqing Ren, Kaiming He, Ross Girshick, and Jian Sun. 2015. Faster r-cnn: Towards real-time object detection with region proposal networks. In *Advances in Neural Information Processing Systems*, pages 91–99.

Ashish Vaswani, Noam Shazeer, Niki Parmar, Jakob Uszkoreit, Llion Jones, Aidan N Gomez, Łukasz Kaiser, and Illia Polosukhin. 2017. Attention is all you need. In *Advances in Neural Information Processing Systems*, pages 5998–6008.

Ramakrishna Vedantam, C Lawrence Zitnick, and Devi Parikh. 2015. Cider: Consensus-based image description evaluation. In *Proceedings of the IEEE Conference on Computer Vision and Pattern Recognition*, pages 4566–4575.

Oriol Vinyals, Alexander Toshev, Samy Bengio, and Dumitru Erhan. 2015. Show and tell: A neural image caption generator. In *Proceedings of the IEEE Conference on Computer Vision and Pattern Recognition*, pages 3156–3164.

Kelvin Xu, Jimmy Ba, Ryan Kiros, Kyunghyun Cho, Aaron Courville, Ruslan Salakhudinov, Rich Zemel, and Yoshua Bengio. 2015. Show, attend and tell: Neural image caption generation with visual attention. In *International Conference on Machine Learning*, pages 2048–2057.

Yanzhi Yi, Hangyu Deng, and Jinglu Hu. 2020. Improving image captioning evaluation by considering inter references variance. In *Proceedings of the 58th Annual Meeting of the Association for Computational Linguistics*, pages 985–994.

Modality-specific Distillation

Woojeong Jin[1*] **Maziar Sanjabi**[2] **Shaoliang Nie**[2] **Liang Tan**[2] **Xiang Ren**[1] **Hamed Firooz**[2]
[1]University of Southern California [2]Facebook AI
{woojeong.jin,xiangren}@usc.edu
{maziars,snie,liangtan,mhfirooz}@fb.com

Abstract

Large neural networks are impractical to deploy on mobile devices due to their heavy computational cost and slow inference. Knowledge distillation (KD) is a technique to reduce the model size while retaining performance by transferring knowledge from a large "teacher" model to a smaller "student" model. However, KD on multimodal datasets such as vision-language datasets is relatively unexplored and digesting such multimodal information is challenging since different modalities present different types of information. In this paper, we propose modality-specific distillation (MSD) to effectively transfer knowledge from a teacher on multimodal datasets. Existing KD approaches can be applied to multimodal setup, but a student doesn't have access to modality-specific predictions. Our idea aims at mimicking a teacher's modality-specific predictions by introducing an auxiliary loss term for each modality. Because each modality has different importance for predictions, we also propose weighting approaches for the auxiliary losses; a meta-learning approach to learn the optimal weights on these loss terms. In our experiments, we demonstrate the effectiveness of our MSD and the weighting scheme and show that it achieves better performance than KD.

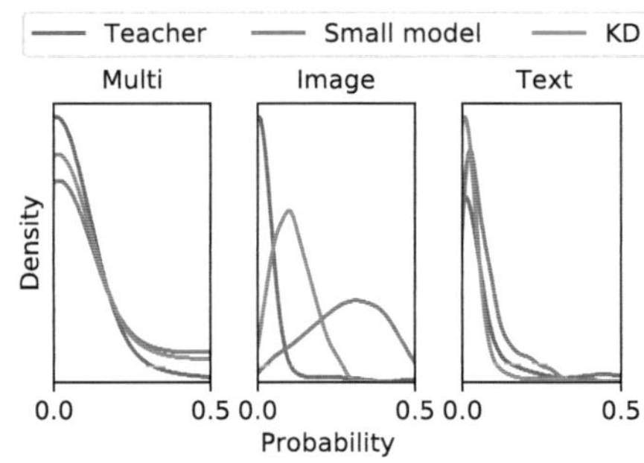

Figure 1: **Density of model outputs on Hateful-Memes:** given multimodality samples as input (Multi), given only image modality as input (Image), and given only text modality as input (Text). KD denotes conventional knowledge distillation and the small model is a model with distillation. We observe that there is still a prediction gap between the teacher and the student trained by KD. To minimize the gap, we propose modality-specific distillation (MSD).

1 Introduction

Recent advances in computer vision and natural language processing are attributed to deep neural networks with large number of layers. Current state-of-the-art architectures are getting wider and deeper with billions of parameters, e.g., BERT (Devlin et al., 2019) and GPT-3 (Brown et al., 2020). In addition to their huge sizes, such wide and deep models suffer from high computational costs and latencies at inference. These shortcomings greatly limit these models practicality and make them unsuitable for many mobile applications.

To mitigate the heavy computational cost and the memory requirement, there have been several attempts to compress a larger model (a teacher) into a smaller model (a student) (Ba and Caruana, 2014; Hinton et al., 2015; Romero et al., 2014; Park et al., 2019; Müller et al., 2020). Among them, *knowledge distillation* (KD) (Hinton et al., 2015) assumes the knowledge in the teacher as a learned mapping from inputs to outputs, and transfers the knowledge by training the student model with the teacher's outputs (of the last or a hidden layer) as targets. Recently, KD has been explored in various studies such as improving a student model (Hinton et al., 2015; Park et al., 2019; Romero et al., 2014; Tian et al., 2019; Müller et al., 2020) and improving a teacher model itself by self-distillation (Xie et al., 2020; Kim et al., 2020; Furlanello et al., 2018).

There has been a surge of interest in distillation in a multimodal setup such as cross-modal

*The work in progress was mainly done during internship at Facebook AI.

Proceedings of the Third Workshop on Multimodal Artificial Intelligence, pages 42–53
June 6, 2021.

distillation (Gupta et al., 2016; Tian et al., 2019). Multimodal problems involve relating information from multiple sources. For example, visual question answering (VQA) requires answering questions about an image (Antol et al., 2015; Goyal et al., 2017; Gurari et al., 2018; Singh et al., 2019) and models should incorporate information from the text and image sources to answer the questions. Multimodal problems are important because many real-world problems requires understanding signals from different modalities to make accurate predictions; information on the web and social media is often represented as textual and visual description. Digesting such multimodal information in an effective manner is challenging due to their different natures, e.g., visual and textual sources present different types of information. Also, they don't have comparable amounts of information in each modality; usually the textual modality tends to dominate and have more information.

While KD approaches can be applied to multimodal applications, student models in these approaches are directly trained to mimic a teacher's outputs without access to teacher's modality-specific behaviors. As a result, the student and teacher models may significantly differ in their outputs using each modality as input. We illustrate the point in Fig 1. The gap verifies that the student's and the teacher's modality-specific behaviors are not well matched. We hypothesize that it may lead to inefficient distillation, because the student does not carefully mimic the teacher's modality-specific predictions.

Thus, we propose *modality-specific distillation* (MSD) which is to mimic the teacher's modality-specific behavior to minimize the gaps. We improve the transfer by splitting the multimodality into separate modalities, using them as additional inputs, and thus distilling modality-specific behavior of the teacher. Our MSD introduces auxiliary losses per modality to encourage each modality to be distilled effectively; we transfer the modality-specific knowledge from the teacher. Furthermore, we propose weighting approaches for weighting the auxiliary losses to take importance of each modality into account; one modality might have more important information. There are two main strategies to weight these auxiliary losses in the objective; population-based and instance-wise weighting schemes. In the population based, the weight of each loss term is fixed for the whole population. But in many cases the samples' modalities might carry different amount of information; one of modalities has more important information for predictions. Thus, we explore an intuitive instance-wise weighting scheme. In the end, we propose a meta-learning approach to find optimal weights.

As we will see in our empirical study on multimodal datasets, MSD significantly improves the performance of student models over KD. Also, our extensive experiments verify that MSD with weighting functions learned by our method shows the best performance among other weighting schemes. In our analysis, we show that datasets are different in the need of population-based or sample-specific weighting; the MM-IMDB dataset, for example, shows less improvement on instance-wise weighting compared to population-based weighting.

2 Background

In this section, we first define notations and revisit conventional knowledge distillation (KD).

2.1 Problem Definition and Notations

Given a trained and frozen teacher model T and a student model S, the output of our task is a trained student model. Our goal is to transfer knowledge from the teacher to the student on multimodal datasets. We let f_T and f_S be functions of the teacher and the student, respectively. t and s refer to softmax output of the teacher and the student. Typically the models are deep neural networks and the teacher is deeper than the student. The function f can be defined using output of the last layer of the network (e.g., logits). X is a multimodal (language-vision) dataset, X^t refers to only the text modality of X, X^v is refers to only the image modality of X, and x_i is a dataset instance. In this work, we focus on one text and one image modalities, but it is easy to extend the work to more/other modalities.

2.2 Conventional Knowledge Distillation

In knowledge distillation (Hinton et al., 2015), a student is trained to minimize a weighted sum of two different losses: (a) cross entropy with hard labels (one-hot encodings on correct labels) using a standard softmax function, (b) cross entropy with soft labels (probability distribution of labels) produced by a teacher with a temperature higher than 1 in the softmax of both models. The temperature controls the softness of the probability distributions.

Thus, the loss for the student is defined as:

$$\mathcal{L}_{\text{student}} = \lambda \mathcal{L}_{\text{CE}} + (1 - \lambda) \mathcal{L}_{\text{distill}}, \quad (1)$$

where $\mathcal{L}_{\text{CE}}$ is a standard cross-entropy loss on hard labels, $\mathcal{L}_{\text{distill}}$ is a distillation loss, which is a cross-entropy loss on soft labels, and $\lambda \in [0, 1]$ controls the balance between hard and soft targets.

To be specific, knowledge distillation (Hinton et al., 2015) minimizes Kullback-Leibler divergence between soft targets from a teacher and probabilities from a student. The soft targets (or soft labels) are defined as softmax on outputs of f_T with temperature τ. The distillation loss is defined as follows:

$$\mathcal{L}_{\text{distill}} = \tau^2 \frac{1}{|X|} \sum_{x_i \in X} \text{KL}(t(x_i; \tau), s(x_i; \tau))), \quad (2)$$

where

$$t(x_i; \tau) = \sigma(\frac{f_T(x_i)}{\tau}), \; s(x_i; \tau) = \sigma(\frac{f_S(x_i)}{\tau}), \quad (3)$$

σ is a softmax functoin. The temperature parameter τ controls the entropy of the output distribution (higher temperature τ means higher entropy in the soft labels). Following (Hinton et al., 2015), we scale the loss by τ^2 in order to keep gradient magnitudes approximately constant when changing the temperature. We omit τ for brevity.

Limitations. This KD can be applied to multimodal setups and student models in this distillation are directly trained to mimic a teacher's outputs without access to teacher's modality-specific behaviors. As a result, the student and teacher models may significantly differ in their modality-specific outputs, which leads to inefficient distillation. To better mimic the teacher's behaviors, we propose modality-specific distillation in the next section.

3 Proposed Method

In this section, we introduce our proposed approach, modality-specific distillation (MSD) for multimodal datasets.

3.1 Modality-specific Distillation

Samples in multimodal datasets are constructed from multiple modalities such as text modality and image modality. In this work, we focus on vision-language datasets. The core idea of MSD is to feed each modality as a separate input into a teacher and a student, and transfer the modality-specific knowledge of the teacher to the student. This will minimize the gap between a teacher and its student with regard to individual modalities predictions and thus the student learns more effectively from a teacher. Fig. 2 illustrates comparison between KD and MSD. From this perspective, MSD serves as a data augmentation strategy (Xie et al., 2019b, 2020), where the augmented data is naturally generated from the modalities of the input. Our approach can be viewed as an extension of Cutout (DeVries and Taylor, 2017) that masks out random sections of input images during training while our approach masks out one of the modalities during distillation. Unlike some other data augmentation techniques such as Mixup (Zhang et al., 2017) where the labels for augmented data is generated through simple interpolation, we use the teacher to guide us for setting soft-labels in MSD.

To be specific, we introduce two loss terms, $\mathcal{L}_{\text{textKD}}$ and $\mathcal{L}_{\text{imageKD}}$ to minimize difference between probability distributions between the teacher and the student given each modality (assuming text and image as the only two modalities).

$$\mathcal{L}_{\text{textKD}} = \tau^2 \frac{1}{|X_t|} \sum_{x_i \in X_t} \text{KL}(t(x_i), s(x_i)). \quad (4)$$

$\mathcal{L}_{\text{imageKD}}$ is similarly defined; the input is image modality instead.

With above two auxiliary losses, the MSD loss for the student is defined as follows:

$$\mathcal{L}_{\text{distill}} = \sum_{x_i \in X} w_i \text{KL}(t(x_i), s(x_i))) + \sum_{x_i \in X^v} w_i^v \text{KL}(t(x_i), s(x_i))) + \sum_{x_i \in X^t} w_i^t \text{KL}(t(x_i), s(x_i))), \quad (5)$$

where we omit the scaling factor $\tau^2 \frac{1}{|X|}$ for brevity. $w_i, w_i^t, w_i^v \in [0, 1]$ control the balance between three distillation losses. These weights determine importance of each modality and they affect the student's performance on multimodal datasets.

Weighting on Each Modality. Samples from multimodal datasets have different information on each modality. Fig. 3 shows the teacher model predictions for samples in Hateful-Memes and MM-IMDB test sets. For each sample, three probabilities are calculated: 1) predictions of samples with both of its modalities, 2) predictions of samples with just its text modality, and 3) predictions of samples with just its image modality. As one can

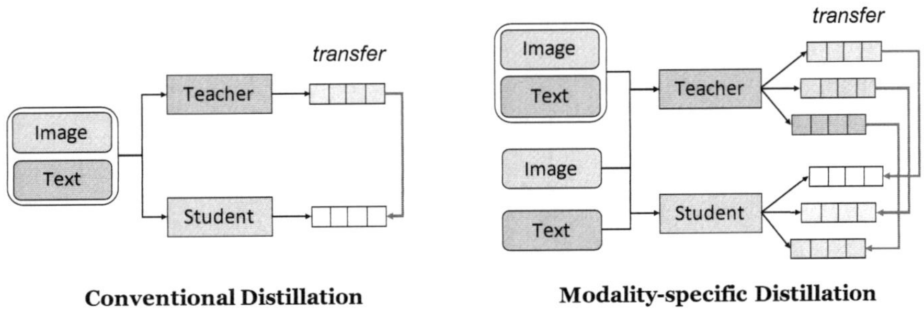

Figure 2: **Comparison between KD and MSD.** In KD, multimodal datasets are taken as a teacher and a student's inputs to compute the distillation loss. However, we factorize the multimodal input into each modality, and use it as a separate input to a teacher and student.

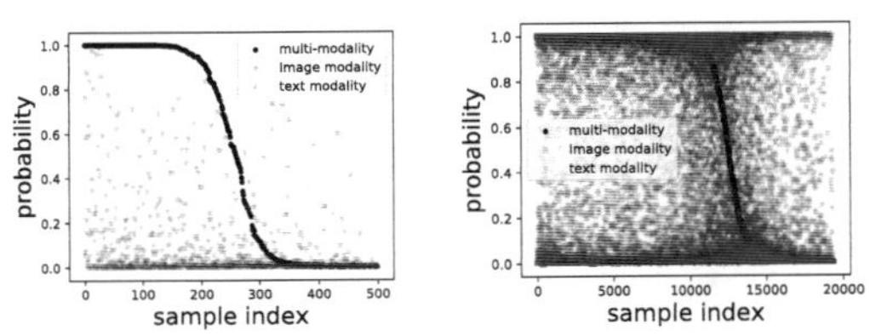

(a) Hateful-Memes (b) MM-IMDB

Figure 3: **Prediction probabilities of test samples for different modalities.** Black points correspond to the predictions of samples with both modalities (original input), red points do with image modality, and blue points do with text modality. The samples are ordered based on their multi modal output probabilities.

see for MM-IMDB there is a strong correlation between multimodal predictions and predictions from text modality, indicating the fact that in MM-IMDB text is a dominant modality. On the other hand, for Hateful-Memes dataset there is no such global pattern but one can observe some correlations for individual instances. This behavior is actually expected based on the way Hateful-Memes is built to include unimodal confounders (Kiela et al., 2020).

Following these observations we propose three weighting schemes for distillation losses, presented in the order of complexity: 1) population-based (Section 3.2), 2) instance-wise (Section 3.3) weighting approaches for the losses, and 3) meta-learning approach (Section 3.4) to find the optimal weights on meta data. We will discuss each of these in the following sections.

3.2 Population-based Weighting

Population-based weighting is to assign weights depending on modality; we give constant weights (w_i, w_i^v, w_i^t) for each loss term in equation (5). This weighting approach assumes the weights are determined by the types of modality. Best weights or coefficients for each loss term are obtained by grid search on the validation set. However, population-based weighting is limited because it does not assign finer-grained weights to each data instance; each data instance might have different optimal weights for the loss terms. This is what we pursue next in the instance-wise weighting.

3.3 Instance-wise Weighting

Instance-wise weighting is to give different weights to each loss term depending on a data sample. The assumption is that each data point has different optimal weights for knowledge distillation. By assigning instance-level weights, we expect a better learning for the student to mimic teacher's modality-specific behavior. In this sense, population-based weighting can be regarded as one version of instance-wise weighting that assigns weights depending on modality. As it is not possible to tune sample-weights as separate hyper-parameters, we instead propose to use simple/intuitive fixed weighting functions, described as follows. We exploit teacher's output as the input to these fixed weighting schemes. Obviously, the next step to this approach would be to learn this weighting function alongside the rest of the model, i.e. meta-learning, which we discuss further in the Section 3.4.

Importance-based weighting. The idea is to weight each loss term based on the importance of its corresponding modality. To measure the importance of each modality, we compute the change in the output of teacher after dropping the other modality:

$$I_{i,t} = \delta(t(x_i), t(x_i^v)), I_{i,v} = \delta(t(x_i), t(x_i^t)), \quad (6)$$

where $t(x_i), t(x_i^v), t(x_i^t)$ is teacher's probabilities (i.e. softmax output), given the multimodal, image alone and text alone inputs, respectively. We use Kullback-Leibler Divergence to measure the difference denoted by δ. Thus weights for loss terms are defined as $w_i^v = g(I_{i,t})$ and $w_i^t = g(I_{i,v})$, where $g = \tanh(\cdot)$ to ensure the weights are in the range $[0, 1]$. In this strategy, we assign $w_i = 1$ for the loss term for multimodality. Note that in this strategy we do not explicitly use the true labels to decide the distillation weights, and we use the teacher's predictions instead.

Correctness-based weighting. Another idea of instance-wise weighting is to weight terms depending on how accurate predictions of the teacher on each modality are. This is to measure the correctness between ground truth and predictions with each modality. If the prediction with one modality is close to the ground truth, then we assign a larger weight to that. To measure the correctness, we adopt cross entropy loss on each instance. We choose the weights proportionally according to the following rule:

$$w_i : w_i^v : w_i^t = 1/h(t(x_i)) : 1/h(t(x_i^v))) : 1/h(t(x_i^t)) \tag{7}$$

where $h(x) = -\sum_{j=1}^{c} y_{i,j} \log x$ and $y_{i,j} \in \{0, 1\}$ are the correct targets for the j-th class of the i-th example. $h(x)$ measures the distance between ground-truth labels and predictions and thus the inverse of $h(x)$ can represent the correctness of the predictions. In order to choose the actual weights, we add a normalization constraint such that, $w_i + w_i^v + w_i^t = 1$. It is worth noting that in this weighting scheme, the actual labels are directly used in deciding the weights unlike the previous one.

3.4 Meta Learning for Weights

Although, the aforementioned weighting schemes are intuitive, there is no reason to believe they are the optimal way of getting value out of modality-specific distillation. Moreover, it is not trivial to get optimal weight functions since it can depend on a dataset. Thus, we propose a meta-learning approach to find optimal weight functions. Inspired by (Shu et al., 2019), we design meta learners to find the optimal coefficients. (w_i, w_i^v, w_i^t) is defined as follows:

$$(w_i, w_i^v, w_i^t) = f(t(x_i), t(x_i^v), t(x_i^t); \mathbf{\Theta}) \tag{8}$$

Algorithm 1: Meta-Learning Algorithm

Input: Training data $\mathcal{D}$, Meta-data set $\hat{\mathcal{D}}$, batch size n, m, learning rates α, β, max iterations T.

for $t \leftarrow 0$ **to** $T - 1$ **do**
- $\{x, y\} \leftarrow \text{SampleMiniBatch}(D, n)$.
- $\{x^{(\text{meta})}, y^{(\text{meta})}\} \leftarrow \text{SampleMiniBatch}(\hat{D}, m)$.
- $\hat{\mathbf{w}}^{(t)}(\mathbf{\Theta}^{(t)}) \leftarrow \mathbf{w}^{(t)} - \alpha \frac{1}{n} \sum_{i=1}^{n} \nabla_{\mathbf{w}} \mathcal{L}_{\text{student}}(\mathbf{w}^{(t)}, \mathbf{\Theta}^{(t)})$
- $\mathbf{\Theta}^{(t+1)} \leftarrow \mathbf{\Theta}^{(t)} - \beta \frac{1}{m} \sum_{i=1}^{m} \nabla_{\mathbf{\Theta}} \mathcal{L}_{\text{meta}}(\hat{\mathbf{w}}^{(t)}(\mathbf{\Theta}^{(t)}))$
- $\mathbf{w}^{(t+1)} \leftarrow \mathbf{w}^{(t)} - \alpha \frac{1}{n} \sum_{i=1}^{n} \nabla_{\mathbf{w}} \mathcal{L}_{\text{student}}(\mathbf{w}^{(t)}, \mathbf{\Theta}^{(t+1)})$

return Network parameters $\mathbf{w}^{(T)}, \mathbf{\Theta}^{(T)}$

where $\mathbf{\Theta}$ defines the parameters for the meta learner network, an Multi-Layer Perceptron (MLP) with a sigmoid layer, which approximates a wide range of functions (Csáji et al., 2001). In general, the meta function for defining weights can depend on any input from the sample; but here we limit ourselves to the teacher's predictions.

Meta-Learning Objective. We assume that we have a small amount of unbiased meta-data set $\{x_i^{(\text{meta})}, y_i^{(\text{meta})}\}_{i=1}^{M}$, representing the meta knowledge of ground-truth sample-label distribution, where M is the number of meta samples and $M \ll N$. In our setup, we use the validation set as the meta-data set. The optimal parameter $\mathbf{\Theta}^*$ can be obtained by minimizing the following cross-entropy loss:

$$\mathcal{L}_{\text{meta}}(\mathbf{w}^*(\mathbf{\Theta})) = -\frac{1}{M} \sum_{i=1}^{M} \sum_{j=1}^{c} y_{i,j} \log(s(x_i; \mathbf{w}^*(\mathbf{\Theta})), \tag{9}$$

where $\mathbf{w}^*$ is an optimal student's parameter, which is defined as follows:

$$\mathbf{w}^*(\mathbf{\Theta}) = \arg\min_{\mathbf{w}} \mathcal{L}_{\text{student}}(\mathbf{w}, \mathbf{\Theta}). \tag{10}$$

w^* is parameterized by Θ, a meta learner's parameter.

The meta learner is optimized for generating instance weights that minimize the average error of the student over the meta-data set, while the student is trained on the training set with the generated instance weights from the meta learner.

Meta-Learning Algorithm. Finding the optimal Θ^* and w^* requires two nested loops; one gradient update of a meta learner requires a trained student on the training set. Thus, we adopt an online strategy following (Shu et al., 2019), which updates the meta learner with only one gradient update of the student. Algorithm 1 illustrates its learning process. First, we sample mini batches from the training and meta-data sets, respectively (lines 2 and 3). Then, we update the student's parameter along the descent direction of the student's loss on a mini-batch training data (line 4). Note that the student's parameter is parameterized by the meta learner's parameter. With the updated parameter, the meta leaner can be updated by moving the current parameter $\Theta(t)$ along the objective gradient of equation (9) on a mini-batch meta data (line 5). After updating the meta-learner, the student's parameter can be updated on a mini-batch training data (line 6).

4 Experiments

In this section, we empirically show the effectiveness of our proposed approaches.

4.1 Experimental Setup

We use VisualBERT (Li et al., 2019), a pre-trained multimodal model, as the teacher model. For a student model, we use TinyBERT (Jiao et al., 2019). VisualBERT consists of 12 layers and a hidden size of 768, and has 109 million number of parameters, while TinyBERT consists of 4 layers and a hidden size of 312, and has 14.5 million number of parameters. We use the region features from images for both the teacher and the student and fine-tune the student on each dataset. For training the meta learner we use the datasets' validation set as meta data. We find the best hyperparameters on the validation set. For comparison, we include various knowledge distillation approaches: Conventional KD (Hinton et al., 2015), FitNet (Romero et al., 2014), RKD (Park et al., 2019), and SP (Tung and Mori, 2019). We empirically show that our MSD approaches, i.e. population-based weighting, instance-wise weighting based on importance of each modality and correctness of predictions of each modality, and meta learning, can improve the performance of the small model compared to other KD approaches. Moreover, meta-learning approach provides the closest performance to the teacher model in all three multimodal datasets by finding the optimal weights per sample for MSD.

4.2 Datasets

To examine our proposed approaches, we use three multimodal datasets: Hateful-Memes (Kiela et al., 2020) MM-IMDB (Arevalo et al., 2017), and Visual Entailment (SNLI-VE) (Xie et al., 2019a; Young et al., 2014).

The Hateful-Memes dataset (Kiela et al., 2020) consists of 10K multimodal memes. The task is a binary classification problem, which is to detect hate speech in multimodal memes. We use Accuracy (ACC), and AUC as evaluation metrics of choice for hateful memes (Kiela et al., 2020).

The MM-IMDB (Multimodal IMDB) dataset consists of 26K movie plot outlines and movie posters. The task involves assigning genres to each movie from a list of 23 genres. This is a multi-label prediction problem, i.e., one movie can have multiple genres and we use Macro F1 and Micro F1 as evaluation metrics following (Arevalo et al., 2017).

The goal of Visual Entailment is to predict whether a given image semantically entails an input sentence. Classification accuracy over three classes ("Entailment", "Neutral" and "Contradiction") is used to measure model performance. We use accuracy as an evaluation metric following (Xie et al., 2019a).

4.3 Results

Table 1 shows our main results on Hateful-Memes, MM-IMDB, and SNLI-VE datasets. The small model refers to the student model without distillation from the teacher. Existing KD approaches improves the student model on all datasets. However, our MSD approaches improve the small model substantially. We observe that among weighting strategies, MSD with meta learning shows the best performance, indicating it finds effective weights for each dataset. We note that population-based weighting shows good improvement, which means weighting based on modality only is still very effective on multimodal datasets. Also, population-based weighting outperforms instance-wise weighting on the MM-IMDB dataset, suggesting all samples are likely to have the same preference or dependency on each modality of the dataset.

In addition, we present improvements over KD approaches with/without our MSD (meta-learning) in Table 2. Here, we use MSD on top of each KD approach. Note that our MSD approach is orthogonal to existing KD approach. The results show the benefits of our MSD method on top of other approaches; MSD improves these KD methods on multimodal datasets.

Table 1: **Main Results.** Mean results (±std) over 5 repetitions are reported. Our MSD outperforms all the KD approaches. Here, we use our MSD on top of conventional KD (Hinton et al., 2015). Also our meta learning for weights shows the best performance.

Method	Hateful-Memes		MM-IMDB		SNLI-VE
	ACC	AUC	Macro F1	Micro F1	ACC
Teacher	65.28	71.82	59.92	66.53	77.57
Small model	60.83 (±0.20)	65.54 (±0.25)	38.78 (±4.03)	58.10 (±1.23)	72.30 (±0.35)
Conventional KD (Hinton et al., 2015)	60.84 (±1.50)	66.53 (±0.27)	41.76 (±4.72)	58.96 (±1.62)	72.61 (±0.55)
FitNet (Romero et al., 2014)	62.00 (±0.26)	67.13 (±0.51)	46.21 (±2.12)	60.46 (±0.30)	73.06 (±0.50)
RKD (Park et al., 2019)	61.43 (±0.40)	67.03 (±0.21)	51.16 (±1.64)	62.52 (±0.70)	73.09 (±0.53)
SP (Tung and Mori, 2019)	61.70 (±1.10)	66.11 (±0.45)	49.07 (±0.82)	61.41 (±0.34)	73.00 (±0.98)
MSD (Population)	62.15 (±1.71)	68.16 (±1.60)	51.85 (±0.34)	62.13 (±0.19)	73.64 (±0.54)
MSD (Instance, Importance)	62.78 (±1.00)	67.94 (±0.52)	49.20 (±1.27)	61.84 (±0.49)	73.34 (±0.48)
MSD (Instance, Correctness)	63.27 (±0.45)	67.72 (±0.82)	51.02 (±0.70)	62.05 (±0.45)	73.52 (±0.54)
MSD (Meta learning)	**63.86 (±1.28)**	**68.30 (±0.62)**	**53.12 (±0.08)**	**63.00 (±0.09)**	**74.04 (±0.15)**

Table 2: **Improvement over KD approaches with MSD.** Our MSD substantially improves existing KD approaches.

Method	Hateful-Memes		MM-IMDB	
	ACC	AUC	Macro F1	Micro F1
KD (Hinton et al., 2015)	60.84	66.53	41.76	58.96
+MSD	**63.86**	**68.30**	**53.12**	**63.00**
FitNet (Romero et al., 2014)	62.00	67.13	46.21	60.46
+MSD	**62.50**	**68.77**	**51.75**	**62.13**
RKD (Park et al., 2019)	61.43	67.03	51.16	62.52
+MSD	**63.10**	**67.58**	**52.36**	**63.24**
SP (Tung and Mori, 2019)	61.70	66.11	49.07	61.41
+MSD	**62.30**	**67.92**	**52.83**	**62.70**

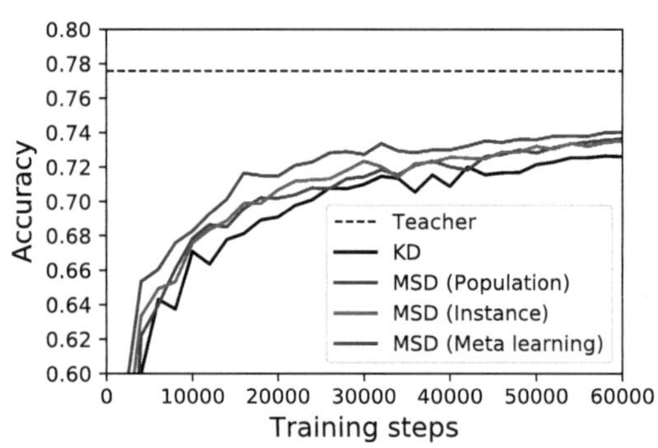

Figure 4: Test accuracy of a student on SNLI-VE during training and comparison between knowledge distillation (KD) and modality-specific distillation (MSD) with population-based weighting, instance-wise weighting, and meta learning for weights.

4.4 Learning Curve

Our proposed MSD approaches can also help with training speed, measured by test metrics over training steps. Fig 4 shows the evolution of accuracy on the *test set* during training on the SNLI-VE dataset. When we train the student with MSD, training progresses faster than KD. Since the teacher provides two additional probabilities with each modality, the student learns faster and the final performance is better than KD. We observe a large performance increase early in training with the meta-learning approach, thus leading to the best accuracy. In this case, the meta learning for sample weighting finds the optimal weights for each data instance, so the student quickly learns from more important modality that is vital for the predictions.

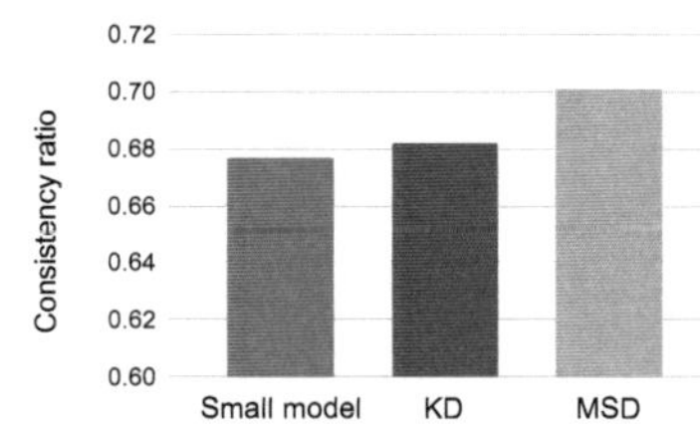

Figure 5: **Teacher-Student consistency ratio.** We investigate the student model's sensitiveness to changes in modalities. Higher ratio indicates its sensitiveness is closer to the teacher's.

4.5 Analysis

In this section, we empirically investigate the benefits of our approach by analyzing MSD.

4.5.1 Teacher-Student Consistency

To showcase that our approach helps the student model to be more sensitive to important changes in modalities, we take examples from the Hateful Memes test set and randomly replace one of the modalities with a modality from another sample. Hateful Memes is a multimodal dataset and changing the modalities might or might not change the final label. In this case, we do not have the ground truth, but we use the teacher's predicted label on the new generated sample as a proxy for ground truth and count the times that the student/small

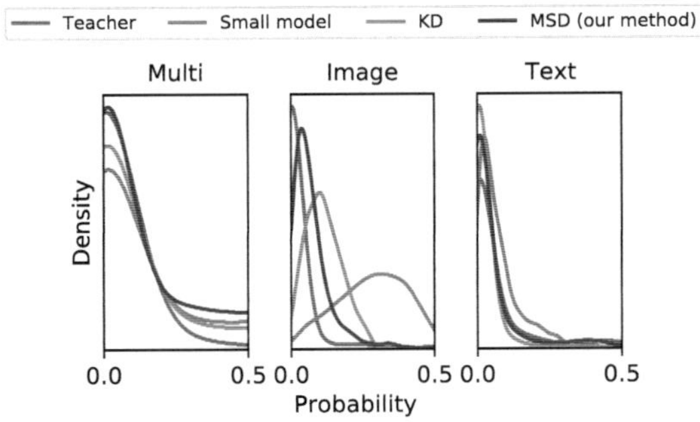

Figure 6: **Density of model outputs on samples of label 0 on the test set of Hateful-Memes:** given multimodal samples as input (Multi), given only image modality as input (Image), and given only text modality as input (Text). Our proposed approach, MSD with the meta-learning approach, minimizes the gap between the teacher and the student trained by KD.

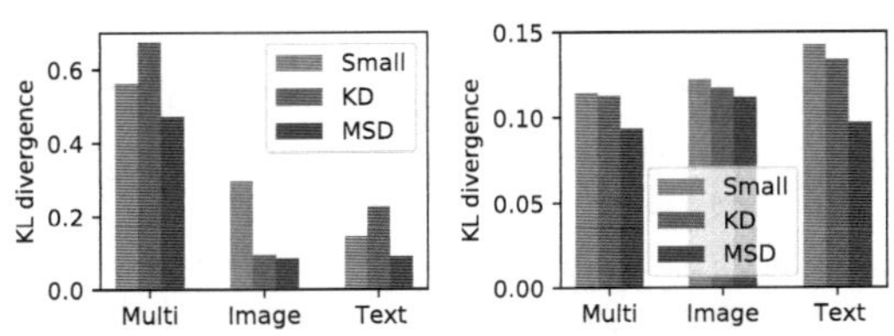

(a) Hateful-Memes (b) MM-IMDB

Figure 7: **Kullback-Leibler divergence on the test set between the teacher's outputs and other models' outputs.** This is a measure of how teacher's probability distribution is different from other models'. The lower divergence is, the closer a model is to the teacher.

model is consistent with the teacher on these generated samples. We define the ratio of such consistent predictions over the total generated samples as "**Teacher-Student consistency ratio**". Note that none of the models have seen these samples during the training. As it can be seen from Fig. 5, our MSD approach has a larger "Teacher-Student consistency ratio" than small model with and without KD. This indicates that MSD not only improves the accuracy but also improves the sensitivity of the student model to better match the teacher on the changes in modalities on unseen data.

4.5.2 Probability Distribution of Model Outputs

There is a performance gap between the teacher model and student model in predicting true labels given a multimodal sample and each of its individual modalities. Fig 6 shows this gap for Hateful-Memes dataset. For example, given only image modality as input (the middle plot in Fig 6), there is a considerable difference between the teacher and the small model for predicting benign samples. KD minimizes the gap and our MSD with the meta-learning approach shows the similar density curve to the teacher's.

In addition, we measure Kullback-Leibler (KL) divergence between the teacher's outputs and other models' outputs on the test set as shown in Fig 7. This is to measure the difference between teacher's probability distribution and others'. As is shown, our MSD approach shows the smallest KL divergence from the teacher which means the student learned with MSD outputs probability distribution close to the teacher's.

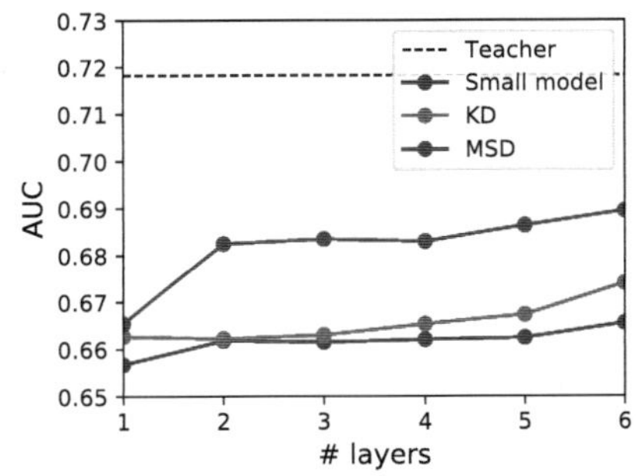

Figure 8: **Test AUC on Hateful-Memes with varying the number of layers in the student model.**

4.5.3 Student Model Size

To examine how the size of student model affects the performance, we evaluate the baselines and our MSD method on the Hateful-Memes dataset, with varying number of layers in the student model. The result is depicted in Fig 8. In this case, the number of layers is proportional to the number of parameters, i.e. student model size. We use the meta-learning weighting as our MSD method of choice here. As is shown, we observe that the AUC score improves as the model size is getting larger. Also the improvement of KD over the small model is marginal and MSD significantly outperforms KD in any number of layers in the student.

5 Related Work

Knowledge Distillation. There have been several studies of transferring knowledge from one model to another (Ba and Caruana, 2014; Hinton et al., 2015; Romero et al., 2014; Park et al., 2019; Müller et al., 2020; Tian et al., 2019; Furlanello et al., 2018; Kim et al., 2020). Ba and Caruana (Ba and

Caruana, 2014) improve the accuracy of a shallow neural network by training it to mimic a deep neural network with penalizing the difference of logits between the two networks. Hinton et al. (Hinton et al., 2015) introduced knowledge distillation (KD) that trains a student model with the objective of matching the softmax distribution of a teacher model at the output layer. Romero et al. (Romero et al., 2014) distill a teacher using additional linear projection layers and minimize L_2 loss at the earlier layers to train a students. Park et al. (Park et al., 2019) focused on mutual relations of data examples instead and they proposed relational knowledge distillation. The transfer works best when there are many possible classes because more information can be transferred, but in cases where there are only a few possible classes the transfer is less effective. To deal with the problem, Müller et al. (Müller et al., 2020) improved the transfer by forcing the teacher to divide each class into many subclasses. Tian et al. (Tian et al., 2019) proposed to distill from the penultimate layer using a contrastive loss for cross-modal transfer. A few recent papers (Furlanello et al., 2018; Kim et al., 2020) have shown that distilling a teacher model into a student model of identical architecture, i.e., self-distillation, can improve the student over the teacher.

Meta Learning for Sample Weighting. Recently, some methods were proposed to learn an adaptive weighting scheme from data to make the learning more automatic and reliable including Meta-Weight-Net (Shu et al., 2019), learning to reweight (Ren et al., 2018), FWL (Dehghani et al., 2017), MentorNet (Jiang et al., 2018), and learning to teach (Fan et al., 2018; Wu et al., 2018; Fan et al., 2020). These approaches were proposed to deal with noisy and corrupted labels and learn optimal functions from clean datasets. They are different in that they adopt different weight functions such as a multilayer perceptron (Shu et al., 2019), Bayesian function approximator (Dehghani et al., 2017), and a bidirectional LSTM (Jiang et al., 2018); and they take different inputs such as loss values and sample features. In our case, we adopt these ideas of meta-learning, and specifically Meta-Weight0Net, and utilize it in a different context, i.e. multimodal knowledge distillation.

Bias in Multimodal Datasets. Different multimodal datasets were proposed to study whether a model uses a single modality's features and the implications for its generalization properties (Agrawal et al., 2018). Different approaches were proposed to deal with such problems where the model overfits to a single modality. Wang et al. (Wang et al., 2020) suggest to regularize the overfitting behavior to different modalities. REPAIR (Li and Vasconcelos, 2019) prevents a model from dataset biases by re-sampling the training data. Cadene et al. (Cadene et al., 2019) proposed RUBi that uses a bias-only branch in addition to a base model during training to overcome language priors. In our study, although we do not directly deal with the overfitting phenomena, we use different weighting schemes to better transfer the modality specific information from the teacher to the student.

6 Conclusion

We studied knowledge distillation on multimodal datasets; we observed that conventional KD may lead to inefficient distillation since a student model does not fully mimic a teacher's modality-specific predictions. To better transfer knowledge from a teacher on the multimodal datasets, we proposed modality-specific distillation; the student mimics the teacher's outputs on each modality. Furthermore, we proposed weighting approaches, population-based and instance-wise weighting schemes, and a meta-learning approach for weighting the auxiliary losses to take importance of each modality into consideration. We empirically showed that we can improve the student's performance with our modality-specific distillation compared to conventional distillation. Our MSD approach results on modality specific outputs that better resemble the teacher's outputs. We showed that the results hold across different student sizes. Moreover, our meta-learning approach is flexible enough to find different effective weighting schemes, depending on the dataset.

References

Aishwarya Agrawal, Dhruv Batra, Devi Parikh, and Aniruddha Kembhavi. 2018. Don't just assume; look and answer: Overcoming priors for visual question answering. In *Proceedings of the IEEE Conference on Computer Vision and Pattern Recognition*, pages 4971–4980.

Stanislaw Antol, Aishwarya Agrawal, Jiasen Lu, Margaret Mitchell, Dhruv Batra, C Lawrence Zitnick, and Devi Parikh. 2015. Vqa: Visual question answering. In *Proceedings of the IEEE international conference on computer vision*, pages 2425–2433.

John Arevalo, Thamar Solorio, Manuel Montes-y Gómez,

and Fabio A González. 2017. Gated multimodal units for information fusion. *arXiv preprint arXiv:1702.01992.*

Jimmy Ba and Rich Caruana. 2014. Do deep nets really need to be deep? In *Advances in neural information processing systems*, pages 2654–2662.

Tom B Brown, Benjamin Mann, Nick Ryder, Melanie Subbiah, Jared Kaplan, Prafulla Dhariwal, Arvind Neelakantan, Pranav Shyam, Girish Sastry, Amanda Askell, et al. 2020. Language models are few-shot learners. *arXiv preprint arXiv:2005.14165.*

Remi Cadene, Corentin Dancette, Matthieu Cord, Devi Parikh, et al. 2019. Rubi: Reducing unimodal biases for visual question answering. In *Advances in neural information processing systems*, pages 841–852.

Balázs Csanád Csáji et al. 2001. Approximation with artificial neural networks. *Faculty of Sciences, Etvs Lornd University, Hungary*, 24(48):7.

Mostafa Dehghani, Arash Mehrjou, Stephan Gouws, Jaap Kamps, and Bernhard Schölkopf. 2017. Fidelity-weighted learning. *arXiv preprint arXiv:1711.02799.*

J. Devlin, Ming-Wei Chang, Kenton Lee, and Kristina Toutanova. 2019. Bert: Pre-training of deep bidirectional transformers for language understanding. In *NAACL-HLT*.

Terrance DeVries and Graham W Taylor. 2017. Improved regularization of convolutional neural networks with cutout. *arXiv preprint arXiv:1708.04552.*

Yang Fan, Fei Tian, Tao Qin, Xiang-Yang Li, and Tie-Yan Liu. 2018. Learning to teach. *arXiv preprint arXiv:1805.03643.*

Yang Fan, Yingce Xia, Lijun Wu, Shufang Xie, Weiqing Liu, Jiang Bian, Tao Qin, Xiang-Yang Li, and Tie-Yan Liu. 2020. Learning to teach with deep interactions. *arXiv preprint arXiv:2007.04649.*

T. Furlanello, Zachary Chase Lipton, Michael Tschannen, L. Itti, and Anima Anandkumar. 2018. Born again neural networks. In *ICML*.

Yash Goyal, Tejas Khot, Douglas Summers-Stay, Dhruv Batra, and Devi Parikh. 2017. Making the v in vqa matter: Elevating the role of image understanding in visual question answering. In *Proceedings of the IEEE Conference on Computer Vision and Pattern Recognition*, pages 6904–6913.

Saurabh Gupta, Judy Hoffman, and Jitendra Malik. 2016. Cross modal distillation for supervision transfer. In *Proceedings of the IEEE conference on computer vision and pattern recognition*, pages 2827–2836.

Danna Gurari, Qing Li, Abigale J Stangl, Anhong Guo, Chi Lin, Kristen Grauman, Jiebo Luo, and Jeffrey P Bigham. 2018. Vizwiz grand challenge: Answering visual questions from blind people. In *Proceedings of the IEEE Conference on Computer Vision and Pattern Recognition*, pages 3608–3617.

Geoffrey Hinton, Oriol Vinyals, and Jeff Dean. 2015. Distilling the knowledge in a neural network. *arXiv preprint arXiv:1503.02531.*

Lu Jiang, Zhengyuan Zhou, Thomas Leung, Li-Jia Li, and Li Fei-Fei. 2018. Mentornet: Learning data-driven curriculum for very deep neural networks on corrupted labels. In *International Conference on Machine Learning*, pages 2304–2313.

Xiaoqi Jiao, Yichun Yin, Lifeng Shang, Xin Jiang, Xiao Chen, Linlin Li, Fang Wang, and Qun Liu. 2019. Tinybert: Distilling bert for natural language understanding. *arXiv preprint arXiv:1909.10351.*

Douwe Kiela, Hamed Firooz, Aravind Mohan, Vedanuj Goswami, Amanpreet Singh, Pratik Ringshia, and Davide Testuggine. 2020. The hateful memes challenge: Detecting hate speech in multimodal memes. *arXiv preprint arXiv:2005.04790.*

Kyungyul Kim, ByeongMoon Ji, Doyoung Yoon, and Sangheum Hwang. 2020. Self-knowledge distillation: A simple way for better generalization. *arXiv preprint arXiv:2006.12000.*

Liunian Harold Li, Mark Yatskar, Da Yin, Cho-Jui Hsieh, and Kai-Wei Chang. 2019. Visualbert: A simple and performant baseline for vision and language. *arXiv preprint arXiv:1908.03557.*

Yi Li and Nuno Vasconcelos. 2019. Repair: Removing representation bias by dataset resampling. In *Proceedings of the IEEE Conference on Computer Vision and Pattern Recognition*, pages 9572–9581.

Rafael Müller, Simon Kornblith, and Geoffrey Hinton. 2020. Subclass distillation. *arXiv preprint arXiv:2002.03936.*

Wonpyo Park, Dongju Kim, Yan Lu, and Minsu Cho. 2019. Relational knowledge distillation. In *Proceedings of the IEEE Conference on Computer Vision and Pattern Recognition*, pages 3967–3976.

Mengye Ren, Wenyuan Zeng, Bin Yang, and Raquel Urtasun. 2018. Learning to reweight examples for robust deep learning. *arXiv preprint arXiv:1803.09050.*

Adriana Romero, Nicolas Ballas, Samira Ebrahimi Kahou, Antoine Chassang, Carlo Gatta, and Yoshua Bengio. 2014. Fitnets: Hints for thin deep nets. *arXiv preprint arXiv:1412.6550.*

Jun Shu, Qi Xie, Lixuan Yi, Qian Zhao, Sanping Zhou, Zongben Xu, and Deyu Meng. 2019. Meta-weight-net: Learning an explicit mapping for sample weighting. In *Advances in Neural Information Processing Systems*, pages 1919–1930.

Amanpreet Singh, Vivek Natarajan, Meet Shah, Yu Jiang, Xinlei Chen, Dhruv Batra, Devi Parikh, and Marcus Rohrbach. 2019. Towards vqa models that can read. In *Proceedings of the IEEE Conference on Computer Vision and Pattern Recognition*, pages 8317–8326.

Yonglong Tian, Dilip Krishnan, and Phillip Isola. 2019. Contrastive representation distillation. *arXiv preprint arXiv:1910.10699.*

Frederick Tung and Greg Mori. 2019. Similarity-preserving knowledge distillation. In *Proceedings of the IEEE/CVF International Conference on Computer Vision*, pages 1365–1374.

Weiyao Wang, Du Tran, and Matt Feiszli. 2020. What makes training multi-modal classification networks hard? In *Proceedings of the IEEE/CVF Conference on Computer Vision and Pattern Recognition*, pages 12695–12705.

Lijun Wu, Fei Tian, Yingce Xia, Yang Fan, Tao Qin, Lai Jian-Huang, and Tie-Yan Liu. 2018. Learning to teach with dynamic loss functions. In *Advances in Neural Information Processing Systems*, pages 6466–6477.

Ning Xie, Farley Lai, Derek Doran, and Asim Kadav. 2019a. Visual entailment: A novel task for fine-grained image understanding. *arXiv preprint arXiv:1901.06706*.

Qizhe Xie, Zihang Dai, Eduard Hovy, Minh-Thang Luong, and Quoc V Le. 2019b. Unsupervised data augmentation for consistency training. *arXiv preprint arXiv:1904.12848*.

Qizhe Xie, Minh-Thang Luong, Eduard Hovy, and Quoc V Le. 2020. Self-training with noisy student improves imagenet classification. In *Proceedings of the IEEE/CVF Conference on Computer Vision and Pattern Recognition*, pages 10687–10698.

Peter Young, Alice Lai, Micah Hodosh, and Julia Hockenmaier. 2014. From image descriptions to visual denotations: New similarity metrics for semantic inference over event descriptions. *Transactions of the Association for Computational Linguistics*, 2:67–78.

Hongyi Zhang, Moustapha Cisse, Yann N Dauphin, and David Lopez-Paz. 2017. mixup: Beyond empirical risk minimization. *arXiv preprint arXiv:1710.09412*.

	Original (Hateful)	Image replaced (Benign)
Teacher	Hateful	Benign
Small	Hateful	Hateful
KD	Hateful	Hateful
MSD	Hateful	Benign

Figure 9: A multimodal violating sample (Left). We further replaced its image modality with a background picture that makes it benign and examined models on both examples (Right).

Table 3: **Dataset Statistics.**

Stat. \ Data	**Hateful-Memes**	**MM-IMDB**	**SNLI-VE**
Type	Binary	Multilabel	Multiclass
# Classes	2	23	3
# Examples	10,000	25,959	565,286
# Training	8,500	15,552	529,527
# Validation	500	2,608	17,858
# Test	1,000	7,799	17,901

A Case Study

We demonstrate the motivation behind our work through an example. Fig. 9 shows an example of a multimodal sample from Hateful Memes test dataset. The sample is violating based on both modalities together, and all models correctly predict that. To further probe the models, we replace the background image of the sample with a picture that makes the label benign. On this artificially generated sample we notice that only the teacher and MSD model correctly predict benign, while the other two models make wrong predictions (presumably by just looking at the text only).

B Hyperparameters

The teacher model is a VisualBERT (Li et al., 2019), and the student model is TinyBERT (Jiao et al., 2019). We used the MMF library and pretrained checkpoints from it for VisualBERT[1] and used a pretrained checkpoint in TinyBERT [2]. VisualBERT consists of 12 layers and a hidden size of 768, and has 109 million number of parameters, while TinyBERT consists of 4 layers and a hidden size of 312, and has 14.5 million number of parameters. For all experiments, we performed a grid search to find the best hyperparameters. We adopt the AdamW optimizer to train networks. We use a linear learning rate schedule that drops to 0 at the end of training with warmup steps of 10% maximum iterations.

Hateful-Memes. We performed a grid search over learning rates (1e-5, 3e-5, **5e-5**, 1e-4), and temperatures (1, 2, **4**, 8), and, batch sizes (**10**, 20, 30, 40, 50, 60), and the meta learner's learning rates (1e-1, 1e-2, **1e-3**, 1e-4). We set the maximum number of iterations to 5000. The balance parameter λ between cross entropy and distillation is set among (0.2, 0.4, **0.5**, 0.6, 0.8).

MM-IMDB. For MM-IMDB experiments, we follow a similar procedure, a grid search, to the Hateful-Memes. The batch size is 20, temperature is 1, and the meta learner's learning rate is 1e-4. We set the maximum number of iterations to 10000. The balance parameter λ is set to 0.5.

SNLI-VE. For Visual Entailment (SNLI-VE), the batch size is 64, temperature is 4, and the meta learner's learning rate is 1e-4. We set the maximum number of iterations to 60000. The balance parameter λ is set to 0.6.

[1] `https://mmf.sh`

[2] `https://github.com/huawei-noah/Pretrained-Language-Model/tree/master/TinyBERT`

Cold Start Problem For Automated Live Video Comments

Hao Wu
ADAPT Centre
School of Engineering
Trinity College Dublin
Dublin, Ireland
hao.wu@adaptcentre.ie

François Pitié
ADAPT Centre
School of Engineering
Trinity College Dublin
Dublin, Ireland
pitief@tcd.ie

Gareth J. F. Jones
ADAPT Centre
School of Computing
Dublin City University
Dublin, Ireland
Gareth.Jones@dcu.ie

Abstract

Live video comments, or "danmu", are an emerging feature on Asian online video platforms. Danmu are time-synchronous comments that are overlaid on a video playback. These comments uniquely enrich the experience and engagement of their users, and have become a determining factor in the popularity of videos on these platforms. Similar to the "cold start problem" in recommender systems, a video will only start to attract attention when sufficient danmu comments have been posted on it. We study this video cold start problem and examine how new comments can be generated automatically on less-commented videos. We propose to predict danmu comments to promote user engagement, by exploiting a multi-modal combination of the video visual content, subtitles, audio signals, and any surrounding comments (when they exist). Our method fuses these multiple modalities in a transformer network which is then trained for different comment density scenarios. We evaluate our proposed system through both a retrieval based evaluation method, as well as human judgement. Results show that our proposed system improves significantly over state-of-the-art methods.

Figure 1: A video frame from bilibili.com with damnu comments overlaid. The lower part of the image shows danmu comment distribution over the video. The subtitle says: "could you publish some danmu?" and the viewers are responding with a *damnu burst*.

1 Introduction

Live video comments, or "danmu", is an emerging feature of video sharing platforms such as Bilibili and Nicovideo, which has been adopted by hundreds of millions of users in Asia. Danmu comments are a time-synchronous commentary subtitle system that displays user comments as streams of moving subtitles overlaid on the video playback screen (see Fig. 1). Danmu comments have become a key feature of these video platforms. So much so, that videos with many danmu comments stand a higher chance of being recommended or searched, and naturally attract more viewers.

This new form of media consumption comes with a vast amount of annotated video data and opens the path to multiple new research strands for video technologies, including automated highlighting, summarization and conversational engagement. The main focus of the research literature (see Section 2) has so far been on the automatic generation of danmu comments (Lv et al., 2019; Ma et al., 2019; Weiying et al., 2020). In particular, Shuming et al. (Ma et al., 2019) recently proposed in "Livebot", a new benchmark with a baseline unified transformer architecture to automatically generate new danmu comments from existing danmu comments and video content. This literature has mostly focused on the analysis of videos that already have many comments. This is however probably not the most critical scenario for automated danmu generation as these videos are already popular. Also, it is easier in these cases to exploit the numerous nearby comments to generate new comments. Similar to the "cold start problem" in recommender systems, the real issue faced by content creators is that videos need many danmu comments to start attracting traffic.

In this paper we propose to solve this "video cold start problem" by a method that can generate danmu comments on videos which have zero, few,

Proceedings of the Third Workshop on Multimodal Artificial Intelligence, pages 54–62
June 6, 2021. ©2021 Association for Computational Linguistics

or many comments. We propose a multi-density cold video transformer (MCVT) that can leverage multi-modal signals including surrounding comments, video frames, but also subtitles and audio signals in an end-to-end neural network (see Section 4). The key idea is then to approach the task globally and train the network for different comment density scenarios (see Section 5). To achieve this, we collect the publishing timestamps of comments from the video platform and look at the sequence of the comment publishing times (see section 3). This allows us to consider different snapshots of a video's commenting lifetime (ie. when the video was freshly uploaded with no comments, then when it had a few comments, and later with many comments). This information has not been exploited in existing work described in the literature, but we show that it can be used effectively in training of danmu generation.

We evaluate our system in Section 6 through both a retrieval based evaluation method and human judgement. Results show that our system is able to produce comments that are close to the quality of human comments. The key contributions of this paper are as follow:

- We are the first to investigate the cold video problem for automated creation of danmu for videos which enables us to create comments for freshly uploaded videos.
- We expand a publicly available danmu video dataset (Ma et al., 2019) by doubling its size and enriching multi-modal features from video embedded subtitles.
- We propose a multi-density cold video transformer (MCVT) architecture and training framework which can generate high quality comments with different comment density and outperforms state-of-the-art method.

To make our work fully reproducible, both the source codes and the dataset used have been made public available. [1]

2 Related Work

In this section we introduce existing work on automated danmu generation, detection of video highlights based both on manually contributed danmu and atomated analysis of video content, and automated creation of descriptive captions for videos.

[1] https://github.com/fireflyHunter/Cold-Video-Danmu-Generation

2.1 Danmu Generation

The earliest work in danmu content generation was based on a generative adversarial model, where the video frames are directly mapped into the comments textual space (Lv et al., 2019). This method, however, does not exploit existing nearby comments. Ma et al. (2019) proposed *LiveBot* which combines both visual and textual contexts in an encoding phase with a Transformer architecture. They also proposed evaluation metrics and released a publicly accessible training set. This work has served as a benchmark for the most recent approaches (Zhang et al., 2020; Chaoqun et al., 2020; Weiying et al., 2020). In previous work, we reworked the baseline implementationof *LiveBot* to address several shortcomings in both the original dataset and implementation (Wu et al., 2020).

We note that *LiveBot*, and its successors, are trained on densely commented videos, and use all available comments to make predictions. Thus, they do not consider what will in practice be the more useful setting for automatec danmu creation of videos with few or no comments, which we refer to as the *cold start* scenario. Also, they do not make use of all of the attributes of the comments. In particular, the *publishing time* of the comments is not included in the training set. This means that the causality between comments is lost and that the target comments could potentially predate the proposed contextual comments. Also, these methods do not consider *where* to publish in the video timeline.

2.2 Highlight Detection

Video highlights could provide pointers for comment generation, some prior work has tried to predict popular segments in videos. Video highlights, as they are called, can be identified by looking at the current distribution of published danmu comments (see plot in Fig. 1). This is the idea exploited in (Xu et al., 2017), where a personalised frame-level recommendation is based on the analysis of published comments. More relevant to the cold start problem is highlight prediction solely from video content, as proposed in (Zheng et al., 2020) using a bi-directional Long-short Term Memory (LSTM) architecture.

2.3 Video Captioning

Related to our application is the task of video captioning, which aims to generate descriptive sen-

Statistics	Training	Dev	Test	Total
#Videos	4,272	200	200	4672
#danmu	2,549,340	123,646	116,374	2,789,360
avg. duration (s)	217	222	216	217
avg. #danmu/s	2.75	2.78	2.69	2.75

Table 1: Training, development and test sets statistics.

tences of a video sequence. Current architectures for this usually follow an encoder-decoder pattern. In the encoder, the sequence of video frames is embedded by a CNN (Subhashini et al., 2014) or RNN (Nitish et al., 2015). The decoder, typically an LSTM, generates captions from the contextual output of the encoder. Techniques like reinforcement learning (Xin et al., 2018), contextual-aware video captioning (Spencer et al., 2018) and semantic attention model (Gan et al., 2017) have also been explored by researchers in this field. What emerges from the recent literature is that the Transformer architecture, as proposed in *Livebot*, has become the state-of-the-art approach for multi-modal text generation applications and thus we adopt this as the baseline for our application.

3 Task Overview

In this section we define our danmu creation task, introduce the dataset used in our work and outline the video content extraction methods used in this investigation.

3.1 Task Definition

To address the cold start problem we aim to be able to generate high quality comments given videos with different comment densities. In order to handle different danmu density scenarios of the cold start problem, we first sort the existing comments $\mathbf{C}$ for a video by their publication time and only keep a subset $\mathbf{C}_p$ consisting of a percentage p of the earliest comments of the video. This strategy is enforced to reconstruct video danmu comments in different phases of their lifetime. Then we define our task as follows: given a video $\mathbf{V} = \{\mathbf{s_0}, \ldots, \mathbf{s_L}\}$ (following accepted convention $\mathbf{V}$ is split into segments of one second duration), the generation module is asked to generate a target comment $\boldsymbol{y}$ using comments from $\mathbf{C}_p$ and the k previous seconds of the video clip $s_{[i-k,i]}$.

Figure 2: Examples of frames from collected videos. The video content features events from daily life.

3.2 Dataset

For our investigation, we constructed a large-scale dataset with 4,672 videos and 2,789,360 danmu comments, which is publicly available [2]. Part of the data (2,322 videos and 857,993 comments) comes from the publicly available automatic danmu generation *Response to Livebot* dataset (Wu et al., 2020). As our task aims to generate comments for videos with low comment densities compared to a general comment creation list, the size of the suitable training data is reduced significantly during the reconstruction of the cold start scenarios . We thus added another 2,350 videos from the same danmu video website (bilibili.com) to the dataset. The Livebot dataset is mainly themed around natural life, to keep it consistent, the appended videos were selected by having a web crawler pick the 100 most popular "Daily Life" category videos of the recent three days everyday for two months. Fig. 2 presents a small subset of the video frames in this dataset. We scale up the data split in previous work (Ma et al., 2019) (2161 / 100 / 100) and have 4272 / 200 / 200 videos in the training / development / test sets, respectively. Table 1 shows damnu statistics for the dataset.

A key contribution of our paper is that we take into account the publication timestamp of each of the danmu comments. The training data for a particular level p, percentage of existing manual comments preserved, is defined as follows. Each target comment for the training set is randomly sampled from the original comment set $\mathbf{C}$ and the corresponding comment's context is defined as the 5 nearest comments from $\mathbf{C}_p$ that precede the target danmu in the video timeline. This follows the observation made in Livebot (Ma et al., 2019), that the semantic and textual similarity of comments

[2]github.com/fireflyHunter/Cold-Video-Danmu-Generation

is correlated to their timeline proximity and that the danmu context should be limited to the 5 nearest comments. We also add a *causality* constraint by applying the constraint that the comments must have been published before the target danmu in natural time.

We sample the training data for $p = 0\%, 5\%, 30\%, 50\%, 70\%$ and 100%, to form a combined training set of 4,800,145 pairs of target comment/context comments. Target comments can be sampled multiple times for different contexts.

For the 200 videos of the test set, we focus on the video highlights by only selecting 1879 comments in the most frequently commented moments in the video timeline. To study the system performance under different comment densities, we build one test set for each of the proposed values of p.

3.3 Video Information Extraction

We further augment the complete danmu commenting dataset multi-modally by extracting the audio and the subtitle information in addition to the visual and textual comment information. We believe that these additional features will help with the cold start problem.

Visual & Audio Signals. We follow standard practice by sampling one video frame per second of video. The frame from the i-th second of the video is denoted as f_i. The audio soundtrack is extracted from a video and uniformly re-sampled using a 16kHz standard.

Subtitles. We observe that human created danmu comments frequently respond to speech in the video. Fig. 1 shows an example of it: viewers are asked in the subtitles, to post danmu comments. This motivates us to transcribe the speech from the videos. Instead of using speech recognition, we opt to use optical character recognition (OCR). We found that the quality of transcripts produced by speech recognition tools was by comparison of poor quality. While most of the videos on the platform embed speech subtitles that OCR tools can accurately identify. Lastly, captions also display non-speech information which could be exploited. For OCR, we use the open-source Tesseract (Kay, 2007) OCR engine on the lower half of the sampled video frames.

Note that only 109 videos out of 4672 videos contained zero recognisable text and each video contains an average of 13.97 unique subtitles (see Fig. 3).

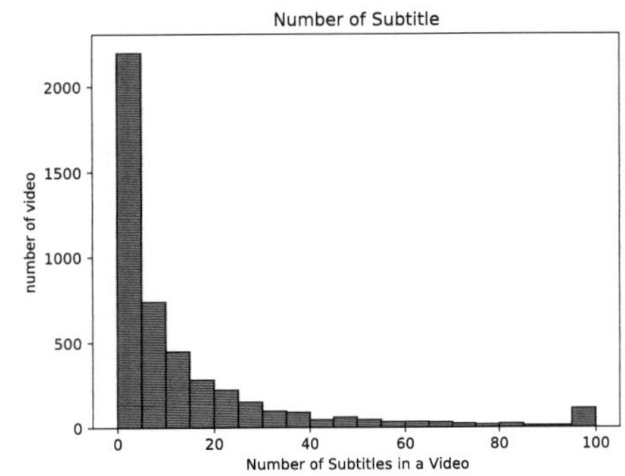

Figure 3: Histogram of the number of subtitles in the videos. For most of the videos there are less than 20 unique subtitles.

4 Network Architecture

Our proposed model, presented in Fig 4, applies standard Transformer modules with an encoder-decoder architecture. During the encoding stage, visual, audio and text features are first encoded respectively, then three transformer modules are used to fuse the information for the three modalities recursively. In the decoder, the target comment is decoded through a transformer layer with multiple multi-head attention modules that attend to three encoded multi-modal representations respectively.

4.1 Video Encoder

As in (Ma et al., 2019), video frames are encoded through a pre-trained 18-layer ResNet. We take the output from the last pooling layer of ResNet as visual feature, the frame vector of the i-th second of the video is denoted as $v_i \in \mathbb{R}^{n_{18}}$, where $n_{18} = 512$ is the size of the resulting ResNet18 features. The frame vectors in the video clip are combined as $\hat{\boldsymbol{v}}_{\boldsymbol{i}} = \{v_{i-k}, \ldots, v_i\}$.

4.2 Audio Encoder

For the audio signal, we use 20-dimensional mel-frequency cepstral coefficients (MFCCs) and another 20-dimensional MFCCs derivatives as audio frame features (Di Gangi et al., 2019). These are extracted with a Hanning window of 40 ms length and 32 ms hop size. We include all audio frames as the audio input, hence we sample 32 audio vectors for each second of the audio. The audio information at time point i is denoted as a_i^j, where j is the j-th audio frame vector in the window analysis at time i. A GRU module (Chaoqun et al., 2020) is applied to recursively encode the input audio sequence. At

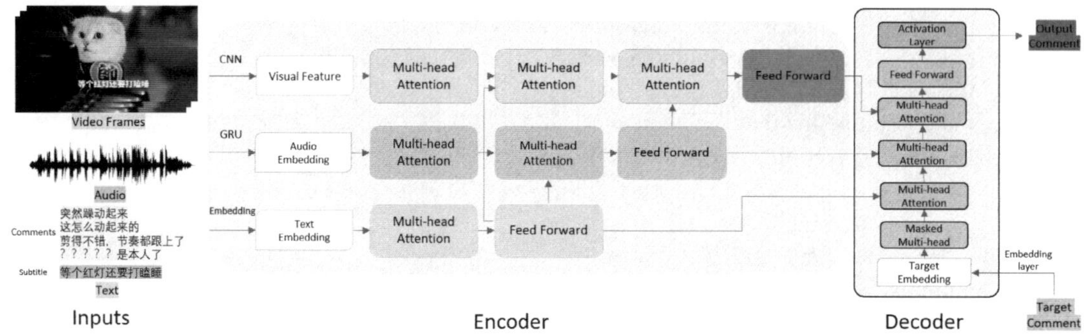

Figure 4: Architecture of the proposed model.

each stage, the current hidden state h_i^j is calculated based on the last hidden state h_i^{j-1} and the current input audio frame vector a_i^j. The sequence of hidden states h_i^j for all audio frames is concatenated into an audio encoder output $\hat{\boldsymbol{a}}_{\boldsymbol{i}} \in \mathbb{R}^{n_a \times 512}$, where $n_a = 32 \times k$ is the number of audio frames in the analysis window and 512 the dimension of the hidden state.

4.3 Text Encoder

Contextual comments are concatenated with a special delimiter token T_d inbetween each comment and then combined with the unique subtitles from the analyzed k second window. As opposed to Livebot (Ma et al., 2019), where there are always 5 context comments, in our cold start scenario we sometimes have less than 5 and even 0 comments. In the extreme case we use a special token T_n with an empty comment field to show that no context comments are available.

All unique subtitles within analysis window $s_{[i-k,i]}$ are also concatenated with the same delimiter token. Finally, we form the text input by combining comment sequence and subtitle sequence with T_d.

We remove the punctuation and segment words using Jieba (an open-sourced Chinese text segmentation tool). Each word of text input is then passed to an embedding layer of size $d \times |V|$, where d is the dimension of the word embedding and $|V|$ is the size of the vocabulary. After embedding, the text input for analysis window $s_{[i-k,i]}$, is now represented as $\hat{\boldsymbol{e}}_{\boldsymbol{i}} \in \mathbb{R}^{n \times d}$.

4.4 Fusion of Modalities

Following the success of the Transformer architecture in multi-modal processing (Ma et al., 2019; Chaoqun et al., 2020), we adopt a multi-unit Transformer module to recursively learn and combine representations from all three modalities. The Transformer unit first encodes the text input $\hat{\boldsymbol{e}}_{\boldsymbol{i}}$ into a transitional hidden state H_e. Then, a second transformer unit combines H_e and the input audio with two multi-head attention modules, the first one attending to $\hat{\boldsymbol{a}}_{\boldsymbol{i}}$ and the second one attending to H_e. Finally, another unit with three multi-head attention modules is used to summarise the video clip representation H_{vae}.

4.5 Decoder

In the model decoder, the output comment is generated through a transformer layer with 4 multi-head attention modules that attend to the target comment $\boldsymbol{y}$, text hidden state H_e, visual hidden state H_{ae} and audio hidden state H_{vae} respectively. Then the probability of output comment is produced with an softmax layer on top of the decoder output.

5 Network Training Regime

5.1 Multi-Density Learning

A key aspect of our method is to consider all the different cold start scenarios together by adopting a multi-task training strategy.

In detail, our training regime is implemented by randomly assigning, at each mini-batch, the percentage p of earlier comments that are kept from a fixed set of values $\{0\%, 5\%, 30\%, 50\%, 70\%, 100\%\}$. Recall that $p = 0\%$ corresponds to the cold start problem, and $p = 100\%$ corresponds to the situation where all other comments are available (such as in Livebot (Ma et al., 2019)). By alternating between these values of p, we are able to train the network for both the cold start and Livebot scenario.

5.2 Training Detail

The video analysis window size k is set to 5 (s). For the text input, we build the vocabulary by selecting the most frequent 50,000 words in the dataset and set the max length of the input text sequence to 50. In the model, the text embedding is of size 512 and is randomly initialized before training. The dimension of the audio's GRU hidden state is set to 512. We apply the same setting for all transformer components used in the network. For each transformer, the hidden state dimension is set to 512, the feed forward network dimension is 2048, the number of heads is 8 and the number of blocks is 6. The loss criterion is cross-entropy. The number of epochs is set to 10, the batch size to 64 and we use the Adam optimizer (Kingma and Ba, 2014) with settings β_1 = 0.9, β_2 = 0.998, weight decay =1×10^{-4}, $\epsilon = 1\times10^{-8}$ and learning rate 1×10^{-4}. All training was done on a Linux server with a single RTX 2080 Ti graphic card, 16 cores Intel(R) Xeon(R) CPU E5-2623 v4 @ 2.60GHz and 256GB RAM. The model is implemented using Pytorch 1.4.0 and Python 3.6. With above settings, it takes around 34 hours to complete the training.

6 Experiments

In this section we report results for our investigation of comment generation. We use the Livebot model (Ma et al., 2019) as a baseline. Specifically, we use the code from (Wu et al., 2020), trained on our full dataset with only video frames and surrounding comments as input. The models proposed in (Chaoqun et al., 2020; Zhang et al., 2020) are very recent and their code is not publicly available yet, so we do not consider these as one of our baseline methods. Other older neural architectures such as LSTM are also not included in this study since it is well established that Transformers are the method of choice for modelling multi-modal signals.

6.1 Evaluation

We note that reference-based metrics for generation tasks like BLEU and ROUGE are not suitable for evaluation of video comments (Das et al., 2017; Ma et al., 2019; Zhang et al., 2020). Hence we follow (Das et al., 2017) and focus on the ability to rank the correct comment originally appearing at this point in the video over other comments taken from the dataset. We evaluate our system through a retrieval based protocol: the model is asked to re-rank a candidate set for each test sample. The comment set for re-ranking is made of 100 comments, including 5 correct groundtruth comments for this point in the video, the 20 most similar comments to the title of the video based on tf-idf score (plausible candidates), the 20 most frequent comments in the dataset and 55 randomly sampled comments.

We report the Recall@k, Precision@k, Mean Rank (MR) and Mean Reciprocal Rank (MRR) as evaluation metrics on this retrieval task. The confidence interval is reported for each of these metrics with confidence level at 95% (for R@k, we use the confidence interval for population proportions).

6.2 Ablation Study

The retrieval task results are reported in Table 3 and Figure 5. In this ablation study, we compare 4 variants of the model.

- **Livebot** (Ma et al., 2019) leverages textual and visual information in a Transformer architecture. It is trained on the extended dataset using the implementation provided in (Wu et al., 2020). The training is done here with p=100%.

- **Livebot-t** applies the same network architecture as textbfLivebot, but is trained with our multi-density training strategy to evaluate the effectiveness of our proposed training regime.

- **MCVT** is the final system proposed in this work, which includes the training regime and the inclusion of the additional audio and subtitle features.

- **MCVT-Zero** is listed to further examine the performance limit in the cold start scenario, i.e. we assume a situation where no comments are present. Thus, we train the MCVT network uniquely on the cold start scenario for $p = 0\%$

The results in Table 3 show that **Livebot-t** outperforms the baseline **Livebot** model in most cases, and thus demonstrates the effectiveness of our training strategy. One exception is found when $p = 100\%$, the **Livebot** model, trained only with densely commented videos, slightly outscores **Livebot-t**, we think this means the information learned from multi-density training strategy produces extra noise when the model only aims to

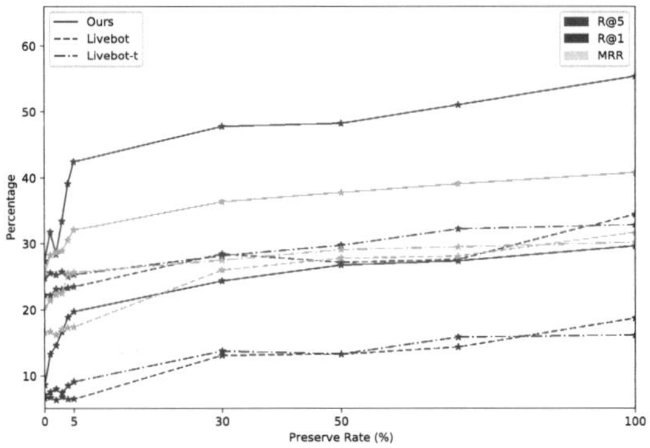

Figure 5: Model performance for R@5, R@1, MRR, at different comment densities p (see Table 3).

generate comments for popular videos. By contrast, from the third and fourth rows of Table 3, we can see that our **MCVT** model has similar performance to **MCVT-zero**, which has been trained specifically for the complete cold start scenario. In this situation, the extra knowledge gained from learning popular videos does not appear to affect the performance in the cold start situation. This comparison between the behaviour of the **Livebot** and **MCVT** systems potentially demonstrates the advantage of our training regime in the case of cold start scenario.

We also see that our model outperforms **Livebot-t** in every scenario, which also supports the idea that integrating the audio signal and subtitle in the generation system can significantly improve the performance of the model.

6.3 Human Evaluation

Additionally, we also use human judgements to obtain a more intuitive and reliable measurement of the generated comments. A subset of 50 videos was randomly sampled from the 200 videos of the test set. Three native Chinese speakers familiar with danmu were asked to rate the quality of the generated comments on three criteria: fluency, relevancy and engagement.

- **Fluency** is intended to measure the language quality of the generated comment.
- **Relevancy** measures the semantic relevancy between the generated comment and the input video and nearby comments.
- **Engagement** should reflect how likely it is that the generated comment will motivate others to respond.

Model	p	Fluency	Relevance	Engagement
MCVT	0%	4.25	3.17	2.76
MCVT	5%	4.33	3.36	2.99
MCVT	50%	4.59	3.78	**3.07**
MCVT	100%	4.47	**3.91**	2.97
Human	-	**4.79**	3.58	3.01

Table 2: Human evaluation on 50 videos from the test set. Each comment is graded between 1 and 5, by 3 reviewers, for their language fluency, relevance to the video content and on how likely they are to provoke other viewers to also comment.

The score for all 3 measurements ranges from 1 (poor) to 5 (excellent). The final score is the average of the scores of the three annotators. The evaluation was conducted on the comments generated by our method for $p \in \{0\%, 5\%, 50\%\}$. For reference, we also evaluate the groundtruth comment set for these videos.

Table 2 reports the results of this human evaluation. We can see that the overall performance of model is almost indistinguishable from real danmu comments. Our relevancy and engagement scores are actually higher when $p \geq 50\%$. The quality of our model degrades slightly for the complete cold start scenario, but the results are still quite close to human comments.

6.4 Case Study

Examples of predicted outputs are shown in Fig. 6. The corresponding video frame shows a groundhog being fed. The subtitle, context comment, generated comments and target comments are reported in the table to the right. We can see that the model generates reasonable comments, which are relevant to the video shot and match the video's positive emotion (e.g. "laugh", "hahaha" and "lol"), even in the case of a complete cold start.

7 Conclusions and Further Development

In this paper we investigate the cold video start problem in automated danmu comment generation. We propose a multi-modal fusion network which includes processing of video frames, already published comments, and also audio and caption text. We train it for different comment density scenarios and perform extensive experiments on an expanded danmu video dataset. Results demonstrate the advantage of our method over the state-of-the-art in solving the cold video start problem.

Table 3: Results of comment generation module, model performance is presented with metrics of R@k, P@k, MRR (higher is better, showed in percentage) and MR (lower is better), p is the percentage of the preserved comments applied in test set.

Model	p	R@1	R@5	R@10	MR	MRR	P@5	P@10
Livebot	0 %	6.56 ± 0.05	22.23 ± 0.22	31.36 ± 0.29	22.15 ± 0.37	16.6 ± 0.48	6.44 ± 0.18	6.58 ± 0.18
Livebot-t	0 %	7.09 ± 0.06	24.78 ± 0.23	37.77 ± 0.36	19.86 ± 0.46	20.4 ± 0.48	6.89 ± 0.18	8.02 ± 0.18
MCVT-zero	0 %	**8.79** ± 0.07	27.25 ± 0.25	45.58 ± 0.44	**18.28** ± 0.33	25.6 ± 0.51	8.45 ± 0.18	**8.85** ± 0.20
MCVT	0 %	8.65 ± 0.07	**27.36** ± 0.25	**47.90** ± 0.44	18.81 ± 0.33	**25.8** ± 0.52	**8.70** ± 0.19	8.68 ± 0.19
Livebot	5 %	6.49 ± 0.05	23.49 ± 0.22	32.88 ± 0.31	21.59 ± 0.34	17.4 ± 0.48	6.15 ± 0.19	6.74 ± 0.18
Livebot-t	5 %	9.13 ± 0.08	25.34 ± 0.23	39.40 ± 0.38	19.51 ± 0.34	25.7 ± 0.48	8.90 ± 0.21	8.59 ± 0.21
MCVT	5 %	**19.74** ± 0.18	**42.44** ± 0.4	**56.70** ± 0.55	**12.90** ± 0.35	**32.1** ± 0.64	**18.75** ± 0.36	**19.11** ± 0.38
Livebot	30 %	13.11 ± 0.13	28.45 ± 0.27	41.50 ± 0.40	19.93 ± 0.37	26.0 ± 0.47	12.88 ± 0.24	11.59 ± 0.24
Livebot-t	30 %	13.75 ± 0.13	28.19 ± 0.27	45.59 ± 0.44	18.71 ± 0.35	27.5 ± 0.48	13.14 ± 0.27	13.07 ± 0.27
MCVT	30 %	**24.36** ± 0.22	**47.77** ± 0.46	**61.38** ± 0.59	**11.87** ± 0.31	**36.4** ± 0.59	**24.85** ± 0.41	**24.15** ± 0.42
Livebot	50 %	13.27 ± 0.12	27.17 ± 0.26	41.98 ± 0.40	20.44 ± 0.37	27.8 ± 0.44	13.37 ± 0.29	13.09 ± 0.27
Livebot-t	50 %	13.31 ± 0.12	29.74 ± 0.29	47.07 ± 0.46	18.39 ± 0.34	29.1 ± 0.51	15.59 ± 0.31	16.23 ± 0.32
MCVT	50 %	**26.75** ± 0.25	**48.23** ± 0.46	**62.57** ± 0.60	**11.23** ± 0.29	**37.8** ± 0.67	**26.17** ± 0.42	**26.89** ± 0.42
Livebot	70 %	14.35 ± 0.14	27.59 ± 0.26	42.09 ± 0.41	19.13 ± 0.36	28.1 ± 0.48	15.15 ± 0.34	14.76 ± 0.34
Livebot-t	70 %	15.85 ± 0.14	32.22 ± 0.31	55.44 ± 0.53	18.11 ± 0.36	29.5 ± 0.48	16.77 ± 0.35	17.01 ± 0.35
MCVT	70 %	**27.38** ± 0.25	**51.04** ± 0.49	**63.21** ± 0.61	**11.10** ± 0.27	**39.1** ± 0.71	**28.25** ± 0.43	**27.65** ± 0.42
Livebot	100 %	18.83 ± 0.16	34.50 ± 0.33	52.17 ± 0.51	17.81 ± 0.36	34.7 ± 0.48	18.88 ± 0.36	18.31 ± 0.36
Livebot-t	100 %	17.17 ± 0.15	32.89 ± 0.31	52.91 ± 0.51	18.09 ± 0.36	33.2 ± 0.48	18.15 ± 0.36	18.11 ± 0.36
MCVT	100 %	**29.65** ± 0.28	**55.36** ± 0.53	**63.90**± 0.62	**10.81** ± 0.29	**40.8** ± 0.65	**29.79** ± 0.43	**29.82** ± 0.43

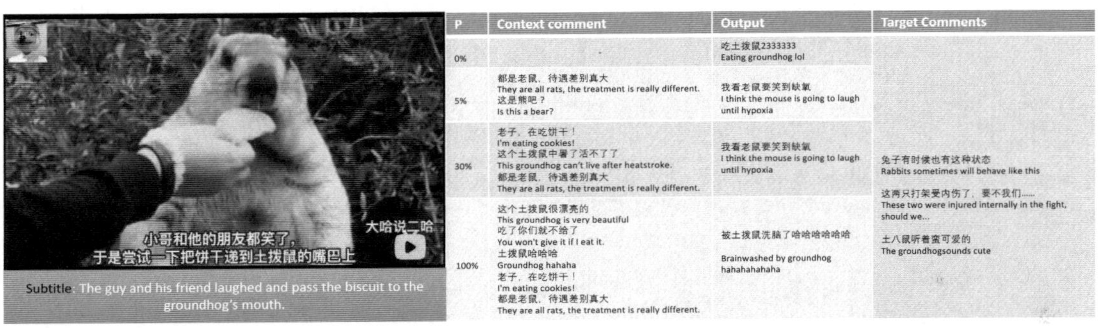

Figure 6: An example from the test set, left side is the video frame and the subtitle translation of the time point. The table on the right shows the target comments, context comments and the generated comment in different preserve rate p.

Our next research goal is to leverage a highlight detection method in this task to seek to further improve the system performance, since this is expected to reveal areas of likely user interest on the video timeline which could provide pointers for preferred locations for the automated creation of danmu comments.

Acknowledgement

This work was supported by Science Foundation Ireland as part of the ADAPT Centre (Grant 13/RC/2106) (www.adaptcentre.ie) at Trinity College Dublin.

References

D. Chaoqun, C. Lei, M. Shuming, W. Furu, Z. Conghui, and Z. Tiejun. 2020. Multimodal matching transformer for live commenting. In *ECAI*.

Abhishek Das, Satwik Kottur, Khushi Gupta, Avi Singh, Deshraj Yadav, José MF Moura, Devi Parikh, and Dhruv Batra. 2017. Visual dialog. In *Proceedings of the IEEE Conference on Computer Vision and Pattern Recognition*, pages 326–335.

Mattia Antonino Di Gangi, Matteo Negri, Roldano Cattoni, Dessi Roberto, and Marco Turchi. 2019. Enhancing transformer for end-to-end speech-to-text translation. In *Machine Translation Summit XVII*, pages 21–31. European Association for Machine Translation.

Z. Gan, C. Gan, X. He, Y. Pu, K. Tran, J. Gao, L. Carin, and D. Li. 2017. Semantic compositional networks for visual captioning. In *CVPR*.

Anthony Kay. 2007. Tesseract: an open-source optical character recognition engine. *Linux Journal*.

Diederik P Kingma and Jimmy Ba. 2014. Adam: A method for stochastic optimization. *ICLR*.

G. Lv, T. Xu, Q. Liu, E. Chen, W. He, M. An, and Z .Chen. 2019. Gossiping the videos: An embedding-based generative adversarial framework for time-sync comments generation. In *Springer*.

S. Ma, L. Cui, D. Dai, F. Wei, and X. Sun. 2019. Livebot: Generating live video comments based on visual and textual contexts. In *AAAI*.

S. Nitish, M. Elman, and S. Ruslan. 2015. Unsupervised learning of video representations using lstms. In *ICML*.

W. Spencer, J. Heng, B. Mohit, C. Shih-Fu, and V. Clare. 2018. Incorporating background knowledge into video description generation. In *EMNLP*.

V. Subhashini, H. Xu, D. Jeff, R. Marcus, M. Raymond, and S. Kate. 2014. Translating videos to natural language using deep recurrent neural networks. *arXiv*.

W. Weiying, C. Jieting, and J. Qin. 2020. Videoic: A video interactive comments dataset and multimodal multitask learning for comments generation. In *ACMMM*.

H. Wu, G. J. F. Jones, and F. Pitié. 2020. Response to livebot: Generating live video comments based on visual and textual contexts. *arXiv*.

W. Xin, C. Wenhu, J. Wu, Y. Wang, and Y. William. 2018. Video captioning via hierarchical reinforcement learning. In *CVPR*.

C. Xu, Z. Yongfeng, A. Qingyao, X. Hongteng, Y. Junchi, and Q. Zheng. 2017. Personalized key frame recommendation. In *SIGIR*, pages 315–324.

Z. Zhang, Z. Yin, S. Ren, X. Li, and S. Li. 2020. Dca: Diversified co-attention towards informative live video commenting. In *CCF NLPCC*.

W. Zheng, Z. Jie, M. Jing, L. Jingjing, A. Jiangbo, and Y. Yang. 2020. Discovering attractive segments in the user-generated video streams. *Information Processing & Management*.

¡Qué maravilla! Multimodal Sarcasm Detection in Spanish: a Dataset and a Baseline

Khalid Alnajjar
Department of Digital Humanities
University of Helsinki
khalid.alnajjar@helsinki.fi

Mika Hämäläinen
Department of Digital Humanities
University of Helsinki
mika.hamalainen@helsinki.fi

Abstract

We construct the first ever multimodal sarcasm dataset for Spanish. The audiovisual dataset consists of sarcasm annotated text that is aligned with video and audio. The dataset represents two varieties of Spanish, a Latin American variety and a Peninsular Spanish variety, which ensures a wider dialectal coverage for this global language. We present several models for sarcasm detection that will serve as baselines in the future research. Our results show that results with text only (89%) are worse than when combining text with audio (91.9%). Finally, the best results are obtained when combining all the modalities: text, audio and video (93.1%).

1 Introduction

Figurative language is one of the most difficult forms of natural language to model computationally and there have been several studies in the past focusing on its subcategories such as metaphor interpretation (Xiao et al., 2016; Hämäläinen and Alnajjar, 2019a), humor generation (Hämäläinen and Alnajjar, 2019b) and analyzing idioms (Flor and Klebanov, 2018). Sarcasm is one of the extreme forms of figurative language, where the meaning of an utterance has little to do with the surface meaning (see Kreuz and Glucksberg 1989).

Understanding sarcasm is difficult even for us humans as it requires certain mental capacities such as a theory of mind (see Zhu and Wang 2020) and it is very dependent on the context and speaker who is being sarcastic. There are also very different view to sarcasm in the literature, for example, according to Kumon-Nakamura et al. (1995) sarcasm requires an allusion to a failed expectation and pragmatic insincerity (see Grice 1975) to be present in the same time. However, Utsumi (1996) highlights that these two preconditions are not enough, as sarcasm needs an ironic context to take place.

Haverkate (1990) argues that, in the context of sarcasm, the meaning difference can either be the complete opposite of the semantic meaning of a sentence or somewhat different as seen in the lexical opposition of the words and the intended meaning. The fact that there are several different theoretical ways of understanding sarcasm, highlights the complexity of the phenomenon.

In this paper, we present an audio aligned dataset for sarcasm detection in Spanish. The dataset containing text and video timestamps has been released openly on Zenodo[1]. An access to the dataset with the video clips[2] can be granted upon request for academic use only. In addition, we will present a baseline model for this dataset to conduct multimodal sarcasm detection in Spanish.

2 Related work

In this section, we will present some of the recent related work on sarcasm detection. There has been some work also on sarcasm generation (Chakrabarty et al., 2020) and interpretation (Peled and Reichart, 2017), but they are rather different as tasks and we will not discuss them in detail.

Badlani et al. (2019) show an approach for sarcasm detection in online reivews. They train a CNN (convolutional neural network) based model on separate feature embeddings for sarcasm, humor, sentiment and hate speech. Similarly, Babanejad et al. (2020) also detect sarcasm in text. They combine an LSTM (long short-term memory) model with BERT. Dubey et al. (2019) also work on text only by detecting sarcastic numbers in tweets. They experiment with rules, SVMs (support vector machines) and CNNs.

Cai et al. (2019) use an LSTM model to detect sarcasm in tweets. Their approach is multimodal in the sense that it takes text and images into account, but it does not deal with audio and video like our

[1]Open access version of the data (contains text only) https://zenodo.org/record/4701383

[2]Access by request version of the data (videos and text) https://zenodo.org/record/4707913

Proceedings of the Third Workshop on Multimodal Artificial Intelligence, pages 63–68
June 6, 2021.

Speaker	Utterance	Translation	Sarcasm
Archer	No, Lana, para nada	No, Lana, not at all	true
Stan	Lo siento chicos, mi papá dice que está muy ocupado con los Broncos, no tiene tiempo	I am sorry guys, my dad says he is very busy with the Broncos, he doesn't have time	false
Lana	Decías algo acerca de un plan	You said something about a plan	true

Table 1: Example sentences from the dataset.

approach.

Castro et al. (2019) present a multimodal sarcasm dataset in English. The dataset consists of annotated videos from TV sitcoms such as Friends and the Big Bang Theory, apart from being in English instead of Spanish, the main difference is that our dataset consists of animated cartoons instead of TV shows played by real people. Another big difference is in the data collection as they opted for querying sarcastic video clips, where as the data we work with represents full episodes. Chauhan et al. (2020) use this data and present a multimodal sarcasm detection framework based on a Bi-GRU model.

Many of the related work has been focusing on text only. Research on multimodal approaches has been carried out only for English data, not unlike the textual approaches.

3 Dataset

We base our work on the sarcasm annotated dataset from the MA thesis of the second author of this paper Hämäläinen (2016)[3]. This dataset is based on two episodes of South Park with voice-overs in Latin-American Spanish and two episodes of Archer with voice-overs in Spanish of Spain. The dataset has the speaker, their utterance and sarcasm annotations for each utterance in all of the episodes. However, the released data has been released shuffled for copyright reasons and it contains text only. Unlike the recent multimodal dataset for English (Castro et al., 2019), this data is expert annotated according to several different theories on sarcasm.

Annotation based on theories is important in order to establish a concrete meaning for sarcasm and to avoid the same mistakes as Castro et al. (2019) had. In their paper, they report that the most sarcastic character in The Big Bang Theory is Sheldon, however this cannot be true as one of the main characteristics of Sheldon is that he does not understand sarcasm. Therefore, their annotations ignore the fundamentally important characteristic of sarcasm, which is speaker intent, and rather they consider sarcasm purely based on subjective intuition.

In order to produce a multimodal dataset out of the existing one, we locate the corresponding videos for the annotations and manually align them with the video. We use our own in-house tool JustAnnotate for this task[4]. This was a time consuming task, but as a result we ended up with a high-quality dataset with audio, video and text aligned. While aligning the dataset, we found several errors in the original transcriptions that we fixed. We did not alter the sarcasm annotations. In addition to the alignment, we introduced scene annotations. An episode of a TV show consists of many different scenes, and sarcasm is typically highly contextual, we indicate in the data which utterances belong to the same scene to better capture the context of each utterance.

Table 1 shows an example of the dataset. The English translation is provided for convenience, but it is not included in the dataset itself. Each line is aligned with audio and video. As we can see from these examples, sarcasm in the dataset is very contextually dependent as the sarcastic sentences presented in the table might equally well be sincere remarks if uttered by someone else or in a different context.

Figure 1: Archer uttering a sarcastic sentence that goes against the common sense

Figure 1 shows an example of a scene in the corpus. In this particular scene, Archer asks sarcastically *¿Dónde se compra la leche materna?* (Where

[3] Available on https://www.kaggle.com/mikahama/the-best-sarcasm-annotated-dataset-in-spanish

[4] https://mikakalevi.com/downloads/JustAnnotate.exe

does one buy breast milk?). This is an example of sarcasm in the corpus where sarcasm violates common sense. Depending on the speaker, the utterance might be sarcastic or the speaker might lack knowledge on the topic.

Figure 2: Cartman uttering a sarcastic sentence that can be resolved only by visual cues.

In Figure 2 Cartman comments on the neckpiece of Stan by saying *Esas corbatas están de moda, tiene suerte de tenerla* (Those neckpieces are fashionable, you are lucky to have one). This is an example of a very different type of sarcasm that cannot be detected just by having common knowledge about the world. In order to understand the sarcastic intent, a system would need to have an access to the video as well to detect the unfashionable neckpiece and the disappointed facial expression of Stan.

4 Method

In this section, we present our method for detecting sarcasm in the multimodal dataset. We experiment with text only, text and audio and all modalities. All models are trained by using the same random train (80%) and test (20%) splits. For the neural model, 10% of the training split is used for validation.

4.1 Text only

For the text only model, we experiment with two models. In the first one, we use an off the shelf OpenNMT (Klein et al., 2017) model. We train the model using a bi-directional long short-term memory (LSTM) based model (Hochreiter and Schmidhuber, 1997) with the default settings except for the encoder where we use a BRNN (bi-directional recurrent neural network) (Schuster and Paliwal, 1997) instead of the default RNN (recurrent neural network). We use the default of two layers for both the encoder and the decoder and the default attention model, which is the general global attention presented by Luong et al. (2015). The model is trained for the default 100,000 steps.

The second model is a Support Vector Machine (SVM) (Schölkopf et al., 2000), due to its efficiency when dealing with a high dimensional space and ability to train a model with small data. We use the SVM implementation provided in Scikit-learn (Pedregosa et al., 2011). Following the work of Castro et al. (2019), we use an RBF kernel and a scaled gamma. The regularization parameter C is set for 1000. This setup is followed in all of our SVM models.

Regarding the textual features of the SVM, we make use of GloVe (Pennington et al., 2014) embeddings[5] trained on the Spanish Billion Words Corpus (Cardellino, 2019) and ELMo (Peters et al., 2018) embeddings provided by (Che et al., 2018). Each textual instance is tokenized using TokTok[6], and then a sentence-level vector is constructed by computing the centroid (i.e., average vector) of all tokens, for each word embeddings type. In the case of ELMo, the vector of each token is the average of the last three layers of the neural network. The input to the SVM model is the concatenation of the two types of sentence embeddings.

4.2 Text and audio

This model is an SVM based model that extends the textual SVM model with audio features. We do not extend the OpenNMT model with audio features as the library does not provide us with audio and video inputters.

For all the audio, we set their sample size into 22 kHz to convert the data into a manageable and consistent size. Thereafter, we extract different audio features using librosa (McFee et al., 2020). These features include short-time Fourier transform (Nawab and Quatieri, 1987), mel-frequency cepstral coefficients (Stevens et al., 1937), chroma, Tonnetz (Harte et al., 2006), zero-crossing rate, spectral centroid and bandwidth, and pitches. In total, 13 features[7] were extracted. By combining all these features, we get the audio vector.

[5] https://github.com/dccuchile/spanish-word-embeddings

[6] https://github.com/jonsafari/tok-tok

[7] We used the following methods from librosa: *stft, mfcc, chroma_stft, spectral_centroid, spectral_bandwidth, spectral_rolloff, zero_crossing_rate, piptrack, onset_strength, melspectrogram, spectral_contrast, tonnetz* and *harmonic*

4.3 All modalities

For videos, instead of trying to represent an entire video as a vector like some of the existing approaches (Hu et al., 2016) to video processing, we extract 3 frames for each video corresponding to an utterance. We extract the frames by dividing the frames of a video clip into three evenly sized chunks and taking the first frame of each chunk. The key motivation behind this is that we are working with animation, where most of the frames are static and changes in between frames are not big. Therefore representing the entire video clip is not important and it would only increase the complexity of the system.

We extract visual features from each of the three frames extracted using a pre-trained ResNet-152 model (He et al., 2016). Features are taken from the last layer in the network, and the overall video vector is the sequence of the three feature embeddings, in the same order. All the vectors described above (i.e., textual, audio and visual vectors) are passed as input to the all-modalities SVM model.

5 Results

In this section, we report the accuracy of predictions by the neural model and the three SVM models that are based on 1) text only, 2) text and audio, and 3) text, audio and video. The results can be seen in Table 2.

Input	Accuracy
Neural Model	
Text	87.5%
SVM	
Text	89.0%
Text + Audio	91.9%
Text + Audio + Video	**93.1%**

Table 2: Accuracies of the predictions by all models for the sarcasm detection task.

As we can see in the results, having more modalities in the training improved the results. The audio features were able to capture more features important for sarcasm than pure text. Having all the three modalities at the same time gave the best results, with a 4.1% gain in the accuracy from the text-based model. The neural model reached to the lowest accuracy, most likely due to the fact that it was not trained with pretrained embeddings, a source of information that was available to the SVM models.

5.1 Error analysis

When we look at the predictions by the model best model (text + audio + video), we can see that the sarcasm detection is not at all an easy task.

An interesting example of a correctly predicted sarcastic utterance is *Lucen bien muchachos. ¡A patear culos!* (You look great, guys. Let's kick some ass!). This is an example of a visually interpretable sarcasm where the kids the sentence was uttered to looked all ridiculous. This would seem, at first, to highlight that the model has learned something important based on the visual features. However, we can see that this is not at all the case as the model predicts incorrectly the following sarcastic utterance: *Sí Stan, es lo que quiere la gente. No te preocupes, luces genial.* (Yes Stan, that is what the people want. Don't worry, you look great.) The context is similar to the one where the model predicted the sarcasm correctly, which means that the visual features are not representative enough for the model to correctly annotate detect this sarcastic utterance.

Interestingly, the model predicted *Sí amigo, es una réplica de la corbata del Rey Enrique V* (Yes friend, it is a replica of the neckpiece of the King Henry V) as sarcastic while in fact the uttrance was not sarcastic. This utterance refers to the same neckpiece as seen in Figure 2. The neckpiece appeared frequently in sarcastic contexts, so the model overgeneralized that anything said about the neckpiece must be sarcastic.

6 Conclusions

We have presented the first multimodal dataset for detecting sarcasm in Spanish. The dataset has been released on Zenodo. Our initial results serve as a baseline for any future work on sarcasm detection on this dataset.

Based on the results, it is clear that multimodality aids in detecting sarcasm as more contextual information is exposed to the model. Despite the improvements when considering multiple modalities, sarcasm detection is a very difficult task to model as it demands a global understanding of the world and the specific context the sarcastic utterance is in, as discussed in our error analysis. Even though the overall accuracy is high, it is clear the model makes errors that indicate that it has learned the data, but not the phenomenon.

References

Nastaran Babanejad, Heidar Davoudi, Aijun An, and Manos Papagelis. 2020. Affective and contextual embedding for sarcasm detection. In *Proceedings of the 28th International Conference on Computational Linguistics*, pages 225–243, Barcelona, Spain (Online). International Committee on Computational Linguistics.

Rohan Badlani, Nishit Asnani, and Manan Rai. 2019. An ensemble of humour, sarcasm, and hate speechfor sentiment classification in online reviews. In *Proceedings of the 5th Workshop on Noisy User-generated Text (W-NUT 2019)*, pages 337–345, Hong Kong, China. Association for Computational Linguistics.

Yitao Cai, Huiyu Cai, and Xiaojun Wan. 2019. Multi-modal sarcasm detection in Twitter with hierarchical fusion model. In *Proceedings of the 57th Annual Meeting of the Association for Computational Linguistics*, pages 2506–2515, Florence, Italy. Association for Computational Linguistics.

Cristian Cardellino. 2019. Spanish Billion Words Corpus and Embeddings.

Santiago Castro, Devamanyu Hazarika, Verónica Pérez-Rosas, Roger Zimmermann, Rada Mihalcea, and Soujanya Poria. 2019. Towards multimodal sarcasm detection (an _obviously_ perfect paper). In *Proceedings of the 57th Annual Meeting of the Association for Computational Linguistics*, pages 4619–4629.

Tuhin Chakrabarty, Debanjan Ghosh, Smaranda Muresan, and Nanyun Peng. 2020. R^3: Reverse, retrieve, and rank for sarcasm generation with commonsense knowledge. In *Proceedings of the 58th Annual Meeting of the Association for Computational Linguistics*, pages 7976–7986, Online. Association for Computational Linguistics.

Dushyant Singh Chauhan, Dhanush S R, Asif Ekbal, and Pushpak Bhattacharyya. 2020. Sentiment and emotion help sarcasm? a multi-task learning framework for multi-modal sarcasm, sentiment and emotion analysis. In *Proceedings of the 58th Annual Meeting of the Association for Computational Linguistics*, pages 4351–4360, Online. Association for Computational Linguistics.

Wanxiang Che, Yijia Liu, Yuxuan Wang, Bo Zheng, and Ting Liu. 2018. Towards better UD parsing: Deep contextualized word embeddings, ensemble, and treebank concatenation. In *Proceedings of the CoNLL 2018 Shared Task: Multilingual Parsing from Raw Text to Universal Dependencies*, pages 55–64, Brussels, Belgium. Association for Computational Linguistics.

Abhijeet Dubey, Lakshya Kumar, Arpan Somani, Aditya Joshi, and Pushpak Bhattacharyya. 2019. "when numbers matter!": Detecting sarcasm in numerical portions of text. In *Proceedings of the Tenth Workshop on Computational Approaches to Subjectivity, Sentiment and Social Media Analysis*, pages 72–80, Minneapolis, USA. Association for Computational Linguistics.

Michael Flor and Beata Beigman Klebanov. 2018. Catching idiomatic expressions in efl essays. In *Proceedings of the Workshop on Figurative Language Processing*, pages 34–44.

H Paul Grice. 1975. Logic and conversation. *1975*, pages 41–58.

Mika Hämäläinen. 2016. Reconocimiento automático del sarcasmo - ¡Esto va a funcionar bien! Master's thesis, University of Helsinki, Finland. URN:NBN:fi:hulib-201606011945.

Mika Hämäläinen and Khalid Alnajjar. 2019a. Let's FACE it. Finnish poetry generation with aesthetics and framing. In *Proceedings of the 12th International Conference on Natural Language Generation*, pages 290–300, Tokyo, Japan. Association for Computational Linguistics.

Mika Hämäläinen and Khalid Alnajjar. 2019b. Modelling the socialization of creative agents in a master-apprentice setting: The case of movie title puns. In *Proceedings of the 10th International Conference on Computational Creativity*. Association for Computational Creativity.

Christopher Harte, Mark Sandler, and Martin Gasser. 2006. Detecting harmonic change in musical audio. In *Proceedings of the 1st ACM workshop on Audio and music computing multimedia*, pages 21–26.

Henk Haverkate. 1990. A speech act analysis of irony. *Journal of pragmatics*, 14(1):77–109.

K. He, X. Zhang, S. Ren, and J. Sun. 2016. Deep residual learning for image recognition. In *2016 IEEE Conference on Computer Vision and Pattern Recognition (CVPR)*, pages 770–778.

Sepp Hochreiter and Jürgen Schmidhuber. 1997. Long short-term memory. *Neural computation*, 9(8):1735–1780.

Sheng-Hung Hu, Yikang Li, and Baoxin Li. 2016. Video2vec: Learning semantic spatio-temporal embeddings for video representation. In *2016 23rd International Conference on Pattern Recognition (ICPR)*, pages 811–816. IEEE.

Guillaume Klein, Yoon Kim, Yuntian Deng, Jean Senellart, and Alexander M. Rush. 2017. OpenNMT: Open-Source Toolkit for Neural Machine Translation. In *Proc. ACL*.

Roger J Kreuz and Sam Glucksberg. 1989. How to be sarcastic: The echoic reminder theory of verbal irony. *Journal of experimental psychology: General*, 118(4):374.

Sachi Kumon-Nakamura, Sam Glucksberg, and Mary Brown. 1995. How about another piece of pie: The allusional pretense theory of discourse irony. *Journal of Experimental Psychology: General*, 124(1):3.

Minh-Thang Luong, Hieu Pham, and Christopher D Manning. 2015. Effective approaches to attention-based neural machine translation. *arXiv preprint arXiv:1508.04025*.

Brian McFee, Vincent Lostanlen, Alexandros Metsai, Matt McVicar, Stefan Balke, Carl Thomé, Colin Raffel, Frank Zalkow, Ayoub Malek, Dana, Kyungyun Lee, Oriol Nieto, Jack Mason, Dan Ellis, Eric Battenberg, Scott Seyfarth, Ryuichi Yamamoto, Keunwoo Choi, viktorandreevichmorozov, Josh Moore, Rachel Bittner, Shunsuke Hidaka, Ziyao Wei, nullmightybofo, Darío Hereñú, Fabian-Robert Stöter, Pius Friesch, Adam Weiss, Matt Vollrath, and Taewoon Kim. 2020. librosa/librosa: 0.8.0.

S. Hamid Nawab and Thomas F. Quatieri. 1987. *Short-Time Fourier Transform*, page 289–337. Prentice-Hall, Inc., USA.

F. Pedregosa, G. Varoquaux, A. Gramfort, V. Michel, B. Thirion, O. Grisel, M. Blondel, P. Prettenhofer, R. Weiss, V. Dubourg, J. Vanderplas, A. Passos, D. Cournapeau, M. Brucher, M. Perrot, and E. Duchesnay. 2011. Scikit-learn: Machine learning in Python. *Journal of Machine Learning Research*, 12:2825–2830.

Lotem Peled and Roi Reichart. 2017. Sarcasm SIGN: Interpreting sarcasm with sentiment based monolingual machine translation. In *Proceedings of the 55th Annual Meeting of the Association for Computational Linguistics (Volume 1: Long Papers)*, pages 1690–1700, Vancouver, Canada. Association for Computational Linguistics.

Jeffrey Pennington, Richard Socher, and Christopher Manning. 2014. GloVe: Global vectors for word representation. In *Proceedings of the 2014 Conference on Empirical Methods in Natural Language Processing (EMNLP)*, pages 1532–1543, Doha, Qatar. Association for Computational Linguistics.

Matthew E. Peters, Mark Neumann, Mohit Iyyer, Matt Gardner, Christopher Clark, Kenton Lee, and Luke Zettlemoyer. 2018. Deep contextualized word representations. In *Proc. of NAACL*.

Bernhard Schölkopf, Alex J. Smola, Robert C. Williamson, and Peter L. Bartlett. 2000. New support vector algorithms. *Neural Comput.*, 12(5):1207–1245.

Mike Schuster and Kuldip K Paliwal. 1997. Bidirectional recurrent neural networks. *IEEE transactions on Signal Processing*, 45(11):2673–2681.

Stanley Smith Stevens, John Volkmann, and Edwin Broomell Newman. 1937. A scale for the measurement of the psychological magnitude pitch. *The journal of the acoustical society of america*, 8(3):185–190.

Akira Utsumi. 1996. A unified theory of irony and its computational formalization. In *COLING 1996 Volume 2: The 16th International Conference on Computational Linguistics*.

Ping Xiao, Khalid Alnajjar, Mark Granroth-Wilding, Kat Agres, Hannu Toivonen, et al. 2016. Meta4meaning: Automatic metaphor interpretation using corpus-derived word associations. In *Proceedings of the Seventh International Conference on Computational Creativity*. Sony CSL Paris.

Ning Zhu and Zhenlin Wang. 2020. The paradox of sarcasm: Theory of mind and sarcasm use in adults. *Personality and Individual Differences*, 163:110035.

Multimodal-Toolkit: A Package for Learning on Tabular and Text Data with Transformers

Ken Gu
Georgian
ken.gu@georgian.io

Akshay Budhkar
Georgian
akshay@georgian.io

Abstract

Recent progress in natural language processing has led to Transformer architectures becoming the predominant model used for natural language tasks. However, in many real-world datasets, additional modalities are included which the Transformer does not directly leverage. We present Multimodal-Toolkit,[1] an open-source Python package to incorporate text and tabular (categorical and numerical) data with Transformers for downstream applications. Our toolkit integrates well with Hugging Face's existing API such as tokenization and the model hub[2] which allows easy download of different pre-trained models.

Age	Title	Review Text	Division Name	Class Name	Department Name
21	Pretty but not for me	This sweater is very pretty, i love the knit a...	General Petite	Sweaters	Tops
36	Beautiful	As beautiful as in the picture. couldn't go wr...	General	Skirts	Bottoms
47	Adorable and comfortable!	Just bought this in black at my local store an...	General	Knits	Tops
29	Must have, elegant, chic	This top! i was hesitant to try this on becaus...	General	Blouses	Tops
38	Very flattering fit	This is a great pair of trousers for work but ...	General Petite	Pants	Bottoms

Figure 1: An example of a clothing review classification dataset. Each row is a data point consisting of text, categorical features, and numerical features.

1 Introduction

In recent years, Transformers (Vaswani et al., 2017) have become popular for model pre-training (Howard and Ruder, 2018; Peters et al., 2018; Devlin et al., 2019) and have yielded state-of-the-art results on many natural language processing (NLP) tasks. In addition, well-documented Transformer libraries such as Hugging Face Transformers (Wolf et al., 2020), and AllenNLP (Gardner et al., 2018) have democratized NLP, making it easier to productionize and experiment on Transformers.

However, there are not a lot of comprehensive tools for Transformers to work with tabular data. Often in real-world datasets, there are tabular data as well as unstructured text data which can provide meaningful signals for the task at hand. For instance, in the small example in Figure 1, each row is a data point. Columns `Title` and `Review Text` contain text features, columns `Division Name`, `Class Name`, and `Department Name` contain categorical features, and the `Age` column is a numerical feature. To the best of our knowledge, no tool exists that makes it simple for Transformers to handle this extra modality. Therefore, given the advances of Transformers for natural language tasks and the maturity of existing Transformer libraries, we introduce Multimodal-Toolkit, a lightweight Python package built on top of Hugging Face Transformers. Our package extends existing Transformers in the Hugging Face's Transformers library to seamlessly handle structured tabular data while keeping the existing tokenization (including subword segmentation), experimental pipeline, and pre-trained model hub functionalities of Hugging Face Transformers. We show the effectiveness of our toolkit on three real-world datasets.

2 Related Work

There have been several proposed Transformer models that aim to handle text features and additional features of another modality. For pre-trained Transformers on images and text, models such as ViLBERT (Lu et al., 2019) and VLBERT (Su et al., 2020) are mainly the same as the original BERT model but treat the extra image modality as additional tokens to the input. These models require pre-training on multimodal image and text data. On the other hand, while treating image features

[1]Github: `https://git.io/JO5a6`
[2]`https://huggingface.co/docs`

Proceedings of the Third Workshop on Multimodal Artificial Intelligence, pages 69–73
June 6, 2021.

as additional input tokens, MMBT (Kiela et al., 2019) proposes to use pre-trained BERT directly and fine-tune on image and text data. This is similar to Multimodal-Toolkit in which no pre-training on text and tabular data is needed.

Likewise, Transformers have been adapted to align, audio, visual, and text modalities in which there is a natural ground truth alignment. MulT (Tsai et al., 2019) is similar to ViLBert in which co-attention is used between pairs of modalities but also includes temporal convolutions so that input tokens are aware of their temporal neighbors. Meanwhile, Rahman et al. (2020) injects cross modality attention at certain Transformer layers via a gating mechanism.

Finally, knowledge graph embeddings have also been effectively combined with input text tokens in Transformers. Ostendorff et al. (2019) combines knowledge graph embeddings on authors with book titles and other metadata features via simple concatenation for book genre classification. On the other hand, for more general language tasks, ERNIE (Zhang et al., 2019) first matches the tokens in the input text with entities in the knowledge graph. With this matching, the model fuses these embeddings to produce entity-aware text embeddings and text-aware entity embeddings.

However, these models do not capture categorical and numerical data explicitly. Hugging Face does include LXMERT (Tan and Bansal, 2019) to handle language and vision modality but this can not be easily adapted for categorical and numerical data. Nevertheless, existing multimodal Transformer models do give good insights into how to combine categorical and numerical features. ViLBERT and VLBERT for example include image modality as input tokens which lead to one of our simple baseline of categorical and numerical features as additional token inputs to the model. Likewise, the gating mechanism Rahman et al. (2020), attention, and different weighting schemes have all been shown to be useful in combining different modalities.

3 Design

The goal of Multimodal-Toolkit is to allow users to quickly adapt state-of-the-art Transformer models for situations involving text and tabular data which occur often in real-world datasets. Moreover, we want to bring the benefits of Transformers to more use cases while making it simple for users

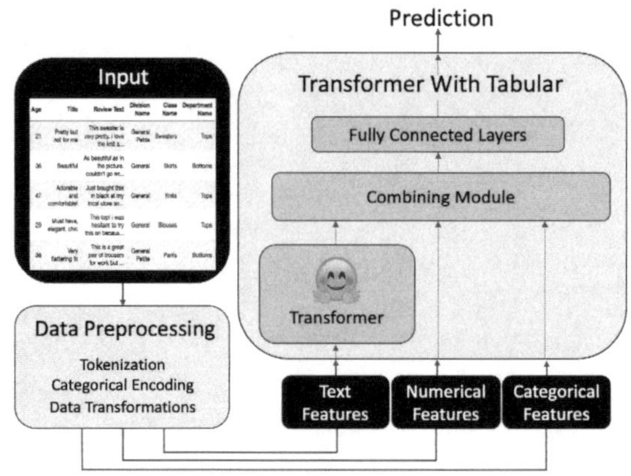

Figure 2: The framework of Multimodal-Toolkit. There is a data processing module that outputs processed text, numerical, and categorical features that are then fed as input to our Transformer With Tabular module consisting of a Hugging Face Transformer and our combining module.

of Hugging Face Transformers to adopt. Therefore, we maintain the existing interface of the popular Hugging Face Transformers library.

This design enables us to easily include more Transformer models, leverage strengths of specific models, use a feature-rich training pipeline, and integrate the thousands of community trained models on Hugging Face's model hub. We support a variety of Transformers (e.g. BERT, ALBERT, RoBERTa, XLNET) for both classification and regression tasks. All together, this becomes a reusable Transformer With Tabular component. We also provide a data preprocessing module for categorical and numerical features. An overview of the system is shown in Figure 2. Currently, the library supports PyTorch Transformers implementations.

3.1 Combining Module

We implement a combining module that is model agnostic that takes as input, $\boldsymbol{x}$, the text features outputted from a Transformer model and preprocessed categorical ($\boldsymbol{c}$) and numerical ($\boldsymbol{n}$) features, and outputs a combined multimodal representation $\boldsymbol{m}$. Although existing multimodal Transformers incorporate cross-modal attention inside middle Transformer layers, we choose the design in which the modality combination comes after the Transformer because this module can be easily included without much adaptation of the existing Hugging Face Transformer interface and can be easily extended to new Transformers included in the future.

Inside the combining module, we implement var-

Combine Feature Method	Equation
Text only	$\boldsymbol{m} = \boldsymbol{x}$
Concat	$\boldsymbol{m} = \boldsymbol{x}\|\|\boldsymbol{c}\|\|\boldsymbol{n}$
Individual MLPs on categorical and-numerical features then concat (MLP + Concat)	$\boldsymbol{m} = \boldsymbol{x}\|\|\text{MLP}(\boldsymbol{c})\|\|\text{MLP}(\boldsymbol{n})$
MLP on concatenated categorical and numerical features then concat (Concat + MLP)	$\boldsymbol{m} = \boldsymbol{x}\|\|\text{MLP}(\boldsymbol{c}\|\|\boldsymbol{n})$
Attention on categorical and numerical features (Attention)	$\boldsymbol{m} = \alpha_{x,x}\boldsymbol{W}_x\boldsymbol{x} + \alpha_{x,c}\boldsymbol{W}_c\boldsymbol{c} + \alpha_{x,n}\boldsymbol{W}_n\boldsymbol{n}$ $\alpha_{i,j} = \frac{\exp(\text{LeakyReLU}(\boldsymbol{a}^T[\boldsymbol{W}_i\boldsymbol{x}_i\|\|\boldsymbol{W}_j\boldsymbol{x}_j]))}{\sum_{k\in\{x,c,n\}}\exp(\text{LeakyReLU}(\boldsymbol{a}^T[\boldsymbol{W}_i\boldsymbol{x}_i\|\|\boldsymbol{W}_k\boldsymbol{x}_k]))}$
Gating on categorical and numerical features and then sum (Rahman et al., 2020) (Gating)	$\boldsymbol{m} = \boldsymbol{x} + \alpha\boldsymbol{h}$ $\boldsymbol{h} = \boldsymbol{g}_c \odot (\boldsymbol{W}_c\boldsymbol{c}) + \boldsymbol{g}_n \odot (\boldsymbol{W}_n\boldsymbol{n}) + b_h$ $\alpha = \min(\frac{\|\|\boldsymbol{x}\|\|_2}{\|\|\boldsymbol{h}\|\|_2} * \beta, 1)$ $\boldsymbol{g}_i = \text{R}(\boldsymbol{W}_{g_i}[\boldsymbol{i}\|\|\boldsymbol{x} + b_i)$ where β is a hyperparameter and R is an activation function
Weighted feature sum on text, categorical, and numerical features (Weighted Sum)	$\boldsymbol{m} = \boldsymbol{x} + \boldsymbol{w}_c \odot \boldsymbol{W}_c\boldsymbol{c} + \boldsymbol{w}_n \odot \boldsymbol{W}_n\boldsymbol{n}$

Table 1: The included combining methods in the combining module. Uppercase bold letters represent 2D matrices, lowercase bold letters represent 1D vectors. b is a scalar bias, $\boldsymbol{W}$ represents a weight matrix, and $||$ is the concatenation operator. Please see Rahman et al. (2020) for details on the gating mechanism.

Dataset	Task	Size	T	C	N
Airbnb	Regression	64k	3	74	15
Clothing	Classification	15k	2	3	3
PetFinder	Classification	28k	2	14	5

Table 2: Statistics of the datasets involved in experiments. T is the number of text columns. C is the number of categorical features, and N is the number of numerical features.

ious methods of combining the different representations in their respective feature spaces into one unified representation. These methods are inspired by the related work in multimodal Transformers as well as straightforward reasonable baselines such as concatenation and multi-layer perceptron (MLP) concatenation. Given a pre-trained Transformer, the parameters of the combining module and Transformer are trained based on the supervised task. In other words, the Transformer is further fine-tuned. The included methods are shown in Table 1.

4 Experiments

In this section, we study the effectiveness of leveraging tabular features on data with text and tabular data. We evaluate Multimodal-Toolkit on three real-world datasets from Kaggle.

4.1 Datasets

Regression: For regression, we use the Melbourne Airbnb Open Data (Airbnb) dataset (Xie, 2019) for the task of listing price prediction. Each data example is an Airbnb listing. Text features include the name of the listing, the summary of the listing, and a host description.

Binary Classification: For binary regression, we use Women's E-Commerce Clothing Reviews (Clothing) (Brooks, 2018). The source of the reviews is anonymous. Data examples consist of a review, a rating, the clothing category of the product etc. The goal is to predict if the review is recommending the product.

Multiclass Classification: Finally, we also include the PetFinder.my Adoption Prediction (PetFinder) dataset (PetFinder.my, 2018). Given the listing information of a pet set for adoption, the goal is to predict the speed at which a pet will be adopted, represented as 5 classes. Text features include the listing description and the pet name.

4.2 Experimental Setting

For experiments, we test each combining feature method described in Table 1. In addition, as mentioned in Section 2 we test a baseline in which the categorical and numerical features are also treated

Method	Airbnb		Clothing		PetFinder	
	RMSE	MAE	F1	AUPRC	$F1_{macro}$	$F1_{micro}$
Text Only	254.0	82.74	0.957	0.992	0.088	0.281
Unimodal	245.2	79.34	**0.968**	**0.995**	0.089	0.283
Concat	239.3	**65.68**	0.958	0.992	0.199	0.362
MLP + Concat	**237.3**	66.73	0.959	0.992	0.244	0.352
Concat + MLP	238.0	65.66	0.959	0.992	0.176	0.344
Attention	246.3	74.72	0.959	0.992	0.254	0.375
Gating (Rahman et al., 2020)	237.8	66.64	0.961	0.994	**0.275**	0.375
Weighted Sum	245.2	71.19	0.962	0.994	0.266	**0.380**

Table 3: Comparison of combining methods with results on regression and classification tasks. For each metric, the best performing model is in bold. For regression we use Root-mean-squared Error (RMSE) and MAE (Mean Absolute Error). In both cases, lower is better. For binary classification, we report F1 score and area under the precision-recall curve (AUPRC). Meanwhile, for multiclass classification, we use $F1_{macro}$ and $F1_{micro}$. In all classification metrics, higher is better.

as text columns. For example, for the situation in Figure 1, the text representing categorical features in `Division Name`, `Class Name`, and `Department Name` as well the numerical value in `Age` would all be tokenized and be treated as additional inputs to the Transformer. We denote this baseline as Unimodal.

For the Clothing Review dataset, we use `bert-base-uncased` as our Transformer and tokenizer. For the Airbnb dataset and Pet Adoption datasets, because there are some data points containing non-English text, we use `bert-base-multilingual`. We keep the training settings consistent for a given dataset. We train for 5 epochs and perform 4-fold-cross-validation, reporting the mean performance. For regression, we use a learning rate of 3e-3 while for classification tasks we use a learning rate of 5e-5. We report the results in Table 3.

4.3 Results

From Table 3, we observe the effectiveness of incorporating tabular features across different tasks and datasets. For each real-world dataset, the text-only baseline is the worst performing model. This shows using only text data with Transformers may be insufficient when extra tabular data is available.

However, how much the performance improves by leveraging Tabular features depends on the dataset. In the case of the Clothing Review dataset, the text of the review was already a very strong signal to the prediction, extra tabular features did not improve the performance much. We hypothesize the strong performance of the text only baseline may be due to the task of classifying review recommendation simplifying to sentiment classification, which the text modality provides the strongest signals. On the other hand, for the PetFinder dataset, the text description of the animal may not be sufficient to predict adoption speed. Rather, it is tabular features such as the age or the breed of the pet. Furthermore, the relative low raw performance of PetFinder dataset could be attributed to the difficulty of the task as a forecasting problem.

Additionally, although the Unimodal baseline is the best for the clothing dataset, this method does not appear to scale well when the number of categorical and numerical features increases or when the extra features' text representation does not reveal obvious semantic meaning.

5 Conclusion

This paper presents Multimodal-Toolkit, an open-source Python library powered by Hugging Face Transformers to learn on data that contains both text and tabular data. We show the effectiveness of incorporating tabular data and treating it as a separate modality with the already powerful Transformers. The modular design and shared API with Hugging Face allow users quick access to Hugging Face's community uploaded Transformer models.

For future work, we aim to include support for more Transformers and integrate the combining module at earlier layers in the Transformer. We hope the toolkit brings more research attention to this data scenario and we welcome open-source contributions to the project.

References

Nick Brooks. 2018. Women's e-commerce clothing reviews.

Jacob Devlin, Ming-Wei Chang, Kenton Lee, and Kristina Toutanova. 2019. BERT: Pre-training of deep bidirectional transformers for language understanding. In *Proceedings of the 2019 Conference of the North American Chapter of the Association for Computational Linguistics: Human Language Technologies, Volume 1 (Long and Short Papers)*, pages 4171–4186, Minneapolis, Minnesota. Association for Computational Linguistics.

Matt Gardner, Joel Grus, Mark Neumann, Oyvind Tafjord, Pradeep Dasigi, Nelson F. Liu, Matthew Peters, Michael Schmitz, and Luke Zettlemoyer. 2018. AllenNLP: A deep semantic natural language processing platform. In *Proceedings of Workshop for NLP Open Source Software (NLP-OSS)*, pages 1–6, Melbourne, Australia. Association for Computational Linguistics.

Jeremy Howard and Sebastian Ruder. 2018. Universal language model fine-tuning for text classification. In *Proceedings of the 56th Annual Meeting of the Association for Computational Linguistics (Volume 1: Long Papers)*, pages 328–339, Melbourne, Australia. Association for Computational Linguistics.

Douwe Kiela, Suvrat Bhooshan, Hamed Firooz, Ethan Perez, and Davide Testuggine. 2019. Supervised Multimodal Bitransformers for Classifying Images and Text. *arXiv e-prints*, page arXiv:1909.02950.

Jiasen Lu, Dhruv Batra, Devi Parikh, and Stefan Lee. 2019. Vilbert: Pretraining task-agnostic visiolinguistic representations for vision-and-language tasks. In *Advances in Neural Information Processing Systems*, volume 32, pages 13–23. Curran Associates, Inc.

Malte Ostendorff, Peter Bourgonje, Maria Berger, Julian Moreno-Schneider, Georg Rehm, and Bela Gipp. 2019. Enriching BERT with Knowledge Graph Embeddings for Document Classification. *arXiv e-prints*, page arXiv:1909.08402.

Matthew Peters, Mark Neumann, Mohit Iyyer, Matt Gardner, Christopher Clark, Kenton Lee, and Luke Zettlemoyer. 2018. Deep contextualized word representations. In *Proceedings of the 2018 Conference of the North American Chapter of the Association for Computational Linguistics: Human Language Technologies, Volume 1 (Long Papers)*, pages 2227–2237, New Orleans, Louisiana. Association for Computational Linguistics.

PetFinder.my. 2018. Petfinder.my adoption prediction.

Wasifur Rahman, Md Kamrul Hasan, Sangwu Lee, AmirAli Bagher Zadeh, Chengfeng Mao, Louis-Philippe Morency, and Ehsan Hoque. 2020. Integrating multimodal information in large pretrained transformers. In *Proceedings of the 58th Annual Meeting of the Association for Computational Linguistics*, pages 2359–2369, Online. Association for Computational Linguistics.

Weijie Su, Xizhou Zhu, Yue Cao, Bin Li, Lewei Lu, Furu Wei, and Jifeng Dai. 2020. Vl-bert: Pre-training of generic visual-linguistic representations. In *International Conference on Learning Representations*.

Hao Tan and Mohit Bansal. 2019. LXMERT: Learning cross-modality encoder representations from transformers. In *Proceedings of the 2019 Conference on Empirical Methods in Natural Language Processing and the 9th International Joint Conference on Natural Language Processing (EMNLP-IJCNLP)*, pages 5100–5111, Hong Kong, China. Association for Computational Linguistics.

Yao-Hung Hubert Tsai, Shaojie Bai, Paul Pu Liang, J. Zico Kolter, Louis-Philippe Morency, and Ruslan Salakhutdinov. 2019. Multimodal transformer for unaligned multimodal language sequences. In *Proceedings of the 57th Annual Meeting of the Association for Computational Linguistics*, pages 6558–6569, Florence, Italy. Association for Computational Linguistics.

Ashish Vaswani, Noam Shazeer, Niki Parmar, Jakob Uszkoreit, Llion Jones, Aidan N Gomez, Ł ukasz Kaiser, and Illia Polosukhin. 2017. Attention is all you need. In *Advances in Neural Information Processing Systems*, volume 30, pages 5998–6008. Curran Associates, Inc.

Thomas Wolf, Lysandre Debut, Victor Sanh, Julien Chaumond, Clement Delangue, Anthony Moi, Pierric Cistac, Tim Rault, Remi Louf, Morgan Funtowicz, Joe Davison, Sam Shleifer, Patrick von Platen, Clara Ma, Yacine Jernite, Julien Plu, Canwen Xu, Teven Le Scao, Sylvain Gugger, Mariama Drame, Quentin Lhoest, and Alexander Rush. 2020. Transformers: State-of-the-art natural language processing. In *Proceedings of the 2020 Conference on Empirical Methods in Natural Language Processing: System Demonstrations*, pages 38–45, Online. Association for Computational Linguistics.

Tyler Xie. 2019. Melbourne airbnb open data.

Zhengyan Zhang, Xu Han, Zhiyuan Liu, Xin Jiang, Maosong Sun, and Qun Liu. 2019. ERNIE: Enhanced language representation with informative entities. In *Proceedings of the 57th Annual Meeting of the Association for Computational Linguistics*, pages 1441–1451, Florence, Italy. Association for Computational Linguistics.

Semantic Aligned Multi-modal Transformer for Vision-Language Understanding: A Preliminary Study on Visual QA

Han Ding* **Li Erran Li*** **Zhiting Hu** **Yi Xu** **Dilek Hakkani-Tur** **Zheng Du** **Belinda Zeng**
Alexa AI, Amazon
{handing, lilimam, huzhitin, yxaamzn, hakkanit, zhengdu, zengb}@amazon.com

Abstract

Recent vision-language understanding approaches adopt a multi-modal transformer pretraining and finetuning paradigm. Prior work learns representations of text tokens and visual features with cross-attention mechanisms and captures the alignment solely based on indirect signals. In this work, we propose to enhance the alignment mechanism by incorporating image scene graph structures as the bridge between the two modalities, and learning with new contrastive objectives. In our preliminary study on the challenging compositional visual question answering task, we show the proposed approach achieves improved results, demonstrating potentials to enhance vision-language understanding.

1 Introduction

Vision-language tasks, such as image captioning (Vinyals et al., 2015), visual question answering (Antol et al., 2015), and visual commonsense reasoning (Zellers et al., 2018), serve as rich test-beds for evaluating the reasoning capabilities of visually informed systems. These tasks require joint understanding of visual contents, language semantics, and cross-modal alignments. In particular, beyond simply detecting what objects are present, models have to understand comprehensively the semantic information in an image, such as objects, attributes, relationships, actions, and intentions, and how all of these are referred to in natural language.

Inspired by the success of BERT (Devlin et al., 2019) on a variety of NLP tasks, there has been a surge of building pretrained models for vision-language tasks, such as ViLBERT (Lu et al., 2019), VL-BERT (Su et al., 2020), and UNITER (Chen et al., 2020). Despite the impressive performance on several vision-language tasks, these models suffer from fundamental difficulties in learning effective visually grounded representations, as they rely solely on cross-attention mechanisms to capture the alignment between image and text features, and learn from indirect signals without any explicit supervisions. Recently, Oscar (Li et al., 2020) introduced object tags detected in images as anchor points to ease the learning of semantic alignments between image regions and word sequences. However, individual object tags in isolation ignore the rich visual information, such as attributes and relationships between objects. Without such information as contextual cues, the core challenge of ambiguity in visual grounding remains difficult to solve. As Figure 1 shows, in order to answer the question correctly, the model needs to reason about object relationships. Without the relation "on" between "cup" and "table", the model mistakenly thinks the "cup" is on the "tray".

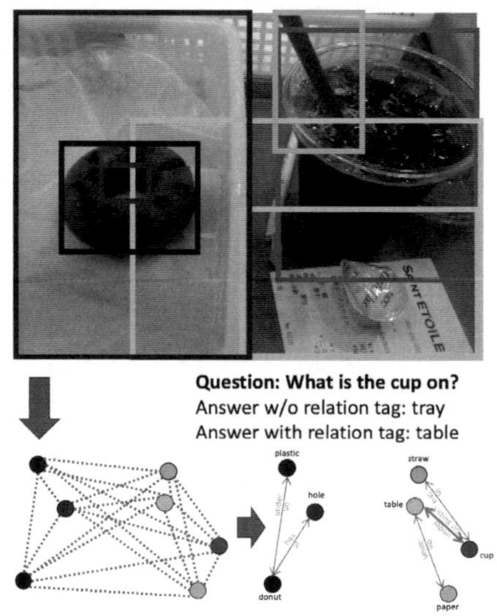

Figure 1: A Visual question-answering example illustrating the effectiveness of using scene graph as the bridge for cross-modal alignment

This work tackles the above challenges by introducing *visual scene graphs* as the bridge to align vision-language semantics. Extracted from the image using modern scene graph generators, a visual

*Equal contribution

Proceedings of the Third Workshop on Multimodal Artificial Intelligence, pages 74–78
June 6, 2021.

scene graph effectively depicts salient objects and their relationships. The visually-grounded intermediate abstraction permits more effective vision language cross attention for disambiguation and finer-grained alignment. Specifically, we propose *Samformer* (Semantic Aligned Multi-modal transFORMER) that learns the alignment between the modalities of text, image, and graphical structure. For each of object-relation labels in the scene graph, the model can easily find the referring text segments in natural language, and then learn to align to the image regions already associated with the scene graph. On the basis of the visually-grounded graph, we apply a contrastive loss and a masked language model loss that explicitly encourage image-text alignment. Furthermore, we propose a per-triplet (object, relation, subject) contrastive loss to align object and relation representations across the two modalities respectively.

We adopt a set of datasets, including Microsoft COCO Captions dataset (Lin et al., 2014), Visual Genome (Krishna et al., 2016), VQA (Antol et al., 2015), GQA (Hudson and Manning, 2019), Flicker 30k (Young et al., 2014), SBU (Ordonez et al., 2011), and Conceptual Caption (Sharma et al., 2018) to pre-train our model and fine-tune it on visual compositional question answering (GQA) (Hudson and Manning, 2019). Our preliminary analyses show improved performance and demonstrate the potential of the proposed approach on broader visual-language applications.

2 Semantic Aligned Vision and Language Transformer

This section presents the proposed semantic aligned multi-modal transformer (Samformer) for vision-language pre-training. Figure 2 provides an overall architectural view of the method.

Given a pair of an image I and a text sequence $\boldsymbol{w}$ describing the image, the goal of vision-language pre-training is to learn a joint representation of the pair which captures the alignment between the words and image regions and can be adapted to assist downstream tasks. Same as the previous vision-language models (Li et al., 2020; Chen et al., 2020), the proposed Samformer first separately encodes each modality into singular embedding features, and then employs a multi-layer self-attention transformer to align the features and obtain a cross-modal contextualized representation.

Samformer differs critically from previous methods in that we incorporate the visual scene graph extracted from the image to enhance the cross-modal representation learning. The structured, visually-grounded graph encodes rich semantic information (e.g., objects, relationships), which, compared to isolated object tags (Li et al., 2020) and bare image text singular features (Chen et al., 2020; Lu et al., 2019; Su et al., 2020), offers valuable cues to resolve ambiguity and *bridge* together text and visual semantics. We describe in details how visual scene graph is integrated to interplay with the text and image modalities for better alignment (section 2.1), and on this basis how contrastive learning strategies are devised for fine-grained alignment supervisions (section 2.2).

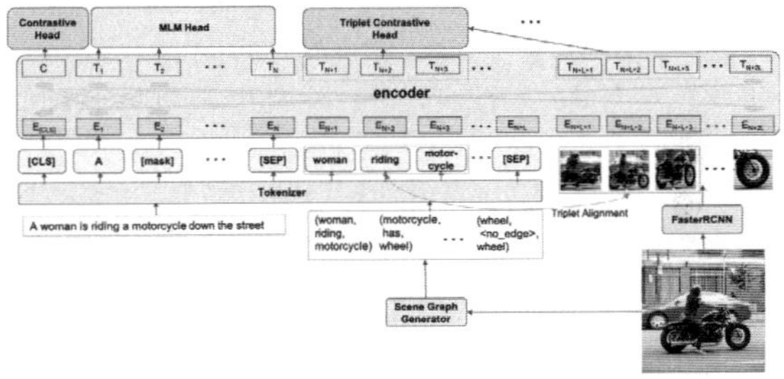

Figure 2: Architecture of the proposed Samformer.

2.1 Cross-modal Alignment with Visual Scene Graph Encoding

Given an image-text pair $(I, \boldsymbol{w})$, we first extract the visual scene graph G from the image with an off-the-shelf scene graph generator (Tang et al., 2020). A scene graph is a directed graph with the nodes representing the objects and the edges depicting their pairwise relationships. We represent the graph as a set of triplets, where a triplet (o_i, r_{ij}, o_j) denotes the relation type r_{ij} between object o_i and object o_j, e.g., ("woman", "riding", "motorcycle") in Figure 2. Crucially, the scene graph is already visually grounded. That is, each of the components in the triplets is associated with the corresponding regions in the image. For example, the object "woman" is associated with the bounding box of woman while the relationship "riding" corresponds to the bounding box that contains both the woman and the motorcycle. With such aligned object/relationship tokens and image regions, the visual scene graph thus serves as a bridge between the original image I and text sequence $\boldsymbol{w}$. That is, the model can easily find the correspondence between the text segments in the sequence $\boldsymbol{w}$ and the triplet tokens in the scene graph, since both are in the text modality. The text segments are then naturally aligned with the respective image regions associated with the scene graph. More importantly, the triplets containing both object and relationship information provide the model with ample contextual cues to resolve ambiguity. For example, Figure 1 shows the relationship "on" between "cup" and "table" resolves the ambiguity whether the cup is on the table or the tray.

In implementation, we first embed tokens in both the text sequence $\boldsymbol{w}$ and scene graph triplets (extracted by SGG (Tang et al., 2020)) with a pre-trained BERT embedder (Devlin et al., 2019). We then extract the visual embedding of each image region and also the union region of each triplet with the Faster R-CNN component (Ren et al., 2015) used in the bottom-up-attention (Anderson et al., 2018). All the embedding vectors are then fed into a transformer network with self-attention mechanisms to infer the alignment, as shown in Figure 2. In particular, to inform the transformer about the known alignment between the scene graph triplet tokens and image regions, we augment each triplet embedding and its corresponding image region embedding with the same position embedding.

2.2 Pre-training

We describe the pre-training method of the model. After pre-training, the model can then be applied to downstream visual-language tasks with efficient finetuning.

2.2.1 Masked Language Modeling (MLM)

This task is very similar to the Masked Language Modeling (MLM) task utilized in BERT (Devlin et al., 2019). The key difference is that visual clues are incorporated to predict the masked words for capturing the dependencies among visual and linguistic contents. During pre-training, each word in the input sentence is randomly masked (at a probability of 15%). For the masked word w_m, its token is replaced with a special token `[MASK]`. The model is trained to predict the masked words, based on the unmasked words $\boldsymbol{w}_{\backslash m}$, the scene graph G, and the visual features $\boldsymbol{v}$ of image regions (Figure 2). During pre-training, the final output feature at the position of the masked word is fed into a classifier over the whole vocabulary, and we minimize the prediction loss:

$$\mathcal{L}_{\mathrm{MLM}}(\boldsymbol{\theta}) = -\mathbb{E}_{\boldsymbol{w},m} \log P_{\theta}\left(\boldsymbol{w}_m \mid \boldsymbol{w}_{\backslash m}, G, \boldsymbol{v}\right) \quad (1)$$

The MLM task learns to use the relevant tokens in triplet tags which effectively aligns the representation between text $\boldsymbol{w}$ and graph G.

2.2.2 Contrastive Losses for Cross-Modal Alignment

As shown in Subsection 2.1, our model aligns the scene graph of an image with paired text using triplet tags as the bridge. We use two Contrastive loss terms. One is at the sequence level to align G and $\boldsymbol{v}$. The other is to align each triplet tag and its region features. For each training example, we randomly decide whether to use the first term or second. As training progresses, we increase the probability of using the first term. The reason to use the sequence level loss is because many downstream visual-language problems directly finetune the sequence level representation.

Specifically, given an image, we sample a object-relation triplet g from its scene graph G. We then replace the scene graph G by G' randomly sampled from the entire dataset with probability 50%. Denote H the resulting scene graph. We apply a fully-connected (FC) layer as a binary classifier on top of the encoder output of `[CLS]` to predict whether the scene graph is original (y = 1 if $H = G$) or has been replaced (y=0 if $H = G'$). The cross-modal contrastive loss at a global level (CMCG) is defined as:

$$\mathcal{L}_{\mathrm{CMCG}}(\boldsymbol{\theta}) = -\mathbb{E}_{\boldsymbol{w},G} \log P_{\theta}\left(y \mid \boldsymbol{w}, H, \boldsymbol{v}\right) \quad (2)$$

The second contrastive loss at the triplet tag level is constructed as follows. For each triplet tag g, we randomly determine with probability 50% whether we replace with another tag, g'. We apply a fully-connected (FC) layer as a binary classifier on top of the encoder output of g' and its region features to predict whether the tag is original (z = 1) or has been polluted (z = 0). The cross-modal contrastive loss for each triplet tag (CMCT) is defined as:

$$\mathcal{L}_{\mathrm{CMCT}}(\boldsymbol{\theta}) = -\mathbb{E}_{\boldsymbol{w},g} \log P_{\theta}\left(z \mid \boldsymbol{w}, G_{\backslash g}, g', \boldsymbol{v}\right) \quad (3)$$

3 Preliminary Experiments

3.1 Experimental Settings

We initialize our model with Oscar (Li et al., 2020) base model weights and pre-train it further on the collected image-text corpus. The scene graph used in our model is extracted using the pretrained model of SGG (Tang et al., 2020).

After pre-training, we conduct our preliminary experiments on GQA (Hudson and Manning, 2019). The task focuses on visual reasoning and compositional question answering in real-world settings

Method	Test-dev	Test-std
Oscar	58.40	59.01
Samformer w/ CMCG	60.46	60.33
Samformer w/ CMCG+CMCT	**60.51**	**60.62**
Improvement	2.11	1.61

Table 1: Comparison of Samformer and Oscar on GQA test sets (fine-tuned on train-bal only).

which involve diverse reasoning skills including spatial reasoning, relational reasoning, logic and comparisons. The task is formulated as a classification problem that chooses an answer from a shared set of 1,852 candidate answers. We select the particular task in our preliminary study because the task would benefit from effective alignment of the text-vision modalities on objects, relationships and attributes. In particular, GQA needs rich scene graph information from images to answer challenging compositional questions.

Since we build our model upon Oscar, we use it as the baseline for comparison. We choose Oscar base which has 12 layers and each layer has 12 attention heads. Both Oscar and ours were fine-tuned on the GQA train-balance dataset. For Oscar, we reproduced it with the official published pretrain model on the smaller balance training set.

3.2 Results

In this section, we study the performance on the downstream GQA task. As shown in Table 1, our Samformer by incorporating scene graphs improves the accuracy by 2.11% on GQA test-dev and 1.61% on test-std. The improvement is stronger if we focus on the challenging open questions (non-binary) in GQA, as shown in Table 2. Specifically, our method achieves 4.09% and 3.45% improvement, respectively, suggesting that including scene graph triplets help with understanding complex scenes and questions. The per-triplet contrastive loss, CMCT further improves the gains.

For fine-grained analysis of our method, we evaluate the performance grouping by the semantic type on the validation set. Among 5 semantic types, our method achieves 3.84% improvement on category type and 2.33% relation type. Although category questions are not directly asking about relation, the question itself sometimes related to a relation, for instance "Who is walking?". A triplet tag such as "man walking on street" would help the model better answer question like this.

To understand the full potential of the proposed approach that makes use of scene graphs, we evaluate the performance of Samformer when *ground-*

Method	Test-dev-open	Test-std-open
Oscar	42.27	43.32
Samformer w/ CMCG	**46.36**	**46.77**
Samformer w/ CMCG+CMCT	45.88	46.26
Improvement	4.09	3.45

Table 2: Comparison of Samformer and Oscar on GQA open questions (fine-tuned on train-bal only).

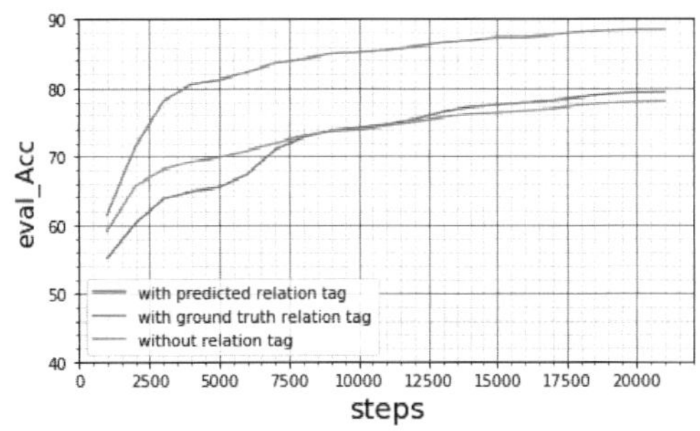

Figure 3: GQA evaluation accuracy curve without relation tags, with predicted relation tags, and with ground-truth relation tags.

truth scene graph is available. Figure 3 shows the results of evaluation accuracy as training proceeds. By including ground-truth scene graph relation tags, we can see significantly improved results compared to the baseline model that does not use relation tags at all. Using predicted relation tags also helps, though the improvement margin is more narrow since the predicted tags can be noisy.

4 Conclusion and Future Work

In this work, we propose Samformer, a novel semantic aligned multi-modal transformer model for vision-language pre-training. We explicitly align the visual scene graphs and text using triplet tags as anchors as well as a contrastive loss between each triplet tags and its paired visual features. We show improved preliminary results on GQA.

As shown in the empirical study, the performance is to some extent capped by the rather limited relations and object categories that can be extracted from off-the-shelf pre-trained scene graph models and object detectors. For future work, we plan to jointly train with scene graph models to more effectively learn from limited labeled data and weak supervision signals from paired text.

References

Peter Anderson, Xiaodong He, Chris Buehler, Damien Teney, Mark Johnson, Stephen Gould, and Lei Zhang. 2018. Bottom-up and top-down attention for image captioning and visual question answering. In *Proceedings of the IEEE/CVF Conference on Computer Vision and Pattern Recognition (CVPR).*

Stanislaw Antol, Aishwarya Agrawal, Jiasen Lu, Margaret Mitchell, Dhruv Batra, C Lawrence Zitnick, and Devi Parikh. 2015. Vqa: Visual question answering. In *Proceedings of the IEEE international conference on computer vision (ICCV).*

Yen-Chun Chen, Linjie Li, Licheng Yu, Ahmed El Kholy, Faisal Ahmed, Zhe Gan, Yu Cheng, and Jingjing Liu. 2020. UNITER: UNiversal Image-TExt representation learning. In *European conference on computer vision (ECCV),*.

Jacob Devlin, Ming-Wei Chang, Kenton Lee, Kristina Toutanova Google, and A I Language. 2019. BERT: Pre-training of deep bidirectional transformers for language understanding. In *North American Chapter of the Association for Computational Linguistics (NAACL).*

Drew A. Hudson and Christopher D. Manning. 2019. GQA: A new dataset for real-world visual reasoning and compositional question answering. In *Proceedings of the IEEE/CVF Conference on Computer Vision and Pattern Recognition (CVPR).*

Ranjay Krishna, Yuke Zhu, Oliver Groth, Justin Johnson, Kenji Hata, Joshua Kravitz, Stephanie Chen, Yannis Kalantidis, Li-Jia Li, David A Shamma, Michael Bernstein, and Li Fei-Fei. 2016. Visual genome: Connecting language and vision using crowdsourced dense image annotations. In *International Journal of Computer Vision (IJCV).*

Xiujun Li, Xi Yin, Chunyuan Li, Pengchuan Zhang, Xiaowei Hu, Lei Zhang, Lijuan Wang, Houdong Hu, Li Dong, Furu Wei, Yejin Choi, and Jianfeng Gao. 2020. Oscar: Object-Semantics aligned pre-training for Vision-Language tasks. In *European conference on computer vision (ECCV).*

Tsung-Yi Lin, Michael Maire, Serge Belongie, James Hays, Pietro Perona, Deva Ramanan, Piotr Dollár, and C Lawrence Zitnick. 2014. Microsoft coco: Common objects in context. In *European conference on computer vision (ECCV).* Springer.

Jiasen Lu, Dhruv Batra, Devi Parikh, and Stefan Lee. 2019. ViLBERT: Pretraining Task-Agnostic visiolinguistic representations for Vision-and-Language tasks. In *Advances in Neural Information Processing Systems (NeurIPS).*

Vicente Ordonez, Girish Kulkarni, and Tamara Berg. 2011. Im2text: Describing images using 1 million captioned photographs. In *Advances in Neural Information Processing Systems (NeurIPS).* Curran Associates, Inc.

Shaoqing Ren, Kaiming He, Ross Girshick, and Jian Sun. 2015. Faster R-CNN: Towards real-time object detection with region proposal networks. In *Advances in Neural Information Processing Systems (NeurIPS).* Curran Associates, Inc.

Piyush Sharma, Nan Ding, Sebastian Goodman, and Radu Soricut. 2018. Conceptual captions: A cleaned, hypernymed, image alt-text dataset for automatic image captioning. In *Annual Meeting of the Association for Computational Linguistics (ACL)*, Melbourne, Australia. Association for Computational Linguistics.

Weijie Su, Xizhou Zhu, Yue Cao, Bin Li, Lewei Lu, Furu Wei, and Jifeng Dai. 2020. VL-BERT: Pre-training of generic Visual-Linguistic representations. In *International Conference on Learning Representations (ICLR).*

Kaihua Tang, Yulei Niu, Jianqiang Huang, and Jiaxin Shi. 2020. Unbiased scene graph generation from biased training. In *Proceedings of the IEEE/CVF Conference on Computer Vision and Pattern Recognition (CVPR).*

Oriol Vinyals, Alexander Toshev, Samy Bengio, and Dumitru Erhan. 2015. Show and tell: A neural image caption generator. In *Proceedings of the IEEE conference on computer vision and pattern recognition (CVPR).*

Peter Young, Alice Lai, Micah Hodosh, and Julia Hockenmaier. 2014. From image descriptions to visual denotations: New similarity metrics for semantic inference over event descriptions. *Transactions of the Association for Computational Linguistics (TACL).*

Rowan Zellers, Mark Yatskar, Sam Thomson, and Yejin Choi. 2018. Neural motifs: Scene graph parsing with global context. In *Proceedings of the IEEE/CVF Conference on Computer Vision and Pattern Recognition (CVPR).*

GraphVQA: Language-Guided Graph Neural Networks for Scene Graph Question Answering

Weixin Liang[1], Yanhao Jiang[1], Zixuan Liu[1]
Stanford University, Stanford, CA 94305
{wxliang, jiangyh, zucks626}@stanford.edu

Abstract

Images are more than a collection of objects or attributes — they represent a web of relationships among interconnected objects. Scene Graph has emerged as a new modality as a structured graphical representation of images. Scene Graph encodes objects as nodes connected via pairwise relations as edges. To support question answering on scene graphs, we propose GraphVQA, a language-guided graph neural network framework that translates and executes a natural language question as multiple iterations of message passing among graph nodes. We explore the design space of GraphVQA framework, and discuss the trade-off of different design choices. Our experiments on GQA dataset show that GraphVQA outperforms the state-of-the-art model by a large margin (88.43% vs. 94.78%). Our code is available at https://github.com/codexxxl/GraphVQA

1 Introduction

Images are more than a collection of objects or attributes. Each image represents a web of relationships among interconnected objects. Towards formalizing a representation for images, Visual Genome (Krishna et al., 2017a) defined scene graphs, a structured formal graphical representation of an image that is similar to the form widely used in knowledge base representations. As shown in Figure 1, scene graph encodes objects (e.g., girl, burger) as nodes connected via pairwise relationships (e.g., holding) as edges. Scene graphs have been introduced for image retrieval (Johnson et al., 2015), image generation (Johnson et al., 2018), image captioning (Anderson et al., 2016), understanding instructional videos (Huang et al., 2018), and situational role classification (Li et al., 2017).

To support question answering on scene graphs, we propose GraphVQA, a language-guided graph

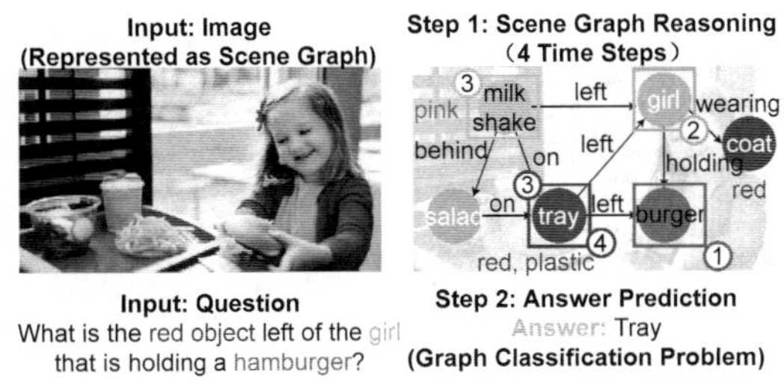

Figure 1: **Scene Graph:** Scene graph encodes objects (e.g., girl, burger) as nodes connected via pairwise relationships (e.g., holding) as edges. **GraphVQA Framework:** Our core insight is to translates and executes a natural language question as multiple iterations of message passing among graph nodes (e.g., hamburger -> small girl -> red tray). The final state after message passing represents the answer (e.g., tray).

neural network framework for Scene Graph Question Answering(Scene Graph QA). Our core insight is to translate a natural language question into multiple iterations of message passing among graph nodes. Figure 1 shows an example question "What is the red object left of the girl that is holding a hamburger". This question can be naturally answered by the following iterations of message passing "hamburger $\rightarrow$ small girl $\rightarrow$ red tray". The final state after message passing represents the answer (e.g., tray), and the intermediate states reflect the model's reasoning. Each message passing iteration is accomplished by a graph neural network (GNN) layer. We explore various message passing designs in GraphVQA, and discuss the trade-off of different design choices.

Scene Graph QA is closely related to Visual Question Answering (VQA). Although there are many research efforts in scene graph generation, Scene Graph QA remains relatively underexplored. Sporadic attempts in scene graph based VQA (Hu et al., 2019; Li et al., 2019; Santoro et al., 2017) mostly propose various attention mechanisms designed primarily for fully-connected graphs, thereby failing to model and capture the important structural information of the scene graphs.

[1]Equal Contribution. Authors listed in alphabetical order.

Proceedings of the Third Workshop on Multimodal Artificial Intelligence, pages 79–86
June 6, 2021. ©2021 Association for Computational Linguistics

We evaluate GraphVQA on GQA dataset (Hudson and Manning, 2019a). We found that GraphVQA with de facto GNNs can outperform the state-of-the-art model by a large margin (88.43% vs. 94.78%). We discuss additional related work in appendix A. Our results suggest the importance of incorporating recent advances from graph machine learning into our community.

2 Machine Learning with Graphs

Modeling graphical data has historically been challenging for the machine learning community. Traditionally, methods have relied on Laplacian regularization through label propagation, manifold regularization or learning embeddings. Today's de facto choice is graph neural network (GNN), which is a operator on local neighborhoods of nodes.

GNNs follow the message passing scheme. The high level idea is to update each node's feature using its local neighborhoods of nodes. Specifically, node i's representation at l-th layer $\boldsymbol{h}_i^{(l)}$ can be calculated using previous layer's node representations $\boldsymbol{h}_i^{(l-1)}$ and $\boldsymbol{h}_j^{(l-1)}$ as:

$$\boldsymbol{h}_{\mathcal{N}_i}^{(l)} = \text{AGG}_{j\in\mathcal{N}_i}\phi^{(l)}(\boldsymbol{h}_i^{(l-1)}, \boldsymbol{h}_j^{(l-1)}, \boldsymbol{e}_{ji}) \quad (1)$$

$$\boldsymbol{h}_i^{(l)} = \gamma^{(l)}(\boldsymbol{h}_i^{(l-1)}, \boldsymbol{h}_{\mathcal{N}_i}^{(l)}) \quad (2)$$

where $\boldsymbol{e}_{ji}$ denotes the feature of edge from node j to node i, $\boldsymbol{h}_{\mathcal{N}_i}^{(l)}$ denotes aggregated neighborhood information, $\gamma^{(l)}$ and $\phi^{(l)}$ denotes differentiable functions such as MLPs, and AGG denotes aggregation functions such as mean or sum pooling.

3 GraphVQA Framework

Figure 2 shows an overview of four modules in GraphVQA: (1) Question Parsing Module translates the question to M instruction vectors. (2) Scene Graph Encoding Module initializes node features X and edge features E with word embeddings. (3) Graph Reasoning Module performs message passing with graph neural networks for each instruction vector. (4) Answering Module summarizes the final state after message passing and predicts the answer.

3.1 Question Parsing Module

Question Parsing Module uses a sequence-to-sequence transformer architecture to translate the question $[q_1, \ldots, q_Q]$ into a sequence of instruction vectors $[\boldsymbol{i}^{(1)}, \ldots, \boldsymbol{i}^{(M)}]$ with a fixed M.

$$[\boldsymbol{i}^{(1)}, \ldots, \boldsymbol{i}^{(M)}] = \text{Seq2Seq}(q_1, \ldots, q_Q) \quad (3)$$

3.2 Scene Graph Encoding Module

Scene Graph Encoding Module first initializes node features $\hat{X} = [\hat{x}_1, ..., \hat{x}_N]$ with the word embeddings of the object name and attributes, and edge features E with the word embedding of edge type. We then obtain contextualized node features X by:

$$\boldsymbol{x}_i = \sigma(\frac{1}{|\mathcal{N}_i|}\sum_{j\in\mathcal{N}_i}(W\text{enc}\ [\hat{\boldsymbol{x}}_j; \boldsymbol{e}_{ij}])) \quad (4)$$

where σ denotes the activation function, $\boldsymbol{e}_{ij}$ denotes the feature of the edge that connects node i and node j, and $X = [x_1, x_2, ..., x_N]$ denotes the contextualized node features.

3.3 Graph Reasoning Module

Graph Reasoning Module is the core of GraphVQA framework. Graph Reasoning Module executes the M instruction vectors step-by-step, with N graph neural network layers. One major difference between our Graph Reasoning Module and standard GNN is that, we want the message passing in layer L conditioned on the Lth instruction vector. Inspired by language model type condition (Liang et al., 2020b), we adopt a general design that is compatible with *any* graph neural network design: Before running the Lth GNN layer, we concatenate the Lth instruction vector to every node and edge feature from the previous layer. Specifically,

$$\hat{\boldsymbol{h}}_i^{(L-1)} = [\boldsymbol{h}_i^{(L-1)}; \boldsymbol{i}^{(L)}] \quad (5)$$

$$\hat{\boldsymbol{e}}_{ij}^{(L-1)} = [\boldsymbol{e}_{ij}^{(L-1)}; \boldsymbol{i}^{(L)}] \quad (6)$$

where $\hat{\boldsymbol{h}}_i^{(L-1)}$ and $\hat{\boldsymbol{e}}_{ij}^{(L-1)}$ denotes the node feature and edge feature as inputs to the Lth GNN layer. Next, we introduce three standard GNNs that we have explored, starting from the simplest one.

3.3.1 Graph Convolution Networks (GCN)

GCN (Kipf and Welling, 2017) treats neighborhood nodes as equally important sources of information, and simply averages the transformed features of neighborhood nodes.

$$\boldsymbol{h}_i^{(L)} = \sigma(\frac{1}{|\mathcal{N}_i|}\sum_{j\in\mathcal{N}_i}(W_{\text{GCN}}^{(L)}\,\hat{\boldsymbol{h}}_j^{(L-1)})) \quad (7)$$

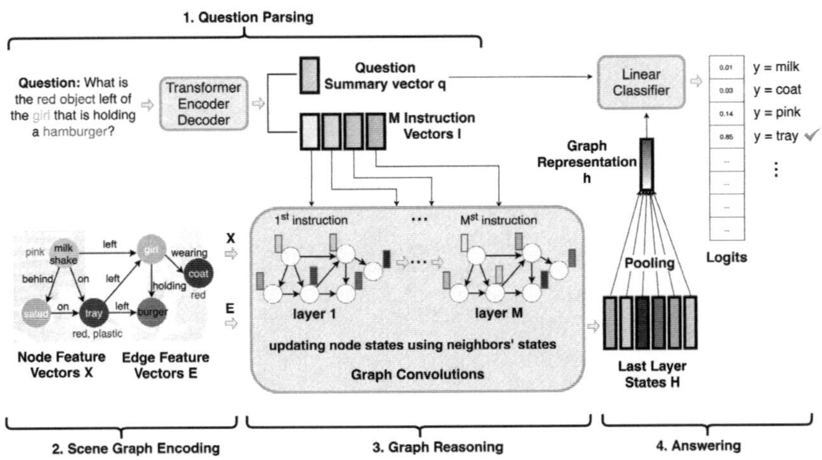

Figure 2: Semantics of the GraphVQA Framework. (1) Question Parsing Module translates the question to M instruction vectors. (2) Scene Graph Encoding Module initializes node features X and edge features E with word embeddings. (3) Graph Reasoning Module perform message passing with graph neural networks for each instruction vector. (4) Answering Module summarizes the final state after message passing and predicts the answer.

3.3.2 Graph Isomorphism Network (GINE)

GIN (Xu et al., 2019) is provably as powerful as the Weisfeiler-Lehman graph isomorphism test. GINE (Hu et al., 2020) augments GIN by also considering edge features during the message passing:

$$\begin{aligned}\boldsymbol{h}_i^{(L)} =& \boldsymbol{\Theta}((1+\epsilon)\hat{\boldsymbol{h}}_i^{(L-1)} + \\ & \sum_{j\in\mathcal{N}(i)} \sigma(\hat{\boldsymbol{h}}_j^{(L-1)} + \hat{\boldsymbol{e}}_{j,i}^{(L-1)}))\end{aligned}$$

where Θ denotes expressive functions such as MLPs, and ϵ is a scale factor for the emphasis of the central node.

3.3.3 Graph Attention Network (GAT)

Different from GIN and GINE, GAT (Veličković et al., 2018) learns to use attention mechanism to weight neighbour nodes differently. Intuitively, GAT fits more naturally with our Scene Graph QA task, since we want to emphasis different neighbor nodes given different instruction vectors. Specifically, the attention score $\alpha_{ij}^{(L)}$ for message passing from node j to node i at L^{th} layer is calculated as:

$$\boldsymbol{\alpha}_{ij}^{(L)} = \text{Softmax}_{\mathcal{N}_i}(\text{MLP}(\hat{\boldsymbol{h}}_i^{(L-1)}, \hat{\boldsymbol{h}}_j^{(L-1)}, \hat{\boldsymbol{e}}_{ij}^{(L-1)})) \tag{8}$$

where $\text{Softmax}_{\mathcal{N}_i}$ is a normalization to ensure that the attention scores from one node to its neighbor nodes sum to 1. After calculating the attention scores, we calculate each node's new representation as a weighted average from its neighbour nodes.

$$\boldsymbol{h}_i^{(L)} = \sigma(\sum_{j\in\mathcal{N}_i} \boldsymbol{\alpha}_{ij}^{(L)}\, \boldsymbol{W}_{\text{GAT}}^{(L)}\, \hat{\boldsymbol{h}}_j^{(L-1)}) \tag{9}$$

where σ denotes the activation function. Similar to transformer models, we use multiple attention heads in practice. In addition, many modern deep learning tool-kits can be incorporated into GNNs, such as batch normalization, dropout, gating mechanism, and residual connections.

3.4 Answering Module

After executing the Graph Reasoning module, we obtain the final states of all graph nodes after M iterations of message passing $[\boldsymbol{h}_1^{(M)}, ..., \boldsymbol{h}_N^{(M)}]$. We first summarize the final states after message passing, and then predict the answer token with the question summary vector q:

$$\boldsymbol{h} = \text{Aggregate}([\boldsymbol{h}_1^{(M)}, \boldsymbol{h}_2^{(M)}, ..., \boldsymbol{h}_N^{(M)}]) \tag{10}$$

$$\boldsymbol{y} = \text{Softmax}(\text{MLP}(\boldsymbol{h}, \boldsymbol{q})) \tag{11}$$

where $\boldsymbol{y}$ is the predicted answer. We note that GraphVQA does not require any explicit supervision on how to solve the question step-by-step, and we only supervise on the final answer prediction.

4 Experiments

Setup We evaluate our GraphVQA framework on the GQA dataset (Hudson and Manning, 2019a) which contains 110K scene graphs, 1.5M questions, and over 1000 different answer tokens. We use the official train/validation split of GQA. Since the scene graphs of the test set are not publicly available, we use validation split as test set. We set the number of instructions $M = 5$. More dataset and training details are included in Appendix C.

	Method	Binary	Open	Consistency	Validity	Plausibility	Distribution	Accuracy
Baseline1	GCN	86.84	84.63	90.21	95.51	94.44	0.13	85.70
Baseline2	LCGN	90.57	88.43	93.88	95.40	93.89	0.16	88.43
Ablation1	Only Questions	61.90	22.69	68.68	96.39	87.30	0.17	41.07
Ablation2	Only Scene Graphs	21.86	17.54	46.98	36.89	32.63	7.22	19.63
Proposed1	GraphVQA-GCN	92.11	88.37	95.44	95.5	94.4	0.12	90.18
Proposed2	GraphVQA-GINE	92.36	88.56	94.79	95.44	94.39	0.13	90.38
Proposed3	**GraphVQA-GAT**	**96.30**	**93.37**	**98.37**	**95.55**	**95.15**	**0.07**	**94.78**

Table 1: Evaluation Results on GQA. All numbers are in percentages. The lower the better for distribution.

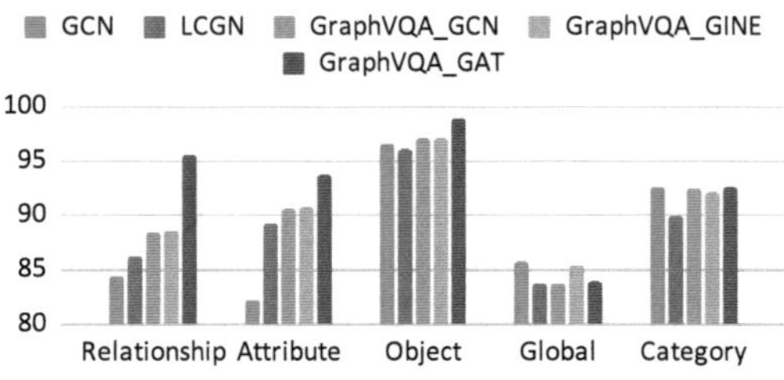

Figure 3: Accuracy breakdown on question semantic types. GraphVQA-GAT achieves significantly higher accuracy in relationship questions (95.53%).

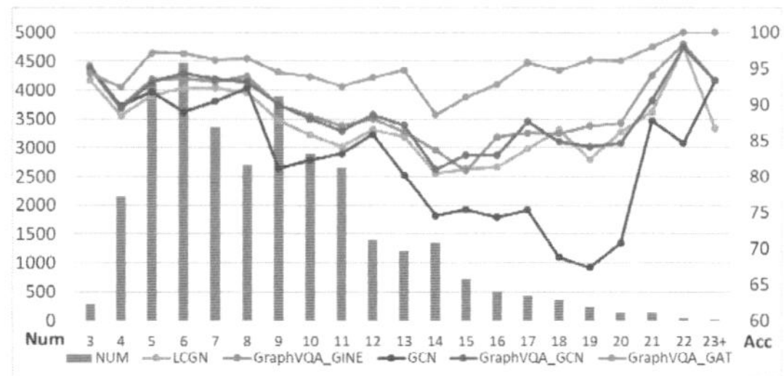

Figure 4: Accuracy breakdown on question word count. Num denotes the number of questions of each length. GraphVQA-GAT shows significant better performance for long question answering tasks.

Models and Metrics We evaluate three instantiations of GraphVQA: GraphVQA-GCN, GraphVQA-GINE, GraphVQA-GAT. We compare with the state-of-the-art model LCGN (Hu et al., 2019). We discuss LCGN in appendix B.3. We also compare with a simple GCN without instruction vector concatenation discussed in § 3.3 to study the importance of language guidance. We report the standard evaluation metrics defined in Hudson and Manning (2019a) such as accuracy and consistency.

Results The first take-away message is that GraphVQA outperforms the state-of-the-art approach LCGN, even with the simplest GraphVQA-GCN. Besides, GraphVQA-GAT outperforms LCGN by a large margin (88.43% vs. 94.78% accuracy), highlighting the benefits of incorporating recent advances from graph machine learning. The second take-away message is that conditioning on instruction vectors is important. Removing such conditioning drops performance (GCN vs. GraphVQA-GCN, 85.7% vs. 90.18%). The third take-away message is that attention mechanism is important for Scene Graph QA, as GraphVQA-GAT also outperforms both GraphVQA-GCN and GraphVQA-GINE by a large margin (94.78% vs. 90.38%), even though GINE is provably more expressive than GAT (Xu et al., 2019).

Analysis Figure 3 shows the accuracy breakdown on question semantic types. We found that GraphVQA-GAT achieves significantly higher accuracy in relationship questions (95.53%). This shows the strength in the attention mechanism in modeling the relationships in scene graphs.

Figure 4 shows the accuracy breakdown on question word count. As expected, longer questions are harder to answer by all models. In addition, we found that as questions become longer, the accuracy GraphVQA-GAT deteriorates drops than other methods, showing that GraphVQA-GAT is better at answering long questions.

5 Conclusion

In this paper, we present GraphVQA to support question answering on scene graphs. GraphVQA translates and executes a natural language question as multiple iterations of message using graph neural networks. We explore the design space of GraphVQA framework, and found that GraphVQA-GAT (Graph Attention Network) is the best design. GraphVQA-GAT outperforms the state-of-the-art model by a large margin (88.43% vs. 94.78%). Our results suggest the potential benefits of revisiting existed Vision + Language multimodal models from the perspective of graph machine learning.

Acknowledgments

We would like to sincerely thank NAACL-HLT 2021 MAI-Workshop Program Committe for their review efforts and helpful feedback. We would also like to extend our gratitude to Jingjing Tian and the teaching staff of Stanford CS 224W for their valuable feedback.

References

Aishwarya Agrawal, Dhruv Batra, and Devi Parikh. 2016. Analyzing the behavior of visual question answering models. In *EMNLP*, pages 1955–1960. The Association for Computational Linguistics.

Saeed Amizadeh, Hamid Palangi, Alex Polozov, Yichen Huang, and Kazuhito Koishida. 2020. Neuro-symbolic visual reasoning: Disentangling "visual" from "reasoning". In *ICML*, volume 119 of *Proceedings of Machine Learning Research*, pages 279–290. PMLR.

Peter Anderson, Basura Fernando, Mark Johnson, and Stephen Gould. 2016. SPICE: semantic propositional image caption evaluation. In *ECCV (5)*, volume 9909 of *Lecture Notes in Computer Science*, pages 382–398. Springer.

Abhishek Das, Harsh Agrawal, Larry Zitnick, Devi Parikh, and Dhruv Batra. 2016. Human attention in visual question answering: Do humans and deep networks look at the same regions? In *EMNLP*, pages 932–937. The Association for Computational Linguistics.

Ronghang Hu, Anna Rohrbach, Trevor Darrell, and Kate Saenko. 2019. Language-conditioned graph networks for relational reasoning. In *ICCV*, pages 10293–10302. IEEE.

Weihua Hu, Bowen Liu, Joseph Gomes, Marinka Zitnik, Percy Liang, Vijay S. Pande, and Jure Leskovec. 2020. Strategies for pre-training graph neural networks. In *ICLR*. OpenReview.net.

De-An Huang, Shyamal Buch, Lucio M. Dery, Animesh Garg, Li Fei-Fei, and Juan Carlos Niebles. 2018. Finding "it": Weakly-supervised reference-aware visual grounding in instructional videos. In *CVPR*, pages 5948–5957. IEEE Computer Society.

Drew A. Hudson and Christopher D. Manning. 2019a. GQA: A new dataset for real-world visual reasoning and compositional question answering. In *CVPR*, pages 6700–6709. Computer Vision Foundation / IEEE.

Drew A. Hudson and Christopher D. Manning. 2019b. Learning by abstraction: The neural state machine. In *NeurIPS*, pages 5901–5914.

Justin Johnson, Agrim Gupta, and Li Fei-Fei. 2018. Image generation from scene graphs. In *CVPR*, pages 1219–1228. IEEE Computer Society.

Justin Johnson, Ranjay Krishna, Michael Stark, Li-Jia Li, David A. Shamma, Michael S. Bernstein, and Fei-Fei Li. 2015. Image retrieval using scene graphs. In *CVPR*, pages 3668–3678. IEEE Computer Society.

Thomas N. Kipf and Max Welling. 2017. Semi-supervised classification with graph convolutional networks.

Ranjay Krishna, Yuke Zhu, Oliver Groth, Justin Johnson, Kenji Hata, Joshua Kravitz, Stephanie Chen, Yannis Kalantidis, Li-Jia Li, David A. Shamma, Michael S. Bernstein, and Li Fei-Fei. 2017a. Visual genome: Connecting language and vision using crowdsourced dense image annotations. *Int. J. Comput. Vis.*, 123(1):32–73.

Ranjay Krishna, Yuke Zhu, Oliver Groth, Justin Johnson, Kenji Hata, Joshua Kravitz, Stephanie Chen, Yannis Kalantidis, Li-Jia Li, David A. Shamma, Michael S. Bernstein, and Li Fei-Fei. 2017b. Visual genome: Connecting language and vision using crowdsourced dense image annotations. *International Journal of Computer Vision*, 123(1):32–73.

Linjie Li, Zhe Gan, Yu Cheng, and Jingjing Liu. 2019. Relation-aware graph attention network for visual question answering. In *ICCV*, pages 10312–10321. IEEE.

Ruiyu Li, Makarand Tapaswi, Renjie Liao, Jiaya Jia, Raquel Urtasun, and Sanja Fidler. 2017. Situation recognition with graph neural networks. In *ICCV*, pages 4183–4192. IEEE Computer Society.

Weixin Liang, Feiyang Niu, Aishwarya N. Reganti, Govind Thattai, and Gökhan Tür. 2020a. LRTA: A transparent neural-symbolic reasoning framework with modular supervision for visual question answering. *CoRR*, abs/2011.10731.

Weixin Liang, Youzhi Tian, Chengcai Chen, and Zhou Yu. 2020b. MOSS: end-to-end dialog system framework with modular supervision. In *AAAI*, pages 8327–8335. AAAI Press.

Weixin Liang and James Zou. 2020. Neural group testing to accelerate deep learning. *CoRR*, abs/2011.10704.

Weixin Liang, James Zou, and Zhou Yu. 2020c. ALICE: active learning with contrastive natural language explanations. In *EMNLP (1)*, pages 4380–4391. Association for Computational Linguistics.

Weixin Liang, James Zou, and Zhou Yu. 2020d. Beyond user self-reported likert scale ratings: A comparison model for automatic dialog evaluation. In *ACL*, pages 1363–1374. Association for Computational Linguistics.

Pramod Kaushik Mudrakarta, Ankur Taly, Mukund Sundararajan, and Kedar Dhamdhere. 2018. Did the model understand the question? In *ACL (1)*, pages 1896–1906. Association for Computational Linguistics.

Jeffrey Pennington, Richard Socher, and Christopher D. Manning. 2014. Glove: Global vectors for word representation. In *EMNLP*, pages 1532–1543. ACL.

Adam Santoro, David Raposo, David G. T. Barrett, Mateusz Malinowski, Razvan Pascanu, Peter W. Battaglia, and Tim Lillicrap. 2017. A simple neural network module for relational reasoning. In *NIPS*, pages 4967–4976.

Petar Veličković, Guillem Cucurull, Arantxa Casanova, Adriana Romero, Pietro Liò, and Yoshua Bengio. 2018. Graph attention networks.

Keyulu Xu, Weihua Hu, Jure Leskovec, and Stefanie Jegelka. 2019. How powerful are graph neural networks? In *ICLR*. OpenReview.net.

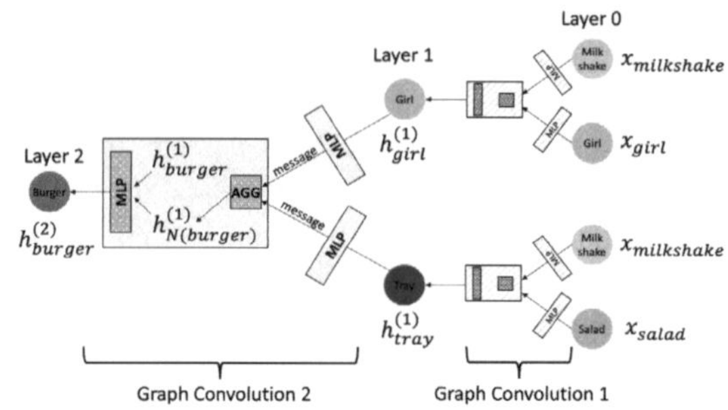

Figure 5: Structure of 2 Layer Graph Neural Network

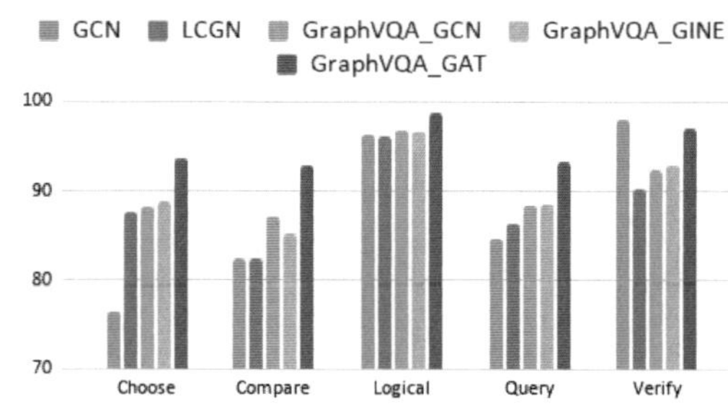

Figure 6: Accuracy breakdown on question structural types. GraphVQA-GAT achieves significantly higher accuracy in all types except for verify.

A Related Work

A.1 Visual Question Answering

VQA requires an interplay of visual perception with reasoning about the question semantics grounded in perception. The predominant approach to visual question answering (VQA) relies on encoding the image and question with a "black-box" neural encoder, where each image is usually represented as a bag of object features, where each feature describes the local appearance within a bounding box detected by the object detection backbone. However, representing images as collections of objects fails to capture relationships which are crucial for visual question answering. Recent study has further demonstrated some unsettling behaviours of those models: they tend to ignore important question terms (Mudrakarta et al., 2018), look at wrong image regions (Das et al., 2016), or undesirably adhere to superficial or even potentially misleading statistical associations (Agrawal et al., 2016). In addition, it has been shown that recent advances are primarily driven by perception improvements (e.g. object detection) rather than reasoning (Amizadeh et al., 2020).

A.2 Scene Graph Question Answering

Although there are many research efforts in scene graph generation, using scene graphs for visual question answering remains relatively underexplored (Hudson and Manning, 2019b; Hu et al., 2019; Li et al., 2019; Liang et al., 2020a). Hudson and Manning (2019b) propose a task-specific graph traversal framework with neural networks. The framework requires specifying the detail ontology of the dataset (e.g., color: red, blue,...; material: wooden, metallic), and thus is not directly generalizable. Other attempts in graph based VQA (Hu et al., 2019; Li et al., 2019) mostly explore attention mechanism on fully-connected graphs, thereby failing to capture the important structural information of the scene graphs.

B Additional Results

B.1 Additional Performances Analysis

Figure 6 provides another set of accuracy breakdown result on question structural types. We found that GraphVQA-GAT achieves the best for all types of questions except for the verify types. Specifically, GraphVQA-GAT outperforms significantly than other methods on answering queries, comparing among objects and making choices. This intuitively matches the principle of attention mechanism and again shows its advantages in modeling structural information in scene graphs.

Scene Graphs Statistics	Validation data	Train data	All
Total Number of Graphs	10,696	74,942	85,638
Total Number of Nodes	174,331	1,231,134	1,405,465
Total Number of Edges	534,889	3,795,907	4,330,796
Average Number of Nodes per Graph	16	16	16
Average Number of Edges per Graph	50	51	51
Total Number of Node Types	1,536	1,702	1,703
Total Number of Edge Types	295	310	310
Total Number of Attributes Types	603	617	617

Table 2: Scene Graphs Statistics of the GQA Dataset

	Level of Classification	Structural	Semantic
Is there apples in the picture?	node	verify	object
What color is the apple?	node	query	attribute
Is the cat to the left or right of the flower?	edge type	choose	relation
Is it sunny or cloudy?	graph	query	global

Table 3: Typical types of questions

B.2 Expressive Ability Analysis of GraphVQA-GINE

As mentioned in Section 3.3.1 and Section 3.3.2, a expressive function Θ is used in GINE layer. When Θ is just a single layer MLP, the corresponding GIN/GINE structure will be very similar to the GCN structure. Since in Section 4 we implemented Θ as a single layer MLP, the performance of GraphVQA-GCN and GraphVQA-GINE stays at very similar stage. As GIN and GINE are now very popular as basic components for large-scale graph neural network design, one may ask if using Θ with more powerful expression ability will help the performance. The short answer is no. We provide a simple ablation study on different choice of Θ, using a two layer MLP-style network with (FC, ReLU, FC, ReLU, BN) structure. Table 4 shows that the result of GraphVQA-GINE-2 degrades to the worst. One possible reason is that the scale for each scen graph is generally small, therefore the expression ability might already be enough for a single layer MLP, and use a more complex Θ may leads to harder optimization problems, and thus leads to a downgrade of the performance. Such guess could possibly be further investigated and evaluated in our future work. In addition, the scene graph-based VQA as in this work might offer an opportunity for further accelerating the real world image-based applications (Liang and Zou, 2020). Exploring such deployment benefits is another direction of future work.

B.3 Brief Introduction of LCGN

Language-Conditioned Graph Networks (LCGN) (Hu et al., 2019) updates node representations recurrently using the same single layer graph neural network. Given a set of instruction vectors $[\boldsymbol{i}_1, \ldots, \boldsymbol{i}_M]$, LCGN uses a single layer attention to convert them into context representations $[\boldsymbol{c}_1, \ldots, \boldsymbol{c}_M]$. Then, given a set of node representations $[\boldsymbol{x}_{loc,1}, \ldots, \boldsymbol{x}_{loc,n}]$, LCGN first randomly initialize another set of context representations $[\boldsymbol{x}_{ctx,1}, \ldots, \boldsymbol{x}_{ctx,n}]$, and then use them to concatenate with node representations to form initial local features, i.e,

$$\tilde{\boldsymbol{x}}_{t,i} = [\boldsymbol{x}_{loc,i}, \boldsymbol{x}_{ctx,i,t-1}, W_1\boldsymbol{x}_{loc,i} \circ W_2\boldsymbol{x}_{ctx,i,t-1}] \quad (12)$$

With the assumption that all nodes are connected, LCGN computes the edge weights $w_{j,i}^{(t)}$ for each node pair (i,j), i.e,

$$\boldsymbol{w}_{j,i}^{(t)} = \text{Softmax}((W_3\tilde{\boldsymbol{x}}_{t,i})^T((W_4\tilde{\boldsymbol{x}}_{t,j}) \circ (W_5c_t))) \quad (13)$$

The messages $m_{i,j}^{(t)}$, are then computed as:

$$\boldsymbol{m}_{j,i}^{(t)} = \boldsymbol{w}_{j,i}^{(t)}((W_6\tilde{\boldsymbol{x}}_{t,j}) \circ (W_7c_t)) \quad (14)$$

Finally, LCGN aggregates the neighborhood message information to update the context local representation $\boldsymbol{x}_{ctx,i,t}$.

$$\boldsymbol{x}_{ctx,i,t} = W_8[x_{ctx,i,t-1}; \sum_{j=1}^{N} m_{j,i}^{(t)}] \quad (15)$$

Method	Binary	Open	Consistency	Validity	Plausibility	Distribution	Accuracy
GraphGQA-GINE-2	86.83	83.85	89.8	95.54	94.25	0.16	85.04

Table 4: Ablation Study Results for 2 layer GraphVQA-GINE. All numbers are in percentages. The lower the better for distribution.

Note that the graph neural structure of LCGN can be regarded as a variant of recurrently-used single standard GAT layer, but with more self-designed learnable parameters. The main difference between LCGN's and other proposed graph neural structure is that the output node and edge features will be recurrently fed into the same layer again for each reasoning step, leading to a RNN-style network structure, instead of a sequential-style network. Moreover, our LCGN implementation is a variant of original LCGN, including a few improvements. Firstly, we use a transformer encoder and decoder to obtain instruction vectors instead of Bi-LSTM (Liang et al., 2020d). Secondly, we incorporate the true scene graph relations as edges instead of densely connected edges. Thirdly, edge attributes are also used in the generation of initial node features.

C Implementation Details

C.1 Data Pre-processing

The edges in the original scene graphs are directed. This means in most of the cases where we only have one directed edge connecting two nodes in the graph, the messages can only flow through one direction. However, this does not make sense in the natural way of human reasoning. For example, an relation of "A is to the left of B" should obviously entail an opposite relation of "B is to the right of A". Therefore, in order to enhance the connectivity of our graphs, we introduce a synthetic symmetric edge for every non-paired edge, making it pointing reversely to the source node. And in order to encode this reversed relationship, we negate the original edge's feature vector and use it as the representation of our synthetic symmetric edge.

C.2 Additional Dataset Information

These scene graphs are generated from 113k images on COCO and Flicker using the Visual Genome Scene Graph (Krishna et al., 2017b) annotations. Specifically, each node in the GQA scene graph is representing an object, such as a person, a window, or an apple. Along with the positional information of bounding box, each object is also annotated with 1-3 different attributes. These attributes are the adjectives used to describe associated objects. For examples, there can be color attributes like "white", size attributes like "large", and action attributes like "standing". Attributes are important sources of information beyond the coarse-grained object classes (Liang et al., 2020c). Each edge in the scene graph denotes relation between two connected objects. These relations can be action verbs, spatial prepositions, and comparatives, such as "wearing", "below", and "taller".

We use the official split of the GQA dataset. We use two files "val_sceneGraphs.json" and "train_sceneGraphs.json" directly obtained on the GQA website as our raw dataset. Since each image (graph) is independent, GQA splits the dataset by individual graphs with rough split percentages of **train/validation: 88%/12%**. In the table 2, we summarize the statistics that we collected from the dataset. We did not report the statistics of the test set since the scene graphs in the test set is not publicly available.

C.3 Training details

We train the models using the Adam optimization method, with a learning rate of 10^{-4}, a batch size of 256, and a learning rate drop(divide by 10) each 90 epochs. We train all models for 100 epochs. Both hidden states and word embedding vectors have a dimension size of 300, the latter being initialized using GloVe (Pennington et al., 2014).The instruction vectors have a dimension size of 512. All results reported are for a single-model settings (i.e., without ensembling). We use cross validation for hyper-parameter tuning.

Learning to Select Question-Relevant Relations for Visual Question Answering

Jaewoong Lee[1]*, **Heejoon Lee**[2]*, **Hwanhee Lee**[1] and **Kyomin Jung**[1]
[1]Dept. of Electrical and Computer Engineering, Seoul National University, Seoul, Korea
[2]SK Hynix, Sungnam, Korea
{hello3196, wanted1007, kjung}@snu.ac.kr
{heejoon1.lee@sk.com}

Abstract

Previous existing visual question answering (VQA) systems commonly use graph neural networks(GNNs) to extract visual relationships such as semantic relations or spatial relations. However, studies that use GNNs typically ignore the importance of each relation and simply concatenate outputs from multiple relation encoders. In this paper, we propose a novel layer architecture that fuses multiple visual relations through an attention mechanism to address this issue. Specifically, we develop a model that uses question embedding and joint embedding of the encoders to obtain dynamic attention weights with regard to the type of questions. Using the learnable attention weights, the proposed model can efficiently use the necessary visual relation features for a given question. Experimental results on the VQA 2.0 dataset demonstrate that the proposed model outperforms existing graph attention network-based architectures. Additionally, we visualize the attention weight and show that the proposed model assigns a higher weight to relations that are more relevant to the question.

1 Introduction

VQA (visual question answering) is a task that aims to output an answer for a given question related to a given image. VQA is a multimodal task that requires an understanding of multiple modalities. Therefore, VQA has received much attention in both computer vision and natural language processing research.

Most related works on VQA focus on the problem of image understanding and various attention mechanisms to fuse textual and image inputs. For example, Bottom-up Top Down Attention (Anderson et al., 2018) uses the features from detection models instead of CNN outputs and demonstrates their effectiveness with VQA tasks. Additionally,

Q: Is the man wearing a tie?

Implicit	Semantic	Spatial	Avg
no	yes	no	no

Q: How many riders are on the motorcycle?

Implicit	Semantic	Spatial	Avg
1	1	0	1

Figure 1: Two examples showing simple weighted sum results in wrong predictions. In both cases, although one relation encoder has given the correct answer, the final model's answer is incorrect, and averaging them result in wrong answer.

variable attention networks such as a stacked attention network (Yang et al., 2016) show that an attention mechanism between visual and text modalities is necessary for solving VQA tasks to find the objects to be focused on to answer a given question.

However, to solve higher-level VQA problems that require multi-hop reasoning, the model must consider various relations, such as geometric relationships between objects in the image. For this reason, researchers try to extract higher-level visual information using a graph neural network(GNN) based relation encoder to aggregate the relational information between the objects in an image.

For example, ReGAT (Li et al., 2019), an existing VQA architecture that uses GNNs, utilizes various relations between objects using graph attention networks (Veličković et al., 2018). Specifically, ReGAT uses three predefined relations: implicit, semantic, and spatial. To capture visual information, ReGAT constructs GNN-based relation encoders for each relation and combines the output probability distributions from the encoders using fixed weights to make the final prediction. However, this process can be problematic because the importance of each relationship for the given question cannot be considered. Figure 1 shows two examples where ReGAT does not make the correct prediction due to using fixed weights. In all cases, even though the

* Equal Contribution

Proceedings of the Third Workshop on Multimodal Artificial Intelligence, pages 87–96
June 6, 2021. ©2021 Association for Computational Linguistics

correct answer is given by one of the relation encoders, ReGAT finally predicts the incorrect answer due to the incorrect answers in the other encoders. For example, in the first example in Figure 1, a semantic relationship is particularly important compared to the other relationships because the model must consider the relation defined as *wearing* between the man and the tie. And the prediction from this semantic relation encoder is correct. However, the other encoders, including implicit and spatial, outputs incorrect answers because these relations are less related to the given question. Therefore, while ReGAT uses various attention mechanisms on objects to obtain relation-aware features, simply using the average or weighted summation with fixed weights to combine the relation-aware features can lead to incorrect predictions when averaging is insufficient to smooth out the noise from the less important relation features.

To resolve this shortcoming of previous models, we propose a novel model that can dynamically select a proper graph representation by considering the input question. We use attention mechanisms to make full use of relation encoders by giving them question-adaptive weights. Specifically, we train all relation encoders concurrently and learn adaptive weights to form a combined joint representation. Using these attention weights, the proposed model assigns higher weights to the relations that are meaningful for a given question. Experimental results demonstrate that the proposed model outperforms the previous existing model. Our model has an accuracy of 64.27%, compared to the existing model with 62.65% in VQA v2.0 dataset. Additionally, the proposed attention module can be easily visualized and has a natural form of interpretability. Thus, we analyze examples through the visualization of attention weights and verify that our model properly assigns attention weights to the relevant relationships for the question. Our contributions can be summarized as follows:

- We propose a novel attention-based VQA model that can dynamically select an essential relation for the given question.
- Experimental results show that the proposed model with adaptive attention weights for each relation outperforms the existing model.
- We also visualize the attention weights given to each relation and show that the proposed model can properly assign higher weights to question-related relations.

2 Related Work

2.1 Visual Question Answering

Models that are designed to solve VQA (Antol et al., 2015) are typically composed of four parts: an image encoder, a question encoder, multimodal fusion, and an answer predictor. In many studies, such as (Yang et al., 2016; Fan and Zhou, 2018; Patro and Namboodiri, 2018; Lu et al., 2016; Teney et al., 2018; Nam et al., 2017; Zhu et al., 2017; Malinowski et al., 2018), CNN-based attention mechanisms are frequently used in image encoders, which use the attention mechanism with images to concentrate on useful objects based on the input questions. Conversely, (Lu et al., 2016; Nam et al., 2017; Fan and Zhou, 2018; Yang et al., 2020) also uses attention mechanisms in question encoders to produce image-adaptive question embeddings.

Many previous works on VQA (Yao et al., 2018; Kipf and Welling, 2016; Santoro et al., 2017; Hu et al., 2018; Cadene et al., 2019; Yang et al., 2018; Teney et al., 2017; Norcliffe-Brown et al., 2018; Wang et al., 2019) use graph attention networks to extract visual features from images. Graph attention networks can more accurately identify various relations, such as semantic relations or spatial relations, between important objects with regard to questions, making the model more accurate and more interpretable. Among those studies, (Li et al., 2019) adds another encoder called an implicit relation encoder and applies each relation encoder directly to images to produce a graph representation for each relation. Then the model uses those representations equally to predict the answer.

Our model also uses relation encoders and graph representations but learns how much from each encoder's output will be used based on each question.

2.2 Relation-aware Graph Attention Network

The relation-aware graph attention network(ReGAT) uses a graph attention network to solve visual question answering tasks. Using a graph network to tackle such tasks was also previously explored in (Yao et al., 2018), where a pretrained semantic relation classifier was used to learn semantic relationships between objects. Using this information, a graph network was created, and graph convolution was used to finally obtain the relation-aware representation of each object. This method has been shown to be successful in image captioning. ReGAT improves this

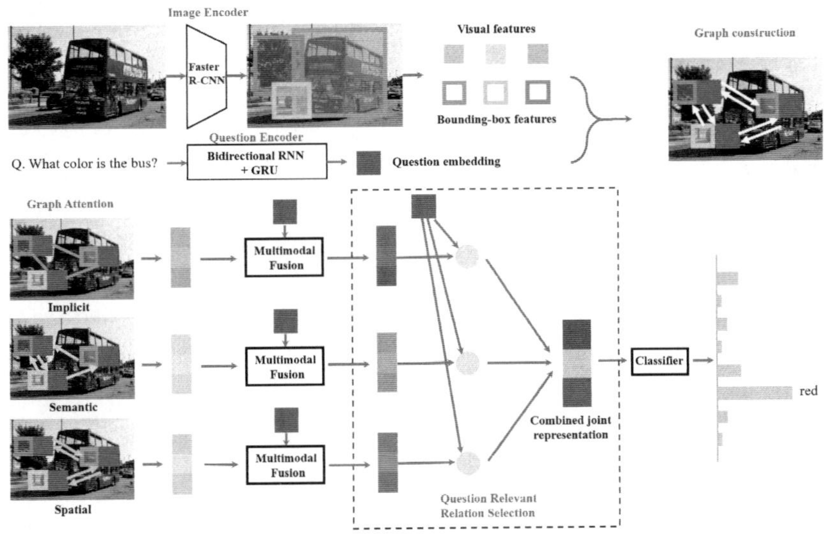

Figure 2: Overall architecture of the proposed model. After the encoders and graph attention layer, the question-relevant relation selection layer efficiently aggregates several visual relationships through an attention mechanism.

graph network using two additional relation types, spatial relations, implicit relations, and graph attention, instead of graph convolution. Spatial relation graphs are similar to semantic relation graphs but use geometric information between the objects to construct the graph. An implicit relation graph, conversely, uses no preexisting relationships between objects. A fully-connected graph is formed with the detected objects as nodes, and the interaction between objects is captured using attention over this graph. Graph attention allows each node in the neighborhood to have different importance and can capture more dynamic information between objects.

3 Model

Our model consists of four major components: a question encoder, an image encoder, a graph attention layer, and a question-relevant relation selection layer. The overall architecture of the proposed model is shown in Figure 2. In this section, we also describe the multimodal fusion method, which is a technique for fusing questions and image information.

3.1 Encoder

Our model uses a bidirectional RNN with a gated recurrent unit(GRU) (Cho et al., 2014) as the question encoder. Bidirectional RNN uses two hidden layers to process the input sequence in both directions. GRU is a simplified variant of LSTM (Hochreiter and Schmidhuber, 1997) that uses fewer parameters. The question encoder is built using these two well-known architectures. The output question embedding is later used as an input to the graph attention layer, multimodal fusion, and question relevant relation selection layer.

For the image, we use Faster R-CNN (Ren et al., 2015), which can identify the image as a set of objects. Each object has a visual feature vector v_i and a bounding-box feature b_i that contains its location information. These objects are forged into a graph that is used as inputs to the graph attention layer.

3.2 Graph Attention Layer

The graph attention (Wang et al., 2019) layer injects visual relationship information between objects into their corresponding visual features. To facilitate this process, we construct a fully-connected graph where each node represents each object from an image. Then, we aggregate the information from each node with the following procedure:
Each node in the neighborhood of v_i including itself, is projected by matrix W; then the edge weight α_{ij} is multiplied. All results are then summed and passed through a nonlinearity function to produce v_i^*, the relation-aware visual feature for object i. To make these relation graphs question-adaptive, question embedding is concatenated to each object's visual feature before applying graph attention. The way the edge weights are calculated differs depend-

ing on the type of relation graph.

Algorithm 1: Graph attention

```
Data: G initial graph, q question embedding, W
      projection matrix
Result: G* relation-aware graph
Let G* be an empty graph;
for each v ∈ G.V do
    Let n be a new node;
    S = 0;
    for each w ∈ G.Adj[v] do
        w_q = [w.visual||q];
        w_q = w_q W;
        α =
          EDGE-WEIGHT(v, w_q, w.bbox, relation type);
        S = S + α * w_q;
    end
    S = RELU(S);
    n.visual = S;
    ADD-VERTEX(G*, n);
end
return G*;
```

Implicit Relation Graph If the model is trained with no predefined edge weights, an implicit relation graph is created, where the model learns the relationship between objects on its own.

The edge weights for the implicit relation graph are learned using both the visual feature v and bounding-box feature b of each object. The detailed equation is as follows (Hu et al., 2018):

$$\alpha_{ij} = \frac{\alpha_{ij}^{b} \cdot \exp(\alpha_{ij}^{v})}{\sum_{j=1}^{K} \alpha_{ij}^{b} \cdot \exp(\alpha_{ij}^{v})} \tag{1}$$

α_{ij}^{v} is calculated by the scaled dot-product of the two visual features:

$$\alpha_{ij}^{v} = (Uv_i^{'})^T \cdot Vv_j^{'} \tag{2}$$

α_{ij}^{b} is computed by the following equation:

$$\alpha_{ij}^{b} = \max(0, w \cdot f_b(b_i, b_j)) \tag{3}$$

,where f_b represents the geometric relationship between objects i and j. Further details are available in (Hu et al., 2018).

However, if certain relationships between objects are known beforehand and the edges are labeled based on this information, the model creates an explicit relation graph (Yao et al., 2018). We use two types of explicit relation graphs in this study.

Semantic Relation Graph The first explicit relation graph used is the semantic relation graph. Semantic relationships between objects are learned beforehand using a semantic relation classifier on a visual relationship dataset. Then, if objects i and j have relationship $p_{i,j}$, the edge between node i and j is labeled $p_{i,j}$. Objects with no semantic relationships have their edges pruned. A total of 15 such semantic relationships are used. The list of relationships used is shown in Table 1.

Relation type	Predicate list
Semantic	wearing, holding, sitting on, standing on, riding, eating, hanging from, carrying, attached to, walking on, playing, covering, lying on, watching, looking at
Spatial	1(inside), 2(covering), 3(overlap with IoU above 0.5), 4-11(overlap with IoU below 0.5)

Table 1: List of predicates used in the construction of semantic and spatial relation graphs.

Edge weights are calculated similarly to the implicit relation case but using only the visual features of each object. However, the direction and label of each edge must be considered. Further details are available in (Li et al., 2019).

Spatial Relation Graph The next explicit relation graph used is the spatial relation graph which encodes positional information between objects. Similar to the semantic relation graph, if two nodes i and j have a semantic relationship p, their edges are labeled $p_{i,j}$. Spatial relations are classified into 11 categories, and the category number and its meaning are shown in Table 1.

Attention weights are calculated in the same as with the semantic relation graph.

3.3 Multimodal Fusion

The graph attention layer produces relation-aware visual features for each object in the image. These features must be fused with question embedding to form a joint representation. The general form of multimodal fusion is computed as follows:

$$J = f(v, q) \tag{4}$$

,where v is the collection of relation-aware visual features of each object, q is the question embedding, and f is the multimodal fusion type. Popular multimodal fusion methods for VQA include bottom-up top-down (Anderson et al., 2018), multimodal Tucker fusion (Ben-Younes et al., 2017) and bilinear attention networks (Kim et al., 2018). We use BUTD and BAN fusion in the proposed model.

Bottom-up Top-down Fusion In the bottom-up top-down (BUTD) fusion method (Anderson et al., 2018), question embedding and visual features are fed into nonlinear layers and joint representation is obtained by elementwise multiplication of the results. However, because there are k object features and just one question embedding for each image-question pair, an attention mechanism is used for each image feature with the question as a query to obtain one overall summary v^* of k objects in the image:

$$v' = \sigma(vW_v + b_v) \tag{5}$$

$$q' = \sigma(qW_q + b_q) \tag{6}$$

$$p = \text{softmax}(\sigma((v' * q')W_h + b_h)) \tag{7}$$

$$v^* = v \cdot p \tag{8}$$

,where $v \in \mathbb{R}^{k \times v}$, $q \in \mathbb{R}^{1 \times q}$, $W_v \in \mathbb{R}^{v \times h}$, $W_q \in \mathbb{R}^{q \times h}$, $W_h \in \mathbb{R}^{h \times 1}$, $b_v \in \mathbb{R}^h$, $b_q \in \mathbb{R}^h$, $b_h \in \mathbb{R}^1$, and σ denote the ReLU nonlinearity function. When calculating the product of v' and q', q' is repeated k times, so that the same question embedding is multiplied to each of the visual features.

After obtaining v^*, it is then fed into nonlinear layers along with q, and the results are multiplied elementwise to compute the joint representation J finally as follows:

$$J = \sigma(v^* W_v' + b_v') * \sigma(qW_q' + b_q') \tag{9}$$

Bilinear Attention Networks The bilinear attention network(BAN) (Kim et al., 2018) fusion method takes a single-channel input and a multichannel input as inputs and combines them to form a single-channel joint representation. In the proposed model, the question vector q is the single-channel input that will be used across the multi-channel input relation-aware visual features v to produce the joint representation J. The detailed equations are as follows:

$$a = ((qU) * (vV))P \tag{10}$$

$$p = \text{softmax}(a) \tag{11}$$

$$v^* = v \cdot p \tag{12}$$

,where $v \in \mathbb{R}^{k \times v}$, $q \in \mathbb{R}^{1 \times q}$, $U \in \mathbb{R}^{q \times h}$, $V \in \mathbb{R}^{v \times h}$, and $P \in \mathbb{R}^{h \times m}$, where m denotes the number of attention heads. These equations indicate that the vector on the left side is repeated k times and multiplied elementwise to the right matrix. When using multiple attention heads($m > 1$), v^* is the concatenation of all the attended outputs.

Once v^* is obtained, the final joint representation J is calculated as follows:

$$J = ((qU') * (v^* V'))P' \tag{13}$$

3.4 Question Relevant Relation Selection

The QRR (question-relevant relation) layer calculates the combined joint representation J^* given the joint representation of each relation, J_{imp}, J_{sem}, J_{spa} and the question embedding q.

Most questions do not use all relations with an equal amount of importance to predict the answer. For example, in the right example of Figure 1, the question requires understanding the spatial relationship between the riders and the motorcycle. Spatial information between objects is primarily encoded in the spatial joint representation, J_{spa}. However, the semantic joint representation J_{sem}, which encodes interactive dynamics between objects, plays nearly no part in answering this question. Thus, using fixed weights for each relation(e.g., 0.3, 0.4, 0.3, respectively in the original model) to predict the answer will not produce the best result due to noise from unnecessary attention given to irrelevant relation encodings like this example. The QRR layer gradually determines which of these relations is the most essential in deriving the correct answer to the given question by feeding the three representations and the given question to an attention network.

More specifically, the QRR layer computes the combined joint representation J^* through the following attention mechanism:

$$h = \tanh((J' W_v + b_v) \oplus (qW_q + b_q)) \tag{14}$$

$$p = \text{softmax}(hW_p + b_p) \tag{15}$$

,where $J' \in \mathbb{R}^{3 \times d}$ is the concatenation of the three joint representations, and $q \in \mathbb{R}^q$ is the question embedding. J' and q are first passed through a linear layer with $W_v \in \mathbb{R}^{d \times k}$, $b_v \in \mathbb{R}^{3 \times k}$, $W_q \in \mathbb{R}^{q \times k}$, and $b_q \in \mathbb{R}^{1 \times q}$, where k is a hyperparameter denoting the dimension of the hidden layer. The operator $\oplus$ indicates that the row of the second operand is to be added to each row of the first operand. The resulting matrix is passed through tanh nonlinearity which yields $h \in \mathbb{R}^{3 \times k}$. The attention distribution over the different relations $p \in \mathbb{R}^3$ are finally obtained by passing h through a linear layer with $W_p \in \mathbb{R}^{k \times 1}$, $b_p \in \mathbb{R}^{3 \times 1}$ and the result is passed through softmax. Each element of $p = [p_{imp} \quad p_{sem} \quad p_{spa}]^T$ represents the optimal weight of each relation given question q. The combined joint representation J^* can then be computed by the inner product of $J^{'}$ and p:

$$J^* = p_{imp}J_{imp} + p_{sem}J_{sem} + p_{spa}J_{spa} \quad (16)$$

This question-adaptive combined joint representation is then fed into the classifier to make a prediction. The combined joint representation J^* is a selective summary of the three relations tailored to the input question q. Compared to the ReGAT, which simply uses fixed weights regardless of the question, the proposed model determines weights dynamically and produces an exclusive representation of the image for the given question. The attention mechanism used in this study is similar to that used in bottom-up top-down multimodal fusion. However, in multimodal fusion, attention values are calculated among the different objects in an image. In the QRR layer, the attention distribution is computed over the three different relations, which allows the model to make more informative predictions and achieve higher accuracy. The QRR layer also adds interpretability to the original model by allowing us to examine the weight of each relation type directly.

Model	Yes/No	Others	Numbers	Overall
BUTD	80.30	55.80	42.80	63.20
MUTAN	**81.45**	47.17	37.32	60.17
Implicit	77.50	52.44	44.21	61.39
Semantic	76.85	51.35	44.19	60.61
Spatial	77.49	52.54	43.79	61.38
ReGAT+BUTD	78.80	45.82	53.57	62.65
ReGAT+BAN	81.22	49.87	55.45	65.02
Ours+BUTD	79.71	46.62	56.01	64.27
Ours+BAN	80.84	49.36	**56.65**	**65.37**

Table 2: Performance on VQA 2.0 dev split with different models.

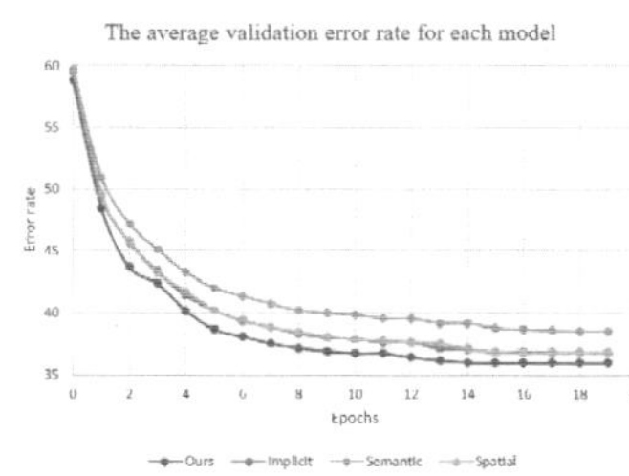

Figure 3: Average validation error rate of four models (the proposed model, implicit only, semantic only, spatial only).

4 Experiments

4.1 Datasets

We evaluate the proposed model using the VQA 2.0 (Goyal et al., 2017) dataset. VQA 2.0 dataset contains real images from MSCOCO (Lin et al., 2014) with questions in 3 categories: *Yes/No*, *Numbers* and *Others*. VQA 2.0 dataset was proposed to counter language priors present in the previous VQA dataset by providing complementary images that are similar but have different answers for the same question. There are 256,016 images and an average of 5.4 questions per image in the dataset. And the dataset has ten answers collected from human annotators for each image.

4.2 Implementation Details

For the question encoder, we set the question embedding dimension and GRU hidden dimension as 1024. We also set 1024 as the dimension of the relation-aware visual features and the QRR hidden layer. We use bottom-up and top-down fusion to fuse the visual features and question embedding.

We pretrain the semantic relation classifier using the Visual Genome dataset (Krishna et al., 2017), which contains 108,000 images with labels for objects, attributes, and relationships. The classifier is trained over the 14 semantic relations that we have defined in Table 1.

In the experiments, we use the PyTorch 1.3.1 (Paszke et al., 2017) framework to implement the proposed model. A batch size of 64 per GPU is used and we train the model for 20 epochs. We use a gradual warm-up learning rate, with the learning rate set initially to 0.0005 and increase linearly to 0.002 in the first 4 epochs. The learning rate is reduced by half every 2 epochs after the 15th epoch. We use the Adamax optimizer (Kingma and Ba, 2014) with weight normalization and dropout (Srivastava et al., 2014). We then train the model using a binary cross-entropy loss.

We measure the accuracy using the following metric:

$$\text{acc}(p) = \min\left(1, \frac{\sum_{i=1}^{10} 1(a_i = p)}{3}\right) \quad (17)$$

,where p is the model's prediction and a_i is the answer provided by human annotators.

4.3 Performance Comparison

Table 2 summarizes the results of the proposed experiment. We compare the results with the results

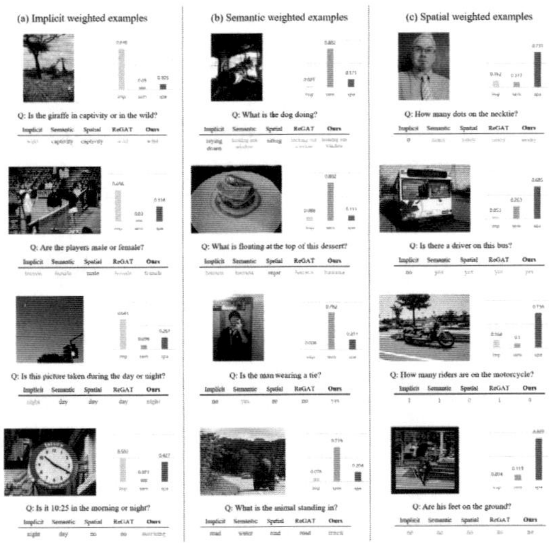

Figure 4: Model output examples and visualization of the attention weights for the QRR layer. Each column represents the cases in which each relation is given the highest weight.

of single relation encoder models and several existing VQA models, including ReGAT, BUTD and MUTAN. We also present a graph that shows the average validation error rate of each relation and our model for each epoch in Figure 3.

When using the BUTD fusion method, the proposed model outperforms ReGAT by 1.62%p in accuracy. We also observe consistent improvement in accuracy when looking at the results for each question type. Our model surpasses ReGAT by 0.91%p in *Yes/No* questions, 0.80%p in *Others* questions, and 2.44%p in *Number* questions. The table also shows the results when using BAN as the multimodal fusion method. The proposed model outperforms ReGAT by 0.35%p in accuracy overall. However, results are somewhat mixed if we consider the accuracy based on each question type. For the *Others* questions, the proposed model yields better accuracy than any other model and outperforms ReGAT by 1.20%p. For *Yes/No* and *Numbers* questions, however, the proposed model fails to achieve the accuracy produced by ReGAT by 0.38%p and 0.51%p, respectively, even though the proposed model surpasses all single relation models. Compared with other existing models, the proposed model with any fusion method outperforms BUTD and MUTAN by more than 1%p. The accuracy of each type of question shows us that the proposed model performs better with *Number* questions, even surpassing the models that outperform

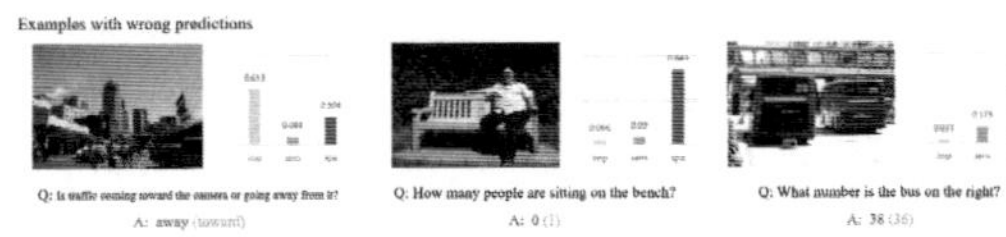

Figure 5: Cases where the model predicts incorrect answers.

the proposed model in overall accuracy.

To interpret the relative importance of each relation type, we analyze the weights used with each relation encoder on the VQA v2.0 validation dataset. On average, the implicit encoder has a weight of 5.78%, the semantic encoder has a weight of 73.70%, and the spatial encoder has a weight of 20.52%. These results show that the three relations are not equally important in answering each question, highlighting our claim that assigning fixed weights of 0.3, 0.4, and 0.3 to each encoder is not optimal. In fact, semantic relation has a much larger weight than the other two relations in most cases. We also define weights above 0.05 as the meaningful usage of that relation. Based on this criterion, 29.88% of the examples show meaningful usage of all three relations, which further highlights that in the remaining 70.12% of the dataset, using two types or one type of relation encoder is sufficient for predicting the correct answer.

4.4 Qualitative Analysis

We visualize the amount of attention given to each relation encoder depending on the input question, as shown in Figure 4. We present certain image-question pairs from the dataset that best demonstrate the usefulness of the QRR layer and visualize the attention given to each relation using a bar graph with each number representing the relative weight. We also show the predictions of the single-relation models and ReGAT below the question along with the proposed model's prediction for comparison.

In Figure 4, we present 12 image-question pairs along with predictions from each model. We organize them into three columns where each column contains examples with the most attention in implicit, semantic, and spatial relations, respectively. Across all examples, we see that the QRR layer has correctly captured the most relevant relation in answering the given question.

The examples for the implicit weighted examples in Figure 4 (a) contain questions that require a thorough understanding of the image to answer.

For example, the first entry asks whether the animal in the picture is in a given state or not. This question cannot be easily answered with only a superficial description of the image. The implicit relation graph has learned this relationship correctly, and the proposed model identified this relation as most important. The third example shows why the proposed model yields higher accuracy than ReGAT. Only the implicit-relation model yields the correct answer, possibly by connecting the small cluster of white pixels in the top left corner to an object seen at night. The other two relations provide incorrect answers; however, ReGAT cannot filter out such misleading information. The proposed model accurately selects the implicit relation as the most critical relation by giving it a weight of 0.641.

The semantically weighted examples in Figure 4 4 contain questions and answers that are heavily related to the 14 semantic relations that we have defined. The first example asks for the action of the dog. In this example, only the semantic-encoder that is most relevant to the question yields the correct answer. Unlike ReGAT that fails to answer correctly, our model gives higher weights to the most important relation to deliver the correct answer. The third example shows that ReGAT is unable to guess correctly due to suboptimal weight distribution. The proposed model blocks out all unnecessary noise by assigning the semantic relation the largest weight for this image-question pair.

The examples in Figure 4 (c) show questions that involve understanding the geometric relationship between objects. The third example demonstrates the effectiveness of the proposed model, which has correctly determined that objects that have an 'on' spatial relation with the motorcycle are the most important in giving the right answer, of which there are none. Other single-relation models and ReGAT possibly suffer from question bias and provide an incorrect answer of 1, which may be correct in many different cases.

The examples in the first and second columns of the last row are interesting in that the proposed model is the only network that has correctly predicted the answer, which shows that the proposed method can derive new answers using optimized weights for each relation type.

4.5 Error Analysis

We explore frequently observed error cases where the proposed model fails to produce the correct answer and present examples in Figure 5. For each example, the prediction of the proposed model is shown in red, and the true label is shown in green. From the examples, we observe the typical reasons for these errors. Most error cases are due to the incorrect prediction of the relation encoder itself, even though our model correctly predicts the type of visual relation. In the first image, the question asks for the direction of motion of the traffic. The bar graph on the right shows that the proposed model determines the implicit relation as the most important relation. However, the implicit relation encoder itself fails to encode such information in the visual features correctly, and our model propagates the incorrect answer to the final output. In the second image, the most important relationship is the semantic relation, where the relation "sitting on" is explicitly encoded between the objects "person" and "bench". However, the proposed model fails to yield the correct result in this case by assigning near-zero weight to the semantic relation. The final prediction then deviates from the correct answer by considering to irrelevant relations. In the last image, the question asks for the number written on the bus on the right. It is clear that the spatial relationship should be used, and indeed, the proposed model assigned the highest weight to the spatial relation. However, the predicted answer '38' is incorrect, which may occur because the quality of the picture is low, and '36' may even be interpreted as '38' by humans. Thus, even if the proposed model correctly identifies the best relation for the given question, it still predicts incorrect results if the optimal encoder itself cannot answer the question correctly.

5 Conclusion

In this paper, we propose a novel stacked attention model that assigns dynamic attention weights for various visual relations with the VQA model. We show that the proposed model yields higher accuracy than existing graph attention network models that equally consider each relation. Additionally, the proposed model, which uses an attention mechanism, has a natural form of interpretability through the visualization of learnable weights multiplied by each encoder's output. By analyzing attention weights, we show that the proposed method provides higher attention to the desired relation encoder.

References

Peter Anderson, Xiaodong He, Chris Buehler, Damien Teney, Mark Johnson, Stephen Gould, and Lei Zhang. 2018. Bottom-up and top-down attention for image captioning and visual question answering. In *Proceedings of the IEEE conference on computer vision and pattern recognition*, pages 6077–6086.

Stanislaw Antol, Aishwarya Agrawal, Jiasen Lu, Margaret Mitchell, Dhruv Batra, C Lawrence Zitnick, and Devi Parikh. 2015. Vqa: Visual question answering. In *Proceedings of the IEEE International Conference on Computer Vision*, pages 2425–2433.

Hedi Ben-Younes, Rémi Cadene, Matthieu Cord, and Nicolas Thome. 2017. Mutan: Multimodal tucker fusion for visual question answering. In *Proceedings of the IEEE international conference on computer vision*, pages 2612–2620.

Remi Cadene, Hedi Ben-Younes, Matthieu Cord, and Nicolas Thome. 2019. Murel: Multimodal relational reasoning for visual question answering. In *Proceedings of the IEEE Conference on Computer Vision and Pattern Recognition*, pages 1989–1998.

Kyunghyun Cho, Bart Van Merriënboer, Caglar Gulcehre, Dzmitry Bahdanau, Fethi Bougares, Holger Schwenk, and Yoshua Bengio. 2014. Learning phrase representations using rnn encoder-decoder for statistical machine translation. *arXiv preprint arXiv:1406.1078*.

Haoqi Fan and Jiatong Zhou. 2018. Stacked latent attention for multimodal reasoning. In *Proceedings of the IEEE Conference on Computer Vision and Pattern Recognition*, pages 1072–1080.

Yash Goyal, Tejas Khot, Douglas Summers-Stay, Dhruv Batra, and Devi Parikh. 2017. Making the v in vqa matter: Elevating the role of image understanding in visual question answering. In *Proceedings of the IEEE Conference on Computer Vision and Pattern Recognition*, pages 6904–6913.

Sepp Hochreiter and Jürgen Schmidhuber. 1997. Long short-term memory. *Neural computation*, 9(8):1735–1780.

Han Hu, Jiayuan Gu, Zheng Zhang, Jifeng Dai, and Yichen Wei. 2018. Relation networks for object detection. In *Proceedings of the IEEE Conference on Computer Vision and Pattern Recognition*, pages 3588–3597.

Jin-Hwa Kim, Jaehyun Jun, and Byoung-Tak Zhang. 2018. Bilinear attention networks. In *Advances in Neural Information Processing Systems*, pages 1564–1574.

Diederik P Kingma and Jimmy Ba. 2014. Adam: A method for stochastic optimization. *arXiv preprint arXiv:1412.6980*.

Thomas N Kipf and Max Welling. 2016. Semi-supervised classification with graph convolutional networks. *arXiv preprint arXiv:1609.02907*.

Ranjay Krishna, Yuke Zhu, Oliver Groth, Justin Johnson, Kenji Hata, Joshua Kravitz, Stephanie Chen, Yannis Kalantidis, Li-Jia Li, David A Shamma, et al. 2017. Visual genome: Connecting language and vision using crowdsourced dense image annotations. *International journal of computer vision*, 123(1):32–73.

Linjie Li, Zhe Gan, Yu Cheng, and Jingjing Liu. 2019. Relation-aware graph attention network for visual question answering. In *Proceedings of the IEEE International Conference on Computer Vision*, pages 10313–10322.

Tsung-Yi Lin, Michael Maire, Serge Belongie, James Hays, Pietro Perona, Deva Ramanan, Piotr Dollár, and C Lawrence Zitnick. 2014. Microsoft coco: Common objects in context. In *European conference on computer vision*, pages 740–755. Springer.

Jiasen Lu, Jianwei Yang, Dhruv Batra, and Devi Parikh. 2016. Hierarchical question-image co-attention for visual question answering. In *Advances in neural information processing systems*, pages 289–297.

Mateusz Malinowski, Carl Doersch, Adam Santoro, and Peter Battaglia. 2018. Learning visual question answering by bootstrapping hard attention. In *Proceedings of the European Conference on Computer Vision (ECCV)*, pages 3–20.

Hyeonseob Nam, Jung-Woo Ha, and Jeonghee Kim. 2017. Dual attention networks for multimodal reasoning and matching. In *Proceedings of the IEEE Conference on Computer Vision and Pattern Recognition*, pages 299–307.

Will Norcliffe-Brown, Stathis Vafeias, and Sarah Parisot. 2018. Learning conditioned graph structures for interpretable visual question answering. In *Advances in neural information processing systems*, pages 8334–8343.

Adam Paszke, Sam Gross, Soumith Chintala, Gregory Chanan, Edward Yang, Zachary DeVito, Zeming Lin, Alban Desmaison, Luca Antiga, and Adam Lerer. 2017. Automatic differentiation in pytorch.

Badri Patro and Vinay P Namboodiri. 2018. Differential attention for visual question answering. In *Proceedings of the IEEE conference on computer vision and pattern recognition*, pages 7680–7688.

Shaoqing Ren, Kaiming He, Ross Girshick, and Jian Sun. 2015. Faster r-cnn: Towards real-time object detection with region proposal networks. In *Advances in neural information processing systems*, pages 91–99.

Adam Santoro, David Raposo, David G Barrett, Mateusz Malinowski, Razvan Pascanu, Peter Battaglia, and Timothy Lillicrap. 2017. A simple neural network module for relational reasoning. In *Advances in neural information processing systems*, pages 4967–4976.

Nitish Srivastava, Geoffrey Hinton, Alex Krizhevsky, Ilya Sutskever, and Ruslan Salakhutdinov. 2014. Dropout: a simple way to prevent neural networks from overfitting. *The journal of machine learning research*, 15(1):1929–1958.

Damien Teney, Peter Anderson, Xiaodong He, and Anton Van Den Hengel. 2018. Tips and tricks for visual question answering: Learnings from the 2017 challenge. In *Proceedings of the IEEE conference on computer vision and pattern recognition*, pages 4223–4232.

Damien Teney, Lingqiao Liu, and Anton van Den Hengel. 2017. Graph-structured representations for visual question answering. In *Proceedings of the IEEE conference on computer vision and pattern recognition*, pages 1–9.

Petar Veličković, Guillem Cucurull, Arantxa Casanova, Adriana Romero, Pietro Liò, and Yoshua Bengio. 2018. Graph attention networks. In *International Conference on Learning Representations*.

Peng Wang, Qi Wu, Jiewei Cao, Chunhua Shen, Lianli Gao, and Anton van den Hengel. 2019. Neighbourhood watch: Referring expression comprehension via language-guided graph attention networks. In *Proceedings of the IEEE Conference on Computer Vision and Pattern Recognition*, pages 1960–1968.

Cheng Yang, Weijia Wu, Yuxing Wang, and Hong Zhou. 2020. Multi-modality global fusion attention network for visual question answering. *Electronics*, 9(11):1882.

Zhuoqian Yang, Jing Yu, Chenghao Yang, Zengchang Qin, and Yue Hu. 2018. Multi-modal learning with prior visual relation reasoning. *arXiv preprint arXiv:1812.09681*, 3(7).

Zichao Yang, Xiaodong He, Jianfeng Gao, Li Deng, and Alex Smola. 2016. Stacked attention networks for image question answering. In *Proceedings of the IEEE conference on computer vision and pattern recognition*, pages 21–29.

Ting Yao, Yingwei Pan, Yehao Li, and Tao Mei. 2018. Exploring visual relationship for image captioning. In *Proceedings of the European conference on computer vision (ECCV)*, pages 684–699.

Chen Zhu, Yanpeng Zhao, Shuaiyi Huang, Kewei Tu, and Yi Ma. 2017. Structured attentions for visual question answering. In *Proceedings of the IEEE International Conference on Computer Vision*, pages 1291–1300.

A Example Appendix

This is an appendix.

Association for Computational Linguistics
209 N. Eighth Street
Stroudsburg, Pennsylvania 18360

ISBN 978-1-7138-3023-8

CURRAN ASSOCIATES INC.
proceedings.com